The Development of Monetary Economics

To John Creedy with thanks

The Development of Monetary Economics

A Modern Perspective on Monetary Controversies

D.P. O'Brien

Emeritus Professor of Economics,
University of Durham, UK

Edward Elgar
Cheltenham, UK · Northampton, MA, USA

Published by
Edward Elgar Publishing Limited
Glensanda House
Montpellier Parade
Cheltenham
Glos GL50 1UA
UK

Edward Elgar Publishing, Inc.
William Pratt House
9 Dewey Court
Northampton
Massachusetts 01060
USA

A catalogue record for this book
is available from the British Library

Library of Congress Cataloguing in Publication Data

O'Brien, D.P. (Denis Patrick), 1939–
    The development of monetary economics : a modern perspective on monetary controversies / by D.P. O'Brien.
        p. cm.
    Includes bibliographical references (p.) and index.
    1. Monetary policy–History. I. Title.

    HG230.3.O27 2007
    332.4–dc22   2007000732

ISBN 978 1 84720 260 4

Printed and bound in Great Britain by MPG Books Ltd, Bodmin, Cornwall

Contents

III   19th Century British Controversies

List of Figures

List of Tables

Preface

In the preparation of this book I owe an enormous debt to John Creedy. First, it was he who undertook the arduous task of welding together my essays into a coherent whole, in the form of camera ready copy. He provided, along the way, all sorts of advice and encouragement as he asked me to look at the intermediate versions which emerged. The volume is dedicated to John; and the work which he has done on it to bring it into a presentable form would have merited that dedication even had that been all.

But in fact the debt is much greater even than that. For every essay in the book was first read by John, commented on by him, and amended in the light of his criticisms. This is true not only of the previously published items but also of those which are new for the book. In particular I have benefited greatly from his comments on my essays on John Law and on John Locke, as well as in many matters of detail elsewhere in the volume, including the question of algebraic notation, and from his arduous work on the presentation of the empirical material in chapter 6.

In the discussions on these and other issues which have taken place between us, I have benefited very greatly from the development of modern communications. We have been able to engage in more or less continuous intellectual dialogue over a distance of 12000 miles. The earlier writers whose work is discussed in the book had not only to contend with the absence of modern computing facilities (though what Thomas Joplin was able to achieve in this respect while equipped with nothing more than pen and paper is astonishing) but also with communications which for long were dependent upon postal facilities of varying degrees of reliability. Though much has occurred in academic life in the last half century which has been extremely damaging, the development of the interchange provided by modern communications has at least been a significant step forward.

I must also thank my wife Julia, who has not only had to put up with a house full of papers and books but who has also read all of the papers appearing in this volume from first draft onwards. Though an intellectual historian herself, economics is not her field, yet she has managed to make valuable comments in every case.

Acknowledgements

Chapter 2 appeared as 'Bodin's Analysis of Inflation', *History of Political Economy* **32**(2), 2000, pp. 367–92. I am grateful to the journal and to Duke University Press for permission. Chapter 5 and Chapter 10 appeared in M. Blaug, W. Eltis, D.P. O'Brien, D. Patinkin, R. Skidelsky, and G. Wood *The Quantity Theory of Money from Locke to Keynes and Friedman*. Aldershot: Edward Elgar, 1995. Chapter 6 appeared as 'Monetary Base Control and the Bank Charter Act of 1844', *History of Political Economy* **29**(4), 1997, pp. 593–633. I am grateful to the journal and Duke University Press for permission. Chapter 7 appeared in *History of Political Economy* **35**(1), 2003, pp. 1–19. I am grateful to the journal and to Duke University Press for permission. Chapter 8 appeared in *The Scottish Journal of Political Economy* **48**(4), 2001, pp. 425–41. I am grateful to the journal and to Blackwell Publishing for permission. Chapter 9 appeared in my book *Thomas Joplin and Classical Macroeconomics. A Reappraisal of Classical Monetary Thought*. Aldershot: Edward Elgar, 1993.

In addition to the help from John Creedy and Julia Stapleton mentioned in the Preface, I am grateful to Roger Backhouse for comments on chapter 2; to Lynne Evans for comments on chapters 5 and 6; to Richard Morley for comments on chapter 6; to Neil Skaggs for comments on chapter 6 which led to a useful slimming down of the original paper; and to David Laidler for comments on chapter 7 which in particular drew my attention to a neglected contribution of Edgeworth. Comments by referees have often been helpful, and the kindness of editors, most notably Craufurd Goodwin of *History of Political Economy*, has been much appreciated.

Part I

Introduction

Chapter 1

Introduction

The literature of monetary economics is perhaps the oldest part of the literature of economics as a whole, with contributions stretching back to the Greeks. It is characterised by a sort of circularity, in which a theory rises, becomes qualified to the point where it remains only as a tautology, and then drops out of sight. It then re-emerges as later generations realise that key truths have been obscured by its eclipse.

Of no part of monetary economics is this more true than the quantity theory of money. It was the mainstream theory up to 1936; but the development by self-styled Keynesians of Keynes's own message led to the relegation of the very idea of the quantity of money to little more than an accounting concept, which was thought to be of no relevance in the consideration of macroeconomic policy. In Britain such an approach found its apogee in the Radcliffe Report, appropriately described by a Nobel Prize winner as 'Neanderthal Keynesianism' (Samuelson, 1986, V, p. 281).

In the 1970s economists suddenly rediscovered the importance of the quantity of money, as inflation accelerated in developed economies – to the point where it threatened social stability. But gradually the focus on the money supply became diluted, so that by the end of the 20th century the focus had shifted entirely to control of the rate of interest. But now, six years in to the new century, with asset price inflation and the bursting of bubbles becoming a feature of developed economies, there are signs that policy makers, at least, are beginning to wonder whether marginalisation of the quantity of money as a concept may not have been premature.

Given this historical experience, it is appropriate that we begin Part II with an account, in chapter 2, of one the earliest proponents of the quantity theory of money, Jean Bodin. Bodin's analysis of inflation, building upon the background of scholastic literature, was an important contribution to understanding the effects of changes in the supply of metallic money, as distinct from debasement of an existing stock of metallic money which had been the main concern of previous writers.

Bodin was quite clear that causality ran from the money supply to the price level. The subject of chapter 3, the celebrated (or notorious) John Law, seems to have regarded the price level as almost an irrelevance. He believed that increasing the money supply was the key to economic growth. A similar belief seems to have motivated some of those advising the British government in the 1970s. In dealing with the case of Law, it is not irrelevant that such advice resulted in a high – and accelerating – level of inflation. For analysis of Law's underlying model demonstrates that, as the great Henry Thornton was to perceive a century after Law, though without spelling out the model in detail, Law's policy prescriptions were in fact prescriptions for inflation.

Law borrowed ideas from a number of previous writers. One of those from whom he borrowed was John Locke, whose work is considered in chapter 4. Locke also argued, though in much more temperate terms than Law, that a plentiful supply of metallic money (not paper money, as envisaged by Law) was a stimulus to economic growth. In the course of this he put forward the proposition that there was a negative relationship between the rate of interest and the money supply, an idea which Law adopted and used for his own purposes. Locke was criticised by both Joseph Massie and David Hume, and the general view has been that his work emerged discredited from their criticisms. However, detailed examination of both these critics and, in particular, of their empirical claims concerning the relationship between the rate of interest and the rate of profit, suggests that historians of economics have in general been rather too generous to them and, correspondingly, less than generous to John Locke.

It was on the foundations provided by this earlier literature that the great monetary controversies of the 19th century, which are the subject of Part III of this book, took place. We begin in chapter 5 with a discussion of the mid-19th century debate between the Currency School, which favoured a counter-cyclical control of the money supply, and the Banking School which – its acceptance of the convertibility of the note issue into gold aside – had more than a little in common with the passive money supply view which underlay the thinking of the authors of the Radcliffe Report. It is argued that, subject to an important qualification concerning the efficacy of monetary base control, the purely theoretical position of the Currency School was much the stronger. It would have been viable had the sole money supply originated with the Bank of England (and it did not) or, alternatively, had the Bank, as keeper of the monetary base, been able to control indirectly the rest of the money supply. Under those circumstances, the price level and balance of payments could have been stabilised by the mechanisms put in place by the 1844 Bank Charter Act.

But as the next chapter, chapter 6, shows, monetary base control did not work. The Bank of England note issue did not control the price level, while the country bank note issue did. In turn the country bank note issue was not controlled by the Bank of England note issue acting as a monetary base. Thomas Joplin's argument that the 1844 Act thus targeted the wrong money supply is vindicated. Indeed his belief that the Act would do nothing to reduce economic fluctuation, and could engender liquidity crises, was justified by the turn of events.

Joplin has other claims to fame. One of these is explored in chapter 7. Walter Bagehot has frequently been credited with nothing less than the invention of the concept of lender of last resort, though more careful discussions have shown that it originated with Francis Baring and Henry Thornton. However it was Joplin, and his intervention in the liquidity crisis of 1825, who developed the whole argument properly, with the idea of penalty rate lending, expanding precautionary balances which had no effect on the price level when lending by the Bank increased in time of crisis, and the essential role of a central reserve. His ideas were taken over – literally overnight – by Bagehot's father-in-law Vincent Stuckey, and while Joplin, as ever, was pushed to one side, and while the Currency School strongly resisted the idea of a lender of last resort (as undermining control over the monetary base), the idea became firmly established along the lines laid down by Joplin, and codified by Bagehot.

Bagehot himself was, however, no mean economist. Part IV of this book deals with macroeconomic models, and chapter 8 outlines Bagehot's own model, which is an important contribution to the literature of economics. Essentially Bagehot switched attention away from the money supply and focused on the interest rate as the core policy tool. Positing a cycle of real income in the economy, his first contribution was a pioneering attempt to explain the existence of a cycle in the economy as a whole as being the result of fluctuations in the agricultural sector. Given endogenous fluctuations, Bagehot then developed a model in which the use of the minimum lending rate of the Bank of England, 'Bank Rate', in anticipation of successive stages of the cycle, would stabilise the economy. It is shown in chapter 8 that the model, when treated formally, does indeed exhibit stability when Bagehot's prescription for the use of Bank Rate is followed.

Bagehot's model is elegant but quite a simple one. That of Thomas Joplin, examined in chapter 9, is a complex model of the neo-Keynesian kind which anticipates the neo-Keynesian synthesis of income-expenditure and monetary models. Joplin's model is characterised by an equilibrium with expenditure equal to income, and by separate treatment of the goods and money markets, with two different LM curves consequent upon the adoption of a dual circulation hypothesis. Specifically, Joplin argued that the Bank of England provided the financial circulation while the country banks provided the money supply which enabled the market in goods and services to function. In the conventional manner, aggregate supply and aggregate demand curves, and a balance of payments function can be used to solve for equilibrium.

Finally, in chapter 10, the question of stability with an inbuilt cycle is again addressed. This time the approach is in terms of the money supply as the controlling variable, as in chapter 5, rather than in terms of the use of Bank Rate as in chapter 8. Employing a formal treatment, it proves possible to demonstrate that the prescriptions of the Currency School would, had they targeted the right money supply, have been stabilising, while those of the Banking School left the price level indeterminate and magnified fluctuations. At best, and only after filling a major gap in the theoretical position of the Banking School, any equilibrium achieved would only be a saddle point.

Viewing the centuries of literature on monetary controversy, three things stand out. The first is the very high quality of many of the contributions. Monetary economics has attracted some of the very best people to have written about economic problems. The second is that, as noted at the beginning of this chapter, there is a cycle in ideas which come and go. The third is the absolutely fundamental importance – and this comes out particularly in chapter 6 – of paying attention to the factual basis of the argument. Indeed, as Mark Blaug has written of the quantity theory of money, in the last resort 'It is facts and not analytical rigour that make the quantity theory good economics. I venture to assert that this so with most if not all economic theories' (Blaug, 1995, p. 44).

Part II

Early Monetary Debates

Chapter 2

Bodin's Analysis of Inflation

The work of Jean Bodin (1530-1596) has been known to economists at least since the mid-19th century (McCulloch, 1862, p. 37), even though his wider fame, by far, lies in political philosophy. But there has been disagreement over precisely what Bodin achieved in his writings on economics.[1]

There is no dispute that the interest of his economic writing lies chiefly in his analysis of the causes of the inflation which was affecting France at the time that he published the two editions of his *Response to Malestroit* (1568 and 1578). But there is considerable dispute about the nature of his achievement. On the one hand we have Schumpeter expressing the clear view that Bodin's:

> [A]nalysis needs but little readjustment or generosity of interpretation to be a correct diagnosis of the historical case as it presented itself in 1568. Even as regards general theoretical content,

---

[1] By far the greater part of the secondary literature relating to Bodin stems from French and German authors. The French contribution includes the work of Baudrillart (1853), Bodin de St. Laurent (1907), Harsin (1928), Hauser (1932) up to Servet (1994). The German contribution has paid more attention to the economic background to Bodin's work and in particular to the depreciation of the precious metals. Detailed references are to be found in Hauser's introduction to Bodin's *Response* (Hauser 1932) and in the excellent account in Spiegel (1991, pp. 700-703). See Baudrillart (1853, pp. 111-144) for a discussion of Bodin's life. This reconsideration of Bodin's work was inspired by the new translation of his *Response to the Paradoxes of Malestroit* by the late Henry Tudor and Dr. R.W. Dyson. This translation is unique in its incorporation of the texts of both the 1568 and the 1578 editions of Bodin's *Response*.

it is superior to much later work. (1954, p. 312)

Similarly, in his study of Bodin's monetary thought, Bodin's descendant, Jean Bodin de St. Laurent, had no difficulty in crediting Bodin with the first correct statement of a metallist version of the quantity theory (Bodin de St. Laurent, 1907, pp. 31-35), while the distinguished French economic historian Henri Hauser expressed astonishment at those who denied Bodin's achievement in formulating, with remarkable clarity, a version of the quantity theory of money (1932, p. xliv).

But, on the other hand, scholars both inside and outside France have been inclined to downplay the extent of Bodin's achievement. Thus Harsin, in a controversial (Hauser, 1932, pp. ix-x) volume, dismissed Bodin's claim to pioneering achievement (Harsin, 1928, pp. 31-44 esp. p. 40). After World War II the Swedish economist Hugo Hegeland also denied Bodin credit on the grounds that in 1568 the quantity theory was not as fully worked out as it was in later centuries. Hegeland also made the claim – which, as we shall see, is baseless – that Bodin believed 'that the price level was solely a function of the quantity of money' (1951, pp. 37n, 153).

The controversy has continued. A recent 'revisionist' interpretation of Malestroit credits him with a formulation of the idea of 'money as a veil' and, correspondingly, downplays Bodin's achievement (Servet, 1994).

It is however worth emphasising that neither critics nor proponents (with the exception of Hauser) call in evidence of their position a detailed examination of the text. It is the contention of this chapter, based on just such an examination, that the dismissal of Bodin's priority rests – where the grounds for such dismissal are clear at all – upon an inappropriate and incomplete statement of the quantity theory. Identifying the theory with five generally accepted propositions associated with it, however, it emerges that Bodin does indeed have a strong claim to be regarded as the pioneer formulator of that theory.

By 'the quantity theory of money' this chapter will take as understood the following propositions: (i) that there is a *demand for money*, dependent primarily on the existing price and income level; (ii) there is a *supply of money* – in the historical context we are discussing this means specie; (iii) the *money market clears*, with demand for money equal to its supply; (iv) a disturbance to *either* demand or supply requires an adjustment in the price (or income) level to enable the money market to clear; and (v) the direction of *causality* is from changes in the money supply to changes in the price level.

In the present context it is an increase in the money supply which is of key interest. In addition it should be recognised that, until quite recently, quantity theorists did not assume completely inelastic aggregate supply, so that there may also be some change in output associated with a change in the money supply.

While it would be completely unreasonable to expect these five key points to be set out clearly by the earliest writers, formulating the issues in this way does make it clear what it is that we are seeking to find in Bodin's work, and indeed in that of other writers distant from us in time. The foundation upon which the analysis rests is the recognition that an increase in the money supply, whatever its source, is likely to raise the price level – and, as we shall see, Bodin has strong claims to have developed this line of argument earlier and better than anybody else.

We begin with an outline of the European experience of precious metal inflow and inflation (section 2.1). Next comes a sketch of the intellectual background enjoyed by Bodin (section 2.2). This is followed by an account of Malestroit's 'Paradoxes', and of Bodin's critique of these, in which he developed his analysis of the causes of inflation (section 2.3). This analysis is then set in the wider context of Bodin's economic thought, covering the gains from trade, Gresham's Law, and the demand for money (section 2.4). Finally we come to the harmful effects of inflation and Bodin's proposals for currency reform, which were designed to limit the damage (section 2.5).

2.1   European Inflation

All governments are faced with a temptation to inflate the money supply to capture resources. The 20th century experience of this has been so all-pervasive that there is a developed literature on 'inflation taxation' (Humphrey, 1993, pp. 190-1). Medieval monarchs, lacking the printing press facilities of modern governments, had instead resort to the process of 'debasement', which involved adding low value metals to the coinage, spreading the supply of gold and silver further. Such a practice was widespread; the history of France contains many examples, while Henry VIII and his successors in England managed to debase the silver coinage to one sixth of its silver content in thirty years (Heaton, 1948, pp. 250-255).

Debasement was essentially a national problem, however, and adjustment of the nominal exchange rate, to reflect the different precious metal content of different currencies, could be relied on to contain at least most of the inflation thus generated within national boundaries. But the 16th century witnessed a different, and far more fundamental, monetary change; a huge increase in the supply of the precious metals themselves, resulting in an inflation which spread across national boundaries and raised prices throughout Europe. The relative value of commodities and the precious metals changed significantly. Thus the author of the hugely impressive study of the Spanish inflation (Hamilton, 1934) estimated that Spanish prices rose by a factor of 4.1 during the 16th century (see also Hauser, 1932, pp. xi-xix, xlvii-xlix). The index of grain prices for New Castille, calculated by Hamilton, rose from 37.05 in 1504 to 102.5 in 1568, the year in which Bodin published the first edition of his *Response* (Hamilton, 1934, pp. 390-1). Hamilton's composite index for silver prices rose from 33.26 in 1501 to 92.44 in 1568 and 137.23 in 1600 (Hamilton, 1934, p. 493).

By modern standards this was a very moderate inflation. (British prices rose almost 20 times between the late 1940s and the early 1990s.) But the

very insidiousness of the process made its causes harder to discern; Malestroit was undoubtedly misled into thinking debasement the more important
problem, and it was Bodin who deserves credit for pinpointing precious metal
increase as the real issue.

Of course, precious metals did not constitute the only means of payment.
Boyer-Xambeu, Deleplace and Gillard (1994) stress the important developments in payment by bills of exchange. But as they state, the use of credit
instruments ('economising expedients' in later terminology) made the coins
'all the more available for internal trade' (p. 151). Indeed they make the
point that 'the bill of exchange did not exclude specie, which had a two-fold
function in intra-European trade: settling accounts and providing reference
rates for exchange. The bill of exchange was a monetary instrument both
because it replaced coins in international relations and because it depended
on them in its relationship with the unit of account' (p. 151). Thus, as under
the gold standard, the bills were not independent of the metallic base.[2]

2.1.1 Inflation in France

The impact of the precious metals was most direct, and earliest, on Spain,
since it was from the Spanish colonies that the metal was coming. But France,
as an immediate neighbour, linked both by trade and by labour mobility, felt
the impact quite soon.[3] There is no doubt that, whatever imperfections
existed in Renaissance markets (Gillard, 1994), there were very many ways

---

[2]See also De Roover (1953, pp. 57 8). The importance of credit instruments has also
been emphasised in the informative review of Boyer-Xambeu, Deleplace and Gillard in
Lowry (1996, pp. 311-12). See also Gómez Camacho (1998, p. 537).

[3]It should be acknowledged that some French economic historians dispute this. In particular Boyer-Xambeu, Deleplace and Gillard (1994, p. 178) contend that the increase in
the precious metals was insignificant in relation to French gross domestic product (GDP).
However, since they only compare the precious metals arriving in the *last decade* of the
16th century with the French GDP, and since a figure for the French GDP in the 16th
century, for which they give no precise figure or source, must, in any case, be highly speculative, not everyone will find such reservations persuasive. In any case, what would be
immediately relevant would not be the total French GDP (however calculated) but that
part of it passing through the market system.

in which the precious metals could find channels of circulation apart from the official ones – including loss, theft and smuggling (Peronnet, 1994, p. 48). The profit opportunities offered by arbitrage were strong enough to ensure that the New World precious metals spread out from Spain by both official and unofficial channels. The official channels were connected, in part, with the pan-European ambitions of the Spanish monarchy (Vilar, 1976, p. 187; Spooner, 1972, pp. 26-9).

In addition there were the normal trade and payments, resulting from a variety of factors which Bodin identifies, in particular French agricultural exports to Spain and remittances to France from Spain by migrant workers. Although Spain and Portugal attempted, in true mercantilist style, to keep full accounting records of the treasure coming in from the New World, a good deal of it will have entered by unofficial channels – 'skimming' by those involved, let alone the piracy which was official policy for Britain, Holland and France in the 16th century (Davies, 1994, p. 185).

The end result of this was perceptible inflation in France.[4] As in the Spanish case, it was very modest by modern standards and thus, correspondingly, harder to analyse. Most estimates show prices rising by 2.5 or 3 times during the 16th century, though some acceleration seems to have occurred in the latter part of the century. Estimates by D'Avenel show rather larger rises in the value of land (D'Avenel, 1894) but wage income lagged behind. A modern study by Phelps Brown and Hopkins indicates this clearly. Taking the third quarter of the 15th century, when prices had fallen, as the base (100), the price of land had risen to 338 by the middle of the next century, to 728 by the third quarter and to 1062 by the end of the century. The wage rate (in the official accounting currency of livre tournois), with the same base, had risen to 156, 179 and 258 over the same period (Phelps Brown and Hopkins,

---

[4]For a violently opposed view see Morineau 1985. However, it should be noted that even sympathetic critics refer to 'la phobie de Michel Morineau pour un "quantitativisme"' (Boyer-Xambeu, Deleplace and Gillard, 1988, p.962).

1959, p. 26). Earlier Hauser, drawing on the work of Levasseur, had reported the price of wheat rising by a factor of 2.5 between the 1520s and the 1580s (Hauser, 1932, p. xx).[5]

This is representative of results obtained by a number of the earlier researchers, which were summarised by Bodin de St. Laurent (1907, p. 4).

This modest inflation thus sets the scene, in terms of contemporary economic experience, for Bodin's analysis of inflation. However there is also a significant intellectual background to his thought.

2.2 Scholastic Contribution

Sixteenth century Spanish scholasticism was an intellectually fertile background. According to Schumpeter, 'The very high level of Spanish sixteenth-century economics was due chiefly to the scholastic contributions' (1954, p. 165). As Schumpeter recognised (1954, p. 101), the roots of what was to become the quantity theory of money are to be found in the writings of the scholastic philosophers. Here the experience of debasement was important; the analysis of this by Nicholas Oresme, writing about 1360, is of particular significance. For Oresme approached the valuation of metallic money in the same way as the valuation of other commodities. This had the important effect of making it subject to the analysis of the Just Price, which was a development of central importance (G. O'Brien, 1920, pp. 145-55; Gordon, 1975, pp. 188-195; see also Monroe, 1924, p. 26 on Antonine). The scholastic analysis of the Just Price had become, largely under the influence of Aquinas (1225-1274), an analysis of price in terms of 'common estimation' – thus pointing in the direction of subjective value theory. In this analysis the Just Price reflected competitive market valuation (where there was not fraud and

---

[5]The picture concerning inflation in France is obscured by a distinction to be made between the unit of account and money in circulation, with the former being the subject of official debasement. Some information, on what is itself a huge topic in detail, is in O'Brien (1997b, pp.14-15). On the recoinage of 1577 in particular, see Boyer-Xambeu, Deleplace and Gillard (1994, pp. 191-3).

monopoly) and it thus reflected relative scarcity. So what had become established, in the universities of late medieval and Renaissance Europe, was an analysis of value founded on relative scarcity, thus clearing the way for an analysis of changes in the values of precious metals which had become much less scarce.

Such ideas are to be found in the 16th century scholastics, notably Dominic de Soto and Luis Molina (Dempsey, 1935).[6] Among these writers was one of particular importance to Bodin's background – Navarrus.

2.2.1   Navarrus

Martín de Azpilcueta Navarro (1493-1586) became a leading member of the School of Salamanca (Grice-Hutchinson, 1952, p. 45; Gordon, 1975, p. 203; Gazier and Gazier, 1978). Indeed Marjorie Grice-Hutchinson has claimed that the first clear statement of the quantity theory of money is in the *Comentario Resolutorio de Usuras* of 1556, by Navarrus (Grice-Hutchinson, 1952, pp. 52, 95; 1978, p. 95). Navarrus argues that relative scarcity determines the value of money, money being a commodity subject to the same analysis of relative scarcity as other commodities. Navarrus then explains:

> That (other things being equal) in countries where there is a great scarcity of money all other saleable goods, and even the hands and labour of men, are given for less money than where it is abundant. Thus we see by experience that in France, where money is scarcer than in Spain, bread, wine, cloth, and labour are worth much less. And even in Spain, in times when money was scarcer, saleable goods and labour were given for very much less than after the discovery of the Indies, which flooded the country with gold and silver. The reason for this is that money is worth

---

[6]See also the outstanding essay by Gómez Camacho (1998).

more where and when it is scarce than where and when it is abundant. (Translated in Grice-Hutchinson, 1952, pp. 94-5)

Thus Navarrus has stated clearly that the purchasing power of money is inversely related to its quantity. He does not however claim (though this claim has been made on his behalf – Grice-Hutchinson, 1952, p. 56) that purchasing power parity exists. Indeed, given the impediments to the distribution of the precious metals, this could only be a long-run equilibrium position.

Bodin was exposed to the influence of these writings in two ways. Firstly, he became a religious novice in his teens and was thus exposed to the detailed intellectual training which would have been the norm (Tooley, 1955, pp. vii-viii). Having abandoned the religious life, Bodin studied law at Toulouse where Navarrus had taught (Franklin, 1968; Hauser, 1932, pp. xxxvi-xliii), though it has been established by H.W. Spiegel that there was a twenty-five year gap between Navarrus leaving Toulouse and Bodin arriving (Spiegel, 1991, pp. 90, 702). But even if Bodin was not directly taught by Navarrus, it is not credible that he would have been uninfluenced by the work of a major writer in a tradition with which he was already familiar from his novitiate, who had taught at the institution, no doubt within the memory of some of those still there.

2.2.2 The Quantity Theory in the 16th Century

While the major influences upon the development of Bodin's thought will have been economic experience and the scholastic background, it has to be recognised that the quantity theory of money, at least in a rudimentary form, was beginning to emerge at the time that he wrote; see Gómez Camacho (1998, pp. 536-54) and Popescu (1998, pp. 580, 582). Most writers will accept that, objectively, Copernicus can claim priority (Spiegel, 1991, pp. 86-8). But Copernicus did not go beyond the idea that 'money usually depreciates when it becomes too abundant' (Grice-Hutchinson, 1952, p. 34), and it is highly unlikely, as Hauser has pointed out, that Bodin owed anything to Copernicus in this matter, even though references elsewhere in his writings show that he was familiar with the astronomical theories of Copernicus. For Bodin had no need to have read what Copernicus wrote about money, given the scholastic background which he already had. Apart from Copernicus, credit has also been given to Nöel du Fail. Bodin de St. Laurent, who drew attention to his work on the effects of the inflow of treasure, dated this at 1548, which would have given him some priority over Bodin.[7] However, as Bodin de St. Laurent points out, du Fail offered a perception, not a developed argument; and in any case it now seems doubtful whether the 1548 work which Bodin de St. Laurent cited contains the relevant material (Harsin, 1928, p. 40, n. 1). At all events there is no evidence that Bodin himself owed anything to du Fail, and it seems reasonable to conclude that his own, remarkably comprehensive, treatment sprang from the scholastic intellectual background combined with something which will become apparent when we look in detail at his text – an exemplary concern with the available data.

An important piece of evidence concerning the scholastic influence on Bodin is indeed to be found in the condemnation of usury in his *Republic*. Bodin saw usury as a source of social inequality and political tension, but he based his condemnation squarely on religious sources (Bodin de St. Laurent, 1907, pp. 149-178).

Bodin's monetary analysis then appeared, in true scholastic style, as a critique (Bodin, 1568a, 1578). In this case it was a critique of two 'paradoxes' put forward by Jean Cherruies (or Cherruier) 'Seigneur de Mallestroit [sic]' one of the 'conseillers-maîtres des comptes' (Servet, 1994, p. 73). It is thus

---

[7]Bodin de St. Laurent has a useful review of precursors of Bodin, including Xenophon, Buridan and Oresme, as well as Copernicus and Nöel du Fail.

necessary to examine Malestroit's argument.[8]

2.3 The Paradoxes

Malestroit's first paradox is a claim that, although prices have risen in terms of the currency, following debasement, the prices of commodities have not risen at all in terms of the precious metals. The rises in price are thus simply changes in the unit of account, resulting from debasement. He insists that prices have not risen in terms of the precious metals during the last 300 years (p. 41).[9] His prime exhibit in support of this claim is the steadiness, as he reports it, of the price of velvet in terms of precious metals, once changes in the precious metal content of the currency have been allowed for. More ambitiously, he extends the claim to perishable commodities, notably corn and wine.

Malestroit's second paradox seems incomprehensible at first sight. It is the claim 'That a significant loss can be made on an ecu or other gold and silver money, although it is paid out at the same price as that at which it was received' (p. 44). The essence of the argument is, however, that rents stated in silver terms now exchange for less gold than they used to – because they are specified in silver *coinage* which has become debased.

Malestroit's aim in publishing these 'paradoxes' is not clear, although it was no doubt in connection with his official position in the public finance machinery, and it may also have been designed to serve the monarchy by damping popular discontent. In advancing them he was clearly hoping to persuade through demonstration of expertise; indeed he employed a rhetorical

---

[8]For the wider context of the debate see Boyer-Xambeu, Deleplace and Gillard (1994, pp. 189-93).

[9]Page references both to Malestroit and to Bodin's *Response* are to the Tudor-Dyson translation (Bodin, 1568b, and note 1 above). It had been intended to include also references to the Hauser edition (Hauser, 1932). Unfortunately this, which is of the first (1568) edition of Bodin, is seriously incomplete with regard to the second edition variants included in an appendix, and it was felt that an incomplete set of page references was of little use.

technique rather similar to that later employed by Sir William Petty, which drew on itself the deserved satirical attention of Swift (Letwin, 1963, pp. 128-140). The technique, as employed by Malestroit, involves describing in words a simple algebraic relationship using ratios. Then, as if by magic, a ratio implied, but not specified, by the verbal expression is appealed to, to give an unexpected result. Thus let $\frac{S}{V}$ be the silver price of velvet and $\frac{S}{G}$ the silver price of gold. Then the ratio $\frac{dS/dV}{dS/dG}$ yields $\frac{dG}{dV}$, so that changes in the gold price of velvet can be appealed to without being specified directly.[10] Such sleight of hand might well have been impressive in 16th century France.

2.3.1   Bodin's Critique

Bodin was able, in his *Response*, to destroy the factual basis of Malestroit's argument. The essential points which he established were these. Firstly, Malestroit's use of data was faulty. Secondly, even after full, and correct, allowance had been made for debasement, this was completely inadequate to explain the rises in price which had actually occurred.

On the first count Bodin was able to advance plausible reasons for doubting whether velvet was even known in 14th century France (pp. 53-4). Given the central claim made by Malestroit about the steadiness of the price of velvet, this was a damaging point. Secondly, Bodin, who was aware that inflation had spread throughout Europe (p. 57), was able, on the basis of the data to which he had access, to identify rises in prices, in terms of the debased silver currency, by a factor of 20. In terms of gold currency, the price of corn had risen by a factor of 2 (p. 55). Malestroit had identified a five-fold debasement, but the remainder of the change required explanation.

To arrive at this view, Bodin carefully based himself on price records

---

[10]Thus, for instance, we find Malestroit stating that in 1328 one gold ecu was worth 20 sols, and a measure (an 'ell') of velvet was worth 4 'livres', which was worth 4 ecus. An ell when Malestroit was writing cost 10 livres, but 10 livres was still worth 4 ecus, equal to 50 sols. 'Therefore, the said ell of velvet is no dearer now than it was then' (quoted in Bodin, 1568b, p. 41).

with which, from his legal work, he was familiar. It is hardly surprising that he immediately encountered the problem which all economists faced until the pioneering work on the construction of widely based index numbers by William Stanley Jevons in the 19th century (Jevons 1863) – that of how to represent a general price change.

Like a number of Jevons's predecessors, Bodin decided that the price of land would provide a good general measure of depreciation. It had the advantage of reflecting (through transfer earnings, though Bodin does not make this point) the prices of a range of commodities. It was, he argued, fixed in amount and of constant fertility in France (p. 55). The price of land had trebled in the last 50 years in terms of gold coin while the gold content of the ecu had only fallen by 10 per cent. The implied inflation was thus around 2.7 times (p. 56).

Casting around for measures of depreciation, Bodin inevitably introduced some confusion into the argument. Later in his *Response* he refers to a rise in the price of property in terms of gold of 3.5 times after correction for debasement (pp. 79-83). He also claims that Crown lands had become worth as much in rental as they were once worth in outright purchase price. Employing the standard mathematics of the value of a perpetual flow (and assuming that the French Crown could borrow at 4 per cent) this implies a 25-fold rise in price (Chiang, 1984, pp. 462-64). This however results from the fact that rents had been specified in silver *coinage* so that the calculation indeed allows both for debasement and for the fall in the value of silver. Land having risen in price by more than commodities, this is consistent with the 20-fold inflation referred to above.

Once the argument is disentangled, it becomes apparent that Bodin's basic estimate of inflation purely in terms of precious metals was in excess of 2.5 times, a remarkably accurate estimate, given the later studies referred to above.

In applying the scholastic technique of criticism to Malestroit's paradoxes,

Bodin had succeeded in establishing that debasement was, on its own, not enough to explain the rise in prices. In itself this was no mean achievement, demonstrating as it did a remarkable grasp of data, a grasp which becomes even more apparent when one looks at his discussion of coinage and exchange rates later in the *Response*.[11]

But having thus established that Malestroit's claims were insupportable, Bodin was then faced with the next stage of his self-imposed task – to explain the causes of the rise in prices. It is in this explanation that the real distinction of his performance lies.

2.3.2   Bodin and the Causes of Inflation

Bodin attributes the rise in prices to five main causes (p. 59). It is worth emphasising that there are five such causes, in view of the claim by Hegeland noted above that Bodin relied solely on changes in the quantity of money. The five main causes are:

1. 'The abundance of gold and silver, which is greater in this kingdom today than it has been in the last 400 years.'

2. Monopolies.

3. 'Scarcity which is caused both by the export trade and by waste.'

4. Fashionable demand for luxuries.

5. Debasement.

Bodin identifies the first cause as, quantitatively, the most important. The historical data (and Bodin was not only enormously well read but the author of an important work on history (Reynolds, 1945)) showed this clearly (pp. 59-60). Following the scholastic analysis, precious metals depended on

---

[11] For Bodin's methodology see Baudrillart (1853, pp. 145-168).

relative scarcity; and the scarcity of both gold and silver, relative to the
supply of commodities, had changed significantly. One piece of evidence
for this was the fact that in past centuries the precious metals had been in
such short supply that there had been serious difficulties in raising ransom
payments for captured royalty. Payments had improved to such an extent
that even the difficulties of liquidity encountered in raising revenue for the
French Crown had now disappeared.

> If Monsieur de Malestroit consults the records of the *Chambre*,
> he will agree with me that more gold and silver has been found
> in France to meet the needs of the king and the commonwealth
> between 1515 and 1568 than could be found in the previous 200
> years. (p. 63)

The key to the change in the liquidity situation lay in the French balance of payments, which had improved remarkably. On the one hand, an
improvement in the terms of trade had resulted from Portugal's development
of trade with the East, enabling France to buy such products as spices on
better terms than those exacted by the Italians during their monopolisation
of this trade. On the other, the increase in French agricultural output, following the arrival of more peaceful times, had resulted in a significant rise
in agricultural exports, earning gold and silver not only from Spain but also
from northern Europe. Thus treasure which had come to Europe from the
New World had found its way into France (pp. 62-5).

To the improvement on current account was added an inflow on capital
account. This was connected with public sector borrowing; the French Crown
paid high interest rates and the City of Paris granted annuities on very
favourable terms. Bodin regarded this capital flow as a healthy development,
and one which could be strengthened by an increase in the size of the banking
sector.

The influx of gold and silver raised prices everywhere – though certainly not far enough to produce uniformity of inflation rates in different countries. The other causes of inflation, while not negligible, were, in practice, of less importance. The importance of monopolies, in both the goods and labour markets, was restricted by law, at least in principle (p. 68). With regard to the third ground, exports, it was true that these could raise the price level – because they both reduced aggregate supply and (since the food was paid for in monetary metal) increased aggregate demand. But Bodin, as we shall see, had an understanding of the benefits of trade which was unusually sophisticated both for his time and his country, and he clearly did not think that this effect, on its own, could produce sustained inflation.

His identification of fashionable demand for luxuries as the fourth cause of high prices may in part reflect the fact that Bodin 'had in his make-up a large measure of Puritanical censoriousness' (Sabine, 1951, p. 343), something which has been evident to the commentators on his political philosophy. Clearly on its own, such demand could explain relative price effects (which would certainly impinge on popular consciousness of 'dearness') but not sustained inflation. It is however extremely interesting that, in analysing the demand for luxuries (pp. 69-72), Bodin used precisely the approach in terms of relative scarcity which underpinned not only his development of the quantity theory but the preceding scholastic analysis of the Just Price.

Bodin understood perfectly well that part of the rise in prices was to be attributed to debasement. He also understood well – unlike some of the more recent defenders of Malestroit – that this was more than a change in the unit of account. The very process of debasement imposed forced saving upon the private sector, at least in the short run. But it was not the fundamental explanation for high prices, for two reasons; firstly, after the State had captured resources, the subsequent long-run equilibrium would indeed represent no more than a change in the unit of account; secondly, it would not explain the *sustained* inflation peculiar to the 16th century, given that debasement itself was a well-established European practice.

Nonetheless, Malestroit himself had attempted to explain all the rises in price by this fifth cause, debasement. Bodin was able to show that Malestroit's demonstration was faulty, both because his understanding of the complex history of French currency was inadequate and also because he had biased his results by selecting particular years.

> It is, therefore, a mistake to take as the basis of our calculations a year when money was strongest and to set aside the years when money was weakest, which were incomparably more frequent than the good years. (p. 79)

Malestroit's attempt to explain everything in terms of debasement was thus fundamentally flawed; the rise in prices had to be explained by the combined effect of debasement and the change in the relative values of commodities and the precious metals. Thus while Malestroit explained a five-fold rise in price by debasement, Bodin's estimate of the rise in prices of different commodities involved figures of 10, 12 or even 20 times (pp. 80-1), as already noted.

Bodin had himself identified five causes of *high prices*. As we have seen he was not convinced that all five causes explain sustained *inflation*. This is true of the third cause, exports. But Bodin's unwillingness to attach significance to the exports argument stemmed in turn from a view of the gains from trade which requires examination.

2.4   Exports and the Gains from Trade

In analysing Bodin's claims to economic sophistication it is important to understand that Bodin showed an appreciation of the gains from trade which was extraordinary, both for the time of his writing and for the fact that his work appeared in the most mercantilist country in Europe. Although the

19th century economist J.R. McCulloch was aware of this aspect of Bodin's writings – McCulloch owned a copy of Knolles's 1606 translation of the *Republic*, as well as Baudrillart's 1853 study of Bodin (McCulloch, 1862, p. 37) – this aspect of Bodin's work seems to have attracted much less attention since McCulloch's day, even though it is integral to the whole argument.

Once again, we need to look at the scholastic writers to understand the background. The earlier Christian writers, even up to the 12th century, were suspicious of trade, and of those engaged in it. As late as 1078 a church council held that merchants (like soldiers) could not hope for eternal salvation (Gordon, 1975, p. 172). But this attitude, which stemmed from Aristotle, was gradually relaxed from the time of Aquinas, who cautiously accepted trade as an occupation which could legitimately be pursued (G. O'Brien, 1920, pp. 145-55). The discussions in the scholastic literature would, for the reasons already given, have been well known to Bodin who, apart from his novitiate, and his decade at Toulouse, was prodigiously well read. But Bodin went much further than the scholastics. Indeed he presented a remarkable case for the wealth-creating effects of trade.

Because France was now able to trade with the Near East directly, France was now wealthier, he argued (p. 66). Like those economists in the 1950s who were emancipating themselves from the sterile general equilibrium interpretation of Heckscher-Ohlin (Kravis, 1956), Bodin argued that trade made available goods which would not otherwise be obtainable. In turn he believed that this was in accordance with natural law, as reflecting God's provision.

> God has with admirable foresight made provision, for He has distributed His favours in such a way that there is no country in the world so well provided for as not to lack many things. (p. 86)

This in turn implied that trade bound nations together in mutual benefit. Indeed, in contradiction of all accepted mercantilist tenets, Bodin argued that imports could be positively beneficial in their effect on the price level, through reducing shortages.

It would be too much to expect that Bodin was entirely consistent in his treatment of trade and its beneficial effects. His suggestion of export duties (pp. 88-9) is not one to which free trade inclined 19th century English classical economists took exception (D.P. O'Brien, 1975, p. 190). But there are undoubtedly mercantilist traces in his writing, as others have observed (MacIver, 1930). In particular, he argued that imports from Italy were unnecessary, given French natural resources, and that they involved luxurious items (p. 69) – Bodin's Puritanism surfaced again. In turn this may reflect the fact that Bodin, for all his generally benevolent attitude towards foreigners (Bodin de St. Laurent's, 1907 Part II, Chapter 2 is entitled 'Bodin xénophile'), disliked Italians. Perhaps this reflected some unfortunate experiences in Toulouse or, more probably, the grasping nature of Italian merchants (Boyer-Xambeu, Deleplace and Gillard, 1994, p. 22); for Bodin, while arguing that foreigners should be treated with kindness, explicitly excluded from this recommendation rogues from Italy (p. 86).

2.4.1 Gresham's Law

Bodin's claims to economic sophistication are further enhanced when we examine his treatment of the proposition which has become known as Gresham's Law. The idea which goes by this name long predates Sir Thomas Gresham (1519-1579) – in whose work it is not to be found. The misattribution is the work of the late 19th century writer H.D. MacLeod who, as one commentator has stated, 'was endowed with a marvelous ability for reading into a text what is not there' (De Roover, 1949, p. 91). The idea is to be found in classical Greek writing, notably in Aristophenes's play *The Frogs*. But the 13th century scholastic writings were associated with a Greek revival, so it is hardly surprising that the idea is to be found therein, not only in the work of Oresme but in earlier writers (Seligman, 1930, pp. 61-2).

Bodin understood the Law not in the sense which it later had – that it is not possible to maintain a bimetallic currency with a fixed Mint ratio, which must necessarily diverge from the relative world price of gold and silver – but in terms of the effects of debasement (pp. 114-115). In this context the Law is summarised by the phrase 'bad money drives out good'. Debased coinage, which still has the same legal value as undebased coinage, will remain in circulation while the (higher market value) undebased coinage flows abroad to take advantage of its higher purchasing power in world markets.

Bodin's understanding of the Law, in the context of debasement but not in the context of a bimetallic currency, is important in two ways. Firstly, since the debate with Malestroit involved the issue of debasement, this was the most direct application of the Law. But it also had the important implication (though Bodin does not spell this out) that the Law in this application explained the shortage of specie in France in the 15th century, to which Bodin did indeed draw attention. For successive debasements of gold and silver coin would have driven out the full weight coin, leaving France short of the precious metals. This would indeed explain why, as Bodin notes, despite successive debasements, on which Malestroit relied for his case, prices had actually fallen in the previous century. Secondly, because Bodin did not appear to understand the Law in the context of a bimetallic currency, he failed – unlike Navarrus – to appreciate that it was not possible to have a fixed silver/gold price ratio of 12:1. Here Bodin's historical methodology and his enormous reading seem to have combined to mislead him; he advocated the retention of a 12:1 ratio, on the grounds that this had been the world price ratio for more than 2,500 years (pp. 109-110). In truth the ratio was changing even as Bodin wrote, as Navarrus showed himself to be aware:

> If there is a shortage of gold coins their value may well increase,
> so that more coins of silver or other metal are given in exchange

for them. Thus we now see that because of the great scarcity of gold money some people will give 23, and even 24 and 25 reales for a [gold] doubloon, which according to the law and price of the kingdom is worth only 22. Similarly, if silver money becomes scarce its value may rise, so that more gold or metal money is given in exchange for it. (Navarrus, 1556, translated in Grice-Hutchinson, 1952, p. 95)

Since Bodin understood perfectly well the analysis of relative scarcity which was being employed here, he should have appreciated that his preference for the historic 12:1 ratio was ill-founded. It has been suggested that his preference reflected a philosophical theory about numbers as the basis for a philosophy of human society (Spooner, 1972, p. 94); but at all events his position sat ill with his analysis of relative scarcity and the effects of changes in the *supply* of money. However, in order to complete our understanding of Bodin's analysis, it is also necessary to look at his treatment of the demand for money.

2.4.2 The Demand for Money

For Bodin to be regarded as having a special claim to a pioneering statement of the quantity theory of money, it is desirable that he should have paid attention to the question of the demand for money. For the quantity theory does not, except in a very simplified form, imply that the price level change resulting from an increase in the money supply should be exactly proportional. Such a position can only be sustained by treating the demand for money as being of unit elasticity with respect to the price level; correspondingly, an analysis of the demand for money is required if such proportionality is to be recognised as simply a special case.

Some commentators have argued that Bodin neglected this issue (Monroe, 1924, p. 198; Schumpeter, 1954, pp. 312-314). But a careful reading of the

Response indicates clearly enough that Bodin understood that the demand for money – and thus the velocity of circulation – was related to the stage of economic development. He is clear that more developed economies would exhibit a greater demand for transactions balances (p. 67). Thus an increase in the money supply would have a smaller effect on the price level than if balances were unimportant. Again, however, this is entirely consistent with Bodin's understanding of the importance of relative scarcity – the demand for balances affected the relative scarcity of money. Thus it is clear, once again, that his analysis of the value of money – commodity money in this context – falls within the general (scholastic) treatment of value.

Whatever the nature of the demand for money, however, it was undeniable that changes in the supply would produce effects on the price level, and that these were likely to be harmful. Bodin both paid attention to the precise nature of the harm and suggested possible remedies.

2.5   Inflation: Effects and Remedies

The prevalence of debasement by medieval monarchs led the scholastic writers, from Aquinas onwards, to explain that the consequent price changes confuse markets and injure trade. This insight was further developed by Copernicus (Monroe, 1924, p. 69). As the inheritor of this tradition, Bodin emphasised the harmful effects of rising prices in his *Response* – both the public and private sectors suffered from the economic uncertainty when the standard of value was no longer stable.

> For if money, which ought to govern the price of everything, is changeable and uncertain no one can truly know what he has: contracts will be uncertain, charges, taxes, wages, pensions and fees will be uncertain, fines and penalties fixed by laws and customs will also be changeable and uncertain; in short, the whole

state of finances and of many public and private matters will be
in suspense. (p. 102)

Following the scholastic analysis, Bodin here directs his remarks at debasement, although the application is much wider.

It was however debasement which Bodin believed to be the only really *re-
mediable* cause of inflation. The other causes could not be countered without
doing more harm than good. There was no sense in trying to drive out the
precious metals; experience showed that both monopoly and extravagance
would be tolerated in practice, and in so far as exports were inflationary, the
gains from trade had also to be taken into account. But debasement could be
attacked, even though this would limit the freedom of the Sovereign, which
Bodin elsewhere argued was absolute (Sabine, 1951, pp. 345-50).[12]

2.5.1 Currency Reform

Debasement made it impossible to stabilise prices (pp. 110-14). It introduced difficulties into foreign exchange markets and trade, since equilibrium
exchange rates ultimately depended upon metallic content but these would
take some time to achieve following debasement (pp. 112-13, 117). To avoid
such effects, a reform of the coinage was necessary.

In discussing this issue, Bodin was able to draw upon his remarkable
reading and to display an astonishing command of the extremely compli-
cated background of European coinage (Hauser, 1932, pp. xxvii-xxxi). He
addressed his discussion to both private and governmental debasement. The
free enterprise version of debasement was subject to horrific penalties which,
however, failed to achieve their end (Bodin de St. Laurent, 1907, p. 77).
Bodin's solution, which anticipates that of Thomas Joplin in the 19th cen-

---

[12]Bodin did however discuss some inherent limitations on sovereignty, notably natural
law (Sabine, 1951, pp. 347-50), and, as Bodin de St. Laurent has pointed out (1907,
pp. 78-84), debasement, to which Bodin was fundamentally opposed, was regarded as a
legitimate exercise of sovereignty by other writers both before and after Bodin.

tury (O'Brien, 1993, p. 24), was to make forgery unprofitable, rather than either impossible or too terrifying to undertake. Were it made unprofitable, it would be reduced to a very small level (pp. 94-7, 118-119). It could be made unprofitable by a reform of the coinage which ensured that ordinary transactors were not easily fooled because the coinage was regular, stable and easily recognised.

Quantitatively, the major problem was not forgery and private debasement but the activity of government in debasing the coinage systematically (just as 20th century forgery of paper currency is of minuscule importance compared with the activities of governments in inflating the money supply). Kings fell prey to the urgings of their courtiers, who recommended debasement (pp. 98-9) and, apparently in search of increased revenues, monarchs carried out this activity on a huge scale (pp. 110-14) and with little public condemnation. What the public sector gained, in command over resources, was correspondingly lost by the private sector, so that, before account is taken of the disruption of markets, what was under consideration was at best a zero sum game (pp. 120, 124-5).

But the confusion engendered by debasement was actually of benefit to the monarchs engaged in this activity; by undermining public awareness of the characteristics of full-weight coin, the monarchs were more easily able to pass off debased coin at full value.

Despite his general defence of the absolute nature of sovereignty, a defence which other writers extended even to debasement, Bodin instead argued that the coinage should be reformed. What was required was a full weight coinage without alloy. The ratio between silver and gold should be 12:1 (pp. 99-108). Such a reformed coinage would make it harder in future for monarchs to pass off coins with a significant proportion of alloy.

> We will also, by these means, prevent all falsification of the coinage; and even the most stupid and ignorant will know the

> worth of any coin by the sight, the sound, and the weight, with-
> out fire, graving-tool or touchstone. (p. 107)

The full weight coin should also have milled edges, to prevent clipping, and it should be cast rather than hammered (pp. 121-3). Such a reform would securely establish the value of gold and silver coinage and would leave inflation to be determined only by those increases in the quantities of the precious metals which were unavoidable.

This would establish the high value coinage (gold and silver) on a firm footing. However, there was a further difficulty. It was the question of the composition of low value coinage for use in retail transactions by poorer people. The problem of the composition of the 'Billon' was a perpetual one for Renaissance governments (Spooner, 1972, pp. 102, 140-2). Perhaps not surprisingly, Bodin was not able to solve a problem which had defeated these governments – indeed there are inconsistencies in the treatment in the *Response*, inconsistencies which are sufficiently serious to suggest that the process of revision between 1568 and 1578 involved some prolonged tinkering with the original text. At one point he even suggested that small value coinage should be phased out (pp. 102-3), while at another he recommended copper coins (or very small silver ones) for the poor (pp. 107-8). Yet he took the (not unusual) view that copper was not suitable for coinage, because it was of varying value, not merely through history but also between different countries (pp. 108-9). Again, towards the end of the *Response* he seems to have veered back towards the view that no Billon should be issued (p. 120).

Unsatisfactory though these vacillations may be, the issue was, from Bodin's point of view, rather a minor one compared with the need to sta-bilise the standard of value – though the poor certainly needed some kind of token for retail transactions, the agricultural sector as a whole was able to use barter to a remarkable extent. Indeed, as English experience demon-strated (pp. 97-8), there was no easy solution; finding a suitable medium for retail transactions in an economy characterised by subsistence agriculture and barter was extremely difficult.

2.6   Conclusions

It should be clear from the account of Bodin's thought given here that Bodin did indeed formulate a recognisable version of the quantity theory of money in his *Response to Malestroit*. Indeed he went on to employ this in his *Republic*, as Bodin de St. Laurent has pointed out (1907, p. 31), in turn incorporating parts of the *Republic* into the second edition of the *Response*. It seems clear that Schumpeter's judgement on Bodin's achievement was substantially correct – and indeed that some reservations which Schumpeter subsequently expressed about Bodin and the quantity theory more narrowly defined (he suggested that Bodin failed to distinguish clearly enough between currency – which could then include paper – and precious metals as commodities (1954, p. 313)) were unnecessary. Bodin's analysis does contain the idea of a demand for money relating to the existing price and income level (treated as the stage of development), a discussion of the supply of money, distinguishing money in coined form, an understanding that the money market clears, with causality running from changes (primarily) in the money supply to changes in the price level, and an appreciation of the operation of markets at both national and international level. Indeed Bodin shows considerable sophistication in his development of the analysis.

Perhaps the clearest testimony to the originality and nature of his contribution is the extent in turn to which his work not only exercised a very considerable, acknowledged, influence, especially in England, but also the extent of its unacknowledged influence – in a word, plagiarism.

His influence in England was particularly marked, as his French editor has noted (Hauser, 1932, p. lxvi). Although no trace has been found of a 16th century English translation referred to by Bodin's publisher when the second edition appeared (G.A. Moore made extensive and scholarly enquiries about it, at the time of his now extremely rare translation of the second edition (Moore, 1948, pp. vii-viii)), Bodin himself did go to England in 1581 and may have been there two years earlier (Bodin de St. Laurent, 1907, p. 44; Baudrillart, 1853, pp. 128-9). In England, too, the process of plagiarisation began early. In 1581 his ideas were appropriated by the anonymous editor of the *Discourse of the Common Weal of this Realm of England* written by John Hales (or Sir Thomas Smith; see Palliser, 1992, pp. 457-58) (Monroe, 1924, p. 59; Schumpeter, 1954, p. 166). Both his descendant Jean Bodin de St. Laurent (1907, pp. 40-51) and his French editor Henri Hauser (1932, pp. lxix-lxxv) noted the extent of the plagiarism which he suffered in France. During the next century his influence became widespread, and it has been traced in considerable detail by Bodin de St. Laurent (1907, pp. 40-51) and by Monroe (1924, pp. 90, 93-5, 99, 101, 113, 117, 120, 144). Monroe (1951, pp. 132-41) also published a partial translation of the *Response*. A particularly interesting manifestation of his impact during the next century is the incorporation of his *Response*, in abstracted form, into the work by Gerrard de Malynes *Englands View, in the Unmasking of Two Paradoxes* (1603). Malynes actually took the argument further; as commentators have noted (De Roover, 1949, p. 247n; Silk, 1972), Malynes makes the excellent point that what is interesting about the quantity theory in the context of international flows is the lagged response of prices across countries.

Both the acknowledged influence and the plagiarisation are testimony to the fact that Bodin's achievement was considerable. He had provided, as early as the mid-16th century, both the first proper analysis and the first clear documentation of that century's inflation. His statement was not in any sense a piece of casual pamphleteering; it drew upon a highly developed scholastic background and reflected intelligence, intellectual training and scholarship. He showed himself fully aware of the implications, in the context of debasement, of Gresham's Law, he not only analysed the effects of changes in the money supply in terms of the Just Price analysis of relative scarcity but also related the demand for money to the degree of economic development, and he capped all this with an appreciation of the benefits of trade which was indeed remarkable, not only for that century but even for the next. When the question of his achievement is related directly to a detailed examination of the content of his *Response*, as has been done here, the extent of his achievement seems undeniable.

Chapter 3

John Law: Money and Trade Considered

The remarkable life of the Scottish adventurer, gambler, duellist and de-
signer of grand financial schemes, John Law (1671-1729) has fascinated generations.[1] However, it is as a monetary theorist that Law has attracted particular attention, with considerable differences of opinion arising with regard
to the merits of his contribution.

Although Law wrote a number of documents on monetary matters, many
of them relating to particular schemes that he was attempting to float, it
is his monetary theory, as encapsulated in his *Money and Trade Considered
with a Proposal for Supplying the Nation with Money*, which was published
in Edinburgh in 1705, which is the subject of this essay. The work brings into
the sharpest possible focus the basic monetary model which Law envisaged.[2]

There are two basic strands to Law's proposals, on the basis of which

---

[1] For a recent account of Law's life, see the fine article by Bonney (2004). Earlier
references will be found in Wasserman and Beach (1934). There is much biographical
material in Murphy (1986), and a full length study by the same author (Murphy, 1997).
This last draws on a much fuller range of Law's published and unpublished writings.
The present chapter is concerned only with Law's 1705 work which is, however, of key
importance in understanding the analytical underpinnings of Law's vision.

[2] A detailed study of the range of Law's documents is to be found in Murphy (1997).
For an account of the hostile reception accorded to Law's ideas in a wide range of historical
documents see Murphy (2000). Page references in this chapter are to Law's *Money and
Trade Considered*.

the model is developed. Neither was in itself original. The first is the idea that increasing the money supply will bring about a rise in real income. This idea dated from the work of William Potter (Potter, 1650, bk. 1, sections iii, iv; Viner, 1937, pp. 37-8). The second is the idea of a land bank. This was a common 17th century idea (Horsefield, 1960, chs 14-17). But it is Law's development of these ideas which has proved of enduring interest. In particular, the idea that inflating the money supply is the key to economic growth is one which has continuously resurfaced in the history of economics.

3.1   Law's Concerns

It is perhaps worth emphasising that Law's thesis is about economic development, not something which would justify reading into his work Keynesian concerns. He argued eloquently that Scotland was suffering from economic under-development because of a shortage of money, not that it was suffering from Keynesian unemployment due to aggregate demand failure (pp. 20, 106, 110-20). Division of labour in the transition from barter is at the core of his model. Like Petty (1690, pp. 104-109), Law was concerned with structural unemployment (pp. 114, 116).

> Our Poor have been computed 200000, our People were then more than now, but our Poor may be as many as then; Suppose only 100000, and by the Addition to our Money 50000 of them were imployed, and only for one half of the year, their Labour to be payed 3 pence, and worth 3 pence more to the Imployer, their Consumption a penny more than now: The yearly value of the Nation would be increas'd by such Labour 208333 lib. 6 sh. and 8 pence. (p. 116)

Again like Petty, Law exhibited the standard Mercantilist concerns. Thus a balance of payments surplus was a policy objective (Petty, 1690, pp. 44,

50-1, 82, 89; O'Brien, 1992, p. 103). It was better to correct the trade balance than to have legislation prohibiting the export of metal (pp. 27-8). But a balance of payments surplus, by increasing the money supply, would stimulate exports; a scarcity of money caused, as well as resulted from, a balance of payments deficit (pp. 25, 115-116). Since Law expected the activities of the note-issuing commission, which he proposed should be established, to be profitable, he believed that the funds thus generated could be used to manage trade, and the weapons of management which he had in mind were not direct controls but tariffs and drawbacks on exports, the latter requiring finance (pp. 55-6, 107-8). In addition to managing trade in this way, it could also be influenced by measures to limit consumption if absorption were too great – in modern terminology, Law envisaged both expenditure variation and expenditure switching (pp. 18-19).

Even more clearly mercantilist (and again strikingly similar to Petty) were Law's concerns with national power and wealth. These depended on population, and on stocks of home and foreign-produced goods; and the greater the money supply, and – in Law's model – the consequent GDP, the greater would these bases of national power be (pp. 59, 100, 101, 117). A nation had to be strong because a weak nation was exposed to its enemies (pp. 98, 119). To allow these enemies some influence on the money supply, the key to national prosperity, was undesirable, and thus paper currency, rather than metal, was part of Law's mercantilist programme (p. 118). With a sufficient money supply leading to increased trade and population, and indeed to increased immigration – Law, like Cantillon (1730, p. 165), assumed international factor mobility – national wealth would be increased. Law follows Petty (1690, pp. 31-3) in multiplying annual wages by '20 years Purchase' in order to make the transition from labour employed to national wealth (p. 19).

3.2   The Role of Money

The opening of Law's work helps to explain why his writings, despite their disastrous practical outcome in France more than a decade later, produced such a favourable impression on later commentators familiar with classical economic literature. For after setting out the basic questions which he wants to answer – the nature of money and the reasons for preferring silver, the effect of money on trade, and possible measures for increasing the money supply – Law begins with a chapter containing a discussion of value which is, in the tradition transmitted to Scotland via the work of Grotius and Pufendorf (O'Brien, 2004, pp. 28-9), distinctly superior to the majority of classical discussions. The diamonds and water paradox is solved by relative scarcity, changes in demand and supply affect value, and price differentials are explained by non-homogeneity. Law then moves on to a discussion of the origins of money as arising from the disadvantages of barter, a view which is reflected in any modern textbook. In the same vein, he explains the advantages of silver as money, contradicting Locke's belief that commodity money has a conventional value.[3]

This leads him to the fundamental theme of the whole work – that output and employment are positive functions of the money supply.

> As Money encreas'd, the Disadvantages and Inconveniencies of
> Barter were removd; The Poor and Idle were employ'd, more of
> the Land was Labour'd, the Product encreas'd, Manufactures and
> Trade improv'd, the Landed-men Lived better, and the People
> with less Dependance on them. (p. 11)

Money is thus essential for economic development. Law considers various measures which have been used by different countries to increase the money

---

[3]Law (p. 9). In this Law was misrepresenting Locke – see chapter 4 below. The passage which provided the basis for the misrepresentation is in Locke (1691, p. 19).

supply, and rules out debasement, as being a device which eventually raises the price level, more or less in proportion to the degree of debasement, though the Law of One Price did not apply immediately and relative international prices took time to adjust (pp. 50-1).[4] Debasement yields no increase in the real money supply, once prices have adjusted, and so does not contribute to economic development. On the other hand, banks were of considerable usefulness. Lending on a fractional reserve basis was an effective way of increasing the money supply, and the recently established Bank of England had produced the same effect through its lending to government (pp. 36-8). Banks were, in any case, a very valuable aid to economic development – the enhanced ease of transactions would on its own, without the benefit of an increased money supply, be enough to justify the risks associated with a fractional reserve banking system (pp. 37-8, 41).

3.3 Silver Coinage

But although a fractional reserve system could help to alleviate the constraints imposed by a commodity money such as silver, it did not by any means overcome the disadvantages of silver as a means of payment. Money was required to be a unit of account, medium of exchange and store of value (p. 61), but silver coinage was of uncertain value, not only because of State debasement (p. 62), but also because of changes in the world values of the precious metals. While the value of perishable commodities remained roughly steady, with output increasing in proportion to the growth of demand, the precious metals fell steadily in value over time. Rather than having a con-

---

[4]Due to his family background no doubt, it is evident from Law's work that he was highly experienced in foreign exchange dealings. Nonetheless the numerical illustrations are unnecessarily opaque as a result of two factors. Firstly, Law takes it for granted that the reader will understand the operation of the gold points, so that the exchange can only deviate from par by about $+/-3$ per cent before metal flows will be actuated. Secondly, the modern reader finds the multiplicity of different types of coin, with Scots coins being different from English ones, a barrier to understanding.

ventional ('imaginary') value, as Law believed Locke to have maintained, the precious metals were subject to the same forces of supply and demand, which determined their relative values, as other commodities. Their output increased more than in proportion to the demand for them, and thus their value fell (pp. 63-4). This argument was, as we shall see, inconsistent with Law's basic thesis that Scottish economic development was hampered by a shortage of money. Variations in the value of metal produced uncertainty in trade, as well as long-run changes over centuries in the value of silver (pp. 61-4). A particularly key argument for Law's general thesis was that silver was less stable in value than land, which was in fixed quantity (pp. 100-2). Land was stable in value because of the variety of uses to which it could be put; silver had, for practical purposes, no transfer earnings.

Law's attack upon silver as a standard of value was tactical rather than fundamental; as we shall see, silver played a key part in the logic of his own proposals. But the tactical purpose was to emphasise that the money supply could best be increased by the use of paper. This was because Law's overriding objective, as becomes clear early in the work, is the stimulation of economic development through monetary growth, using a paper currency, over the supply of which there was national control.

3.4   The Monetary Growth Model

The basic argument is this:

> Domestick Trade depends on the Money. A greater Quantity
> employes more People than a lesser Quantity. A limited Sum can
> only set a number of People to Work proportion'd to it, and 'tis
> with little success Laws are made, for Employing the Poor or Idle
> in Countries where Money is scarce; Good Laws may bring the
> Money to the full Circulation 'tis capable of, and force it to those
> Employments that are most profitable to the Country: But no

Laws can make it go furder, nor can more People be set to Work, without more Money to circulate so, as to pay the Wages of a greater number. They may be brought to Work on Credit, and that is not practicable, unless the Credit have a Circulation, so as to supply the Workman with necessaries; If that's suppos'd, then that Credit is money, and will have the same effects, on Home, and Forreign Trade. (p. 13)

Thus Law is asserting that an increase in the money supply can raise GDP.

The next stage of the argument is that exports also depend upon the money supply. Increasing national income will automatically increase exports, he maintained, foreshadowing the later 'Vent for Surplus' thesis to be found in the literature of Classical Economics (O'Brien, 2004, p. 207). According to Law:

The first Branch of Forreign Trade, which is the Export and Import of Goods, depends on the Money. If one half of the People are employ'd, and the whole Product and Manufacture consum'd; More Money, by employing more People, will make an Overplus to Export: If then the Goods imported ballance the Goods exported, a greater Addition to the Money will imploy yet more People, or the same People before employed to more Advantage; which by making a greater, or more valuable Export, will make a Ballance due. So if the Money lessens, a part of the People then imployed are set idle, or imployed to less advantage; the Product and Manufacture is less, or less valuable, the Export of Consequence less, and a Ballance due to Forreigners. (pp. 14-15)

Basically the argument is that exports, which are output minus absorption, depend on the size of output, which in turn depends on the size of the money supply (p. 14). Because increases in the money supply support further economic development – and thus further division of labour – it is even possible that the price level is a negative function of output, though Law's failure to deal explicitly with this aspect is strange, and poses problems for interpreting his analysis.[5] It is this positive relationship between the money supply and GDP which explains Law's confidence that increases in the money supply would increase exports (p. 75). Indeed the balance of trade was positively related to the money supply (pp. 14, 41-2, 115-16).

> If Trade can be carried on with a 100000 lib. and a Ballance then
> due by Forreigners; the same measures, and a greater Quantity
> of Money, would make the Ballance greater. (p. 42)

Not only did increases in the money supply support greater division of labour; by lowering the rate of interest they further stimulated economic activity (p. 15). A fall in the rate of interest indeed indicated that the money supply had been increased more than in proportion to the demand (pp. 67, 71) – Law was thus following part of Locke's theory of the determination of the rate of interest – and, if lower interest rates were desired, monetary policy rather than recourse to the Usury Laws was the correct way forward (p. 20).

To buttress the argument, Law also put forward an additional reason; he asserted that exports were a positive function of the money supply, because merchants collecting domestic output for export needed credit, and this increased in availability with the money supply (p. 116). Furthermore, raw material imports, re-exported as worked-up manufactures, depended upon the available money supply, as did invisible exports (pp. 16-17).

Law makes clear the mechanisms which he had in mind in a key passage (pp. 97-100) containing a parable about the economic development of an island. This shows certain key features of his thesis. Firstly, it shows that

---

[5]This possibility is considered by T.M. Humphrey, for instance (1993, p. 235).

Law's argument is built on the advantages of money in providing a transition from a barter to a specialised monetary economy; secondly, that in an under-developed economy there is substantial unemployment (on the island there are 300 'Poor or Idle, who live by Charity', p. 97). There is also under-employment (p. 98) (a widely recognised characteristic of under-developed economies). Raising activity levels will provide import substitution, and thus strengthen the balance of payments. If the income rises which occur are such that they would take employment beyond the full employment level, factor imports will occur. The end result will be an increase in power, wealth and strength. It is also clear from this that Law was not reasoning in some kind of proto-Keynesian way about an economy in which unemployment existed because of a preceding fall in the money supply. He was dealing with a case of economic development.

3.5 Development and the Price Level

Needless to say Law's thesis raises (as it raised for his successors such as Thornton – 1811, pp. 341-2) problems about the effects on the price level of an increase in the money supply. As we have already seen, Law simply ignored the issue of the price level, though as already noted one possible interpretation of his essay is that he believed that the price level would actually fall as a result of increased division of labour. This is however completely implausible. The picture which David Hume presented in his classic account of inflation – a picture set in 18th century Scotland be it noted – is far more reasonable at a micro level. When the quantity of money increased, Hume wrote, 'At first no alteration is perceived; by degrees the price rises, first of one commodity, then of another; till the whole at last reaches a just proportion with the new quantity of specie which is in the kingdom' (Hume, 1752, p. 38). Law's vision of economic development clearly required price signals to operate – not least because he envisaged a situation in which a tight Scottish labour market led to immigration (pp. 19, 117). Moreover he clearly expected that labour would be re-allocated, as income rose with an increased money supply (pp. 13-14); and such re-allocation would necessarily involve some prices rising without any guarantee that others would fall. With the issue of notes geared to the 'needs of trade', there would be no pressure for some prices to fall as others rose.

But Law does not seem to have envisaged any loss of purchasing power as new money was created. His basic thesis with regard to money-market clearing was that demand for money would increase as the initial increase in the money supply stimulated economic development (pp. 117-18) and that, if the money supply were demand-determined, this would ensure that money retained its value.

> It cannot well be known what Sum will serve the Occasions of the Nation, for as Manufacture and Trade advance, the Demand for Money will increase; but the many Poor we have always had, is a great Presumption we have never had Money enough. (p. 117)

> If Money were given to a People in greater Quantity than there was a Demand for, Money would fall in its value; but if only given equal to the Demand, it will not fall in value. (p. 117)

> At present perhaps 3 or 40000 lib. is more than there is a Demand for; but as Trade and Manufacture increase, the Demand for Money will be greater. (pp. 117-118)

He apparently envisaged issues of notes according to demand, without any reference to the relationship between the lending rate of interest and the marginal rate of profit, simply holding that lending should be 'at the ordinary Interest' (p. 85) – a position (and in Law's case a practice) which was to attract Thornton's criticism at the beginning of the next century (Thornton, 1802, p. 342). All that Law seems to have envisaged was that a note-issuing commission would supply money on demand on the security of land pledged (pp. 86, 90), though the actual amount of notes 'coined' should be limited to batches of £50,000 (p. 86). Money supply would thus be in equilibrium proportion to GDP (p. 76).[6]

3.6 Paper Money

Such an active, expansionist monetary policy clearly required the introduction of paper money. Law dismissed the idea that convertibility of paper money into metal was necessary for the success of such money (pp. 94-5); paper money had significant advantages of its own, especially portability, divisibility and transportability (p. 93). There was a further advantage – that paper could not, unlike metal, be drained abroad as a result of an adverse balance of payments (pp. 102, 104, 107).

Law's plan involved notes as legal tender and – and this is of key importance – the issue of notes against security of land (pp. 85-6), so that the total value of the notes issued would be equal to the total value of land (p. 89). Law considered land to be a better basis for issue than silver, contrasting the rising long-run value of land with the falling long-run value of silver (pp. 67-70). He believed that this was due to agricultural improvements yielding greater output, as well as the fixity in supply. His view involved a basic fallacy, since it made the value of land independent of the money supply (pp. 67-70), which it clearly was not, as the fiasco of the Assignats in revolutionary France was to demonstrate conclusively.

---

[6]In the case of silver money, at least, Law was prepared to argue that if the money supply increased beyond the optimal level in relation to the national income, this would still be of benefit to the country; Spain had benefited in this way from the inflow of precious metals, while the loss through depreciation had been diffused over the whole of Europe (p. 76).

3.7   The Land Standard

It is when we examine this question that Law's scheme starts to fall apart. For Law argued that a given amount of paper should represent a given amount of land value; but the land value in turn was expressed in terms of silver .

> The Paper-money propos'd will be equal in value to Silver, for it will have a value of Land pledg'd, equal to the same Sum of Silver-money, that it is given out for. (p. 89)

If Law had been serious about this, his whole argument would have collapsed; for he would really have been talking about a silver standard, with the intervening land simply a term which dropped out of the equation.

Writing P for the value of paper currency issued and L for the value of land as valued in silver S, Law proposes that $\frac{P}{L} = \frac{S}{L}$. But then $\frac{P}{L}\frac{L}{S} = \frac{P}{S}$ and the intervening land valuation would be redundant. Thus all the scorn which Law had poured upon silver as a standard would be to no purpose. Yet Law seems quite explicit about this:

> What I have propos'd to supply the Country with Money, may be reduc'd to this. If an Estate of a 100 l. Rent is worth 2000 l. in Silver-money, and this Estate can be convey'd by Paper, and this Paper be capable of being divided; then that Estate may be made current Money for 2000 lib. and any person who receives such Paper-money, receives a value equal to the same Sum of Silver-money, as Silver is valued now. If it is coin'd for 15 years purchase, then that Paper-money will be more valuable than Silver, for 1500 lib. in that Paper will purchase Land worth 2000 lib. Silver-money. If it is coin'd for 25 years purchase, then that Paper-money will not be so valuable as Silver, for 2000 lib. in Silver will buy als [sic] much land as 2500 lib. in Paper. (p. 118)

But now we have a further complication. Law seems to be arguing that the amount of paper issued, for a given amount of land backing, may be arbitrarily varied, and the value of the paper will vary (inversely) accordingly. The value of paper is free to depart from that of silver.

The argument is obscured by Law's own familiarity with banking pratice, and his assumption of an equal familiarity on the part of his readers. The explanation lies in the standard proposition that the value of a piece of land, expressed as a multiple of its annual rental, is dependent on the interest rate.[7]

Thus value V is equal to the ratio of rent R to the interest rate r.

$$V = \frac{R}{r} \tag{3.1}$$

With a falling interest rate, due (through Law's acceptance of Locke's theory) to an increase in the money supply, the reciprocal $\frac{1}{r}$ rises and with it the value of land. With $r = 0.04$ the land is worth 25 years purchase, and with $r = 0.0667$ the land is worth 15 years rental.

But herein lies a fundamental difficulty with the whole scheme. Under the scheme, the demand for loans and the supply of loans will be identically equal, as notes are issued to satisfy the 'needs of trade', as determined by the value of land offered as collateral. But as the note issue swells the money supply, so the rate of interest, in the 'Lockean' theory, will fall, raising the value of land (the number of years purchase), leading to increased value of the collateral offered for loans, leading in turn to yet more note issues.[8]

Of course, as assumed in Section 3.8 of this chapter, the rate of interest will not fall indefinitely but approach a lower limit. But the price of land will still continue to rise since, as Law himself emphasised, its amount is fixed. While other factor shortages could be remedied through migration, as Law

---

[7]For a standard demonstration see Chiang (1984, p. 464).

[8]As is shown below (chapter 4), Locke's theory of the rate of interest, in the context of his macroeconomic model as a whole, did not posit a unidirectional relationship between changes in the money supply and those in the rate of interest.

envisaged, the price of land would necessarily rise, as demand for its services increased with rising income.

3.8   A Formal Statement of Law's Model

Law's model can be summarised in the following equations. The demand for loans, L_t^D, is equal to L_t^S, the supply of loans in meeting the 'needs of trade'. The issue of new notes, N, is the form in which the loans are supplied, to the value of the quantity of land L offered as security, at a price P_L, so that:

$$L_t^D = L_t^S = N_t = L_t P_t \qquad (3.2)$$

$$L_t = \alpha_1 \left(\pi_t - \bar{r} \right) \qquad (3.3)$$

with $\alpha_1 > 0$. The supply of land offered as security depends upon the profit rate π and the 'ordinary' lending rate $\bar{r}$ at which Law envisages loans being made.

$$P_{L,t} = \frac{R_t}{r_t} \qquad (3.4)$$

The price of land depends on annual rental R_t and the market rate of interest r_t.

$$r_t = \alpha_2 k \left(M_{t-1}^S \right)^{-\beta} \qquad (3.5)$$

with $\alpha_2, \beta > 0$. The market rate of interest is inversely related to the money supply (M^s) following Locke's general approach.

$$Y_t = \alpha_3 M_{t-1}^S \qquad (3.6)$$

The level of income, Y, depends upon the money supply. If the money supply is set at a particular level at the start of a period, income will respond over the period, to attain a level appropriate to the money supply.

$$M_t^S - M_{t-1}^S = N_t + (S_t - S_{t-1}) \qquad (3.7)$$

The change in the money supply between $t-1$ and t is made up of new notes issued, and additional silver currency.

Law believed, like the 19th century Banking School, that (some of) the notes issued in one period would subsequently be returned to the issuer, because of the interest charge for the loan. However, as Thornton was later to point out (1811, pp. 341-2), this is incorrect. Firstly, the loan will not be repaid as long as $(\pi - r) > 0$. Secondly if, as we shall argue in conformity with the grounds already given, a rising price level followed additions to the money supply, the extra notes would be required to support the same volume of transactions at a higher absolute price level. In addition we may note that such price inflation would both inflate the nominal profit level and reduce the real value of the lending rate of interest. Finally if, as Law believed, an increased money supply would call forth an increased level of real income, the extra note issue would be required for the extra volume of real transactions, even without a rise in the price level.

$$S_t - S_{t-1} = B_t = X_t - M_t \tag{3.8}$$

The change in the stock of silver coin is equal to the balance of payments B, which is the difference between exports X and imports, M.

$$\begin{aligned} X_t &= \alpha_4 Y_t - \alpha_5 \frac{P_{n,t}}{P_{s,t}} E_t \\ &= \alpha_4 \alpha_3 M_{t-1}^S - \alpha_5 \frac{P_{n,t}}{P_{s,t}} E_t \end{aligned} \tag{3.9}$$

with $\alpha_4, \alpha_5 > 0$. Exports depend upon income Y and upon the ratio of the world (silver) prices (in index form) P_s (to which the Law of One Price applies) to domestically priced exports, where prices are expressed in paper money, P_n. The term E_t is the exchange rate expressed as foreign currency units per unit of home currency.

The second term in equation (3.9) reflects the fact that Law had observed, apparently from his own experience of the foreign exchange market, that the effect of currency debasement on domestically priced exports was not immediately cancelled out by adjustment of the exchange rate.

$$P_t - P_{t-1} = \alpha_6 (Y_t - Y_{t-1}) - \alpha_7 (T_t - T_{t-1}) \tag{3.10}$$

with $\alpha_6, \alpha_7 > 0$. The general domestic price level, P, reflecting the prices of both traded and non-traded goods, is positively related to the level of output Y, and negatively related to gains in productivity T, such as those resulting from improved labour allocation as income rises.

$$T_t - T_{t-1} = \alpha_8 (Y_t - Y_{t-1}) \tag{3.11}$$

Thus the productivity gains are, as envisaged by Law, themselves the result of rises in the level of income.

Substituting 3.11 into 3.10 we have:

$$
\begin{aligned}
P_t - P_{t-1} &= \alpha_6 (Y_t - Y_{t-1}) - \alpha_7 [\alpha_8 (Y_t - Y_{t-1})] \\
&= \alpha_6 (Y_t - Y_{t-1}) - \alpha_7 \alpha_8 (Y_t - Y_{t-1}) \\
&= (\alpha_6 - \alpha_7 \alpha_8) (Y_t - Y_{t-1}) \tag{3.12}
\end{aligned}
$$

Thus, unless the productivity gains are sufficient to offset the upward pressure on the prices of factors, and the scope for this would necessarily diminish over time (in the absence of technological change, on which Law is silent), as opportunities to realise static gains through labour re-allocation are used up, a rising income level will produce a rising price level.

Unfortunately there is ticking away in all this an explosive development. As the money supply increases, the interest rate falls (3.5), so the price of land rises (3.4), which enables more notes to be issued (3.2). The money supply rises, the interest rate falls further, and the price of land rises higher. We have a cumulative process.

This monetary expansion will initially be damped by a reduction in the money supply through the loss of silver, unless, as Law envisaged, the rise in income generated extra exports and thus avoided a balance of payments deficit – and possibly, indeed, produced a net silver inflow; see (3.8) and (3.9).

But such an increase in exports depends upon the potential for productivity gains which, as already noted, are likely to become exhausted. Silver will drain out, and eventually the country will be on a paper standard, with a floating exchange rate and continuing inflation.

The curve relating the interest rate to the money supply has a positive second derivative, and the interest rate will approach a lower limit. But the increased monetary demand generated previously will feed through to rising profit opportunities, rising land prices (due to land shortages rather than a falling interest rate) and rising labour prices (triggering inward migration, as Law envisaged). These effects will lead in turn to further demand for loans, to be met in accordance with the 'needs of trade', and so on in an endless upward spiral.

Neglecting the balance of payments effects as of secondary importance, we have, substituting (3.3), (3.4), and (3.5) into (3.2):

$$
\begin{aligned}
N_t &= L_t P_{L,t} \\
&= \alpha_1 \left(\pi_t - r \right) P_{L,t} \\
&= \alpha_1 \left(\pi_t - \bar{r} \right) \frac{R_t}{r_t} \\
&= \alpha_1 \left(\pi_t - \bar{r} \right) \frac{R_t}{\alpha_2 k \left(M_{t-1}^S \right)^{-\beta}} \\
&= \alpha_1 \left(\pi_t - \bar{r} \right) \frac{R_t}{\alpha_2 k} \left(M_{t-1}^S \right)^{\beta}
\end{aligned}
\tag{3.13}
$$

The term $\alpha_1 \left(\pi_t - \bar{r} \right) R_t / \alpha_2 k \equiv G$ will be not only positive, so long as the lending rate is below the marginal rate of profit, but large, due to the rental value term R_t.

The solution to the difference equation is:

$$
N = G^t \left(M_0^S \right)^{\beta}
\tag{3.14}
$$

which for $G > 0$ is explosive.[9]

---

[9]For a simple and elegant solution to the problem of the time path of the note issue in Law's model, see Humphrey (1993, p. 24). The present model explores the mechanisms envisaged by Law in much more algebraic detail, but the end result is consistent with Humphrey's well-judged intuitive short cuts.

For the general price level we also have an explosive situation, one which is even more alarming, as it is related to changes rather than merely to the level of prices.

From 3.12:

$$P_t - P_{t-1} \equiv \Delta P_t \tag{3.15}$$
$$= (\alpha_6 - \alpha_7 \alpha_8)(Y_t - Y_{t-1}) \tag{3.16}$$

and using (3.6):

$$P_t - P_{t-1} = (\alpha_6 - \alpha_7 \alpha_8)\alpha_3 \left\{ M_{t-1}^S - M_{t-2}^S \right\}$$
$$= (\alpha_6 - \alpha_7 \alpha_8)\alpha_3 N_{t-1} \tag{3.17}$$

ignoring the secondary effect on the money supply arising from changes in the balance of payments.

The solution to the difference equation is:

$$\Delta P_t = [\alpha_3 (\alpha_6 - \alpha_7 \alpha_8)]^t N_0 \tag{3.18}$$

Thus, unless the productivity gains $\alpha_7 \alpha_8$ are sufficient to achieve $(\alpha_6 - \alpha_7 \alpha_8) < 0$ which, as argued above, is basically implausible, we have the prospect not merely of rising prices but of prices rising by increasing amounts.

3.9   Conclusions

Law's model, though superficially persuasive, was thus a fundamentally flawed mercantilist proposal for increasing national strength and wealth. In practice, both in France under Law's management, and in the appalling episode of the Assignats in revolutionary France in the 1790s, the fundamental flaws in Law's argument were to prove disastrous in practice. But the model which he had put forward still involved analytical propositions of considerable interest and it seems likely that, despite Smith's insistence on distancing himself from Law, the author of the *Wealth of Nations* was influenced to some extent by

Money and Trade Considered. The model, if we write down the equations, is incomplete unless we introduce an aggregate supply function of an illegitimate kind in which long-run forces (increased division of labour) are cited in support of the proposition that increasing the money supply will lower the price of output. But on a purely intellectual level, Law's achievement should not be underestimated.

Chapter 4

The Rate of Interest: Locke and His Critics

Locke's vision of the macroeconomic operation of the 17th century economy, and in particular of the rate of interest, developed over a long period from 1668 (Letwin, 1963, pp. 273-300; Kelly, 1991), reaching its apogee in the second (1696) edition of his *Some Considerations of the Consequences of the Lowering of Interest and Raising the Value of Money*.

At one level, Locke's lengthy essay is simply a well-developed argument against lowering the maximum rate of interest permissible under the usury laws. We shall examine those specific elements in Locke's thought first. However, the arguments which Locke deployed against lowering the maximum legal rate of interest were founded on an implicit, though not fully articulated, model of the economy, and to that we shall turn next.

A key element in that model was the proposition that the rate of interest was closely connected with the money supply, and this part of the argument was later subject to criticism by Joseph Massie and by David Hume. The two critics approached the proposition in different ways, but both came to the conclusion that the rate of interest depended on (Massie), or was equalised with (Hume), the rate of profit, and that the money supply was irrelevant to its determination. The criticisms of Massie and Hume are examined in order, below.

Finally we attempt to evaluate Locke's model as a whole, and to see how far it was undermined by subsequent criticism. This is particularly important because that criticism was to lay the foundation for the treatment of the rate of interest, not merely by the classical economists but also by the majority of later writers (Humphrey, 1993, pp. 35-43).

4.1   Locke and the Usury Laws

Locke starts from the proposition that there is a market rate of interest which depends upon the supply of, and demand for, loans (1691, p. 4). This he calls the 'natural Use'. It is defined as follows: 'by natural Use, I mean that Rate of Money which the present scarcity of it makes it naturally at, upon an equal distribution of it' (p. 7).

The phrase 'upon an equal distribution of it' means, for Locke, simply that the market for loanable funds has cleared. If usury laws are effective, they interfere with the market clearing. This in turn interferes with trade (both foreign and domestic), and thus with the level of income (pp. 4-5). This is because they reduce the supply of loanable funds so that trading in them takes place at the short end of the market, with interest below its equilibrium rate (pp. 6-7). Those with loanable funds are prepared to let them lie idle, rather than lend them at an interest rate which is insufficient to compensate for risk. In addition, foreigners will be reluctant to lend in England, thus further reducing the supply of funds (p. 14). Taken together, these effects are damaging to economic activity. In particular a shortage of loanable funds will damage trade, both because foreign capital will be repatriated and because the domestic capital holders will be reluctant to lend (pp. 10, 12, 25). It was true that a reduction in the rate of interest would reduce the service charge on foreign held debt, thus reducing withdrawals from the money stock over the balance of payments but, Locke pointed out, that gain had to be balanced against the loss of money earned through exports, as trade was reduced (pp.

12-14).

Thus lowering of the maximum rate of interest, through its effect upon the money supply, and through its effect upon willingness to lend with a given money supply, was damaging to economic activity.

In addition, there were distributive effects which were of no economic or social benefit. Loan-deposit rates would be widened, as specialist lenders enjoyed a rent on their expertise in placing funds within a restricted market (pp. 6-7). The unsophisticated would lose and the sharp money-market operator would gain (pp. 4-5, 9-10). In addition, the 'profligate' would be able to bid for funds, and encouraged to waste their inheritance, when the rate of interest was lower (pp. 63-4).

None of these distributive effects would be completely effective in lowering the rate which some traders had to pay for loans; they would be forced to pay whatever was necessary to secure funds (p. 7). It is thus apparent that it is only in the legitimate market that Locke expects trading at the short end of the market. So even though trade might be interest sensitive, it would not be assisted by lowering of the legal maximum that traders would have to pay. Moreover, to the extent that lowering the rate of interest was successful, the reduced interest charge would not compensate traders for the difficulties posed by rationing of funds (p. 10).

Locke clearly envisaged that lowering of the rate of interest would damage the market framework – he anticipated the growth of perjury which was already common in some parts of trade (pp. 5-6). Nor could there be any benefit to be expected in the form of lower prices of commodities through a lower rate of interest; relative prices depended upon demand and supply, while the absolute price level could only be altered through monetary effects – which, as we have seen, Locke expected to be damaging, if the money supply fell (pp. 27-8).

Of course Locke was here opposing a great deal of vested interest. In particular Sir Josiah Child (1668) had argued strongly for measures to reduce the interest rate to the level of that in Holland; and Nicholas Barbon, an operator in the speculative building trade, was also keen to promote the idea of lowering and fixing the rate of interest (Barbon, 1690).

Locke argued resolutely against this. The interest rate was low in Holland, he held, because Holland enjoyed a developed capital market, a large money supply, and a liquid public debt at a low rate of interest (pp. 56-8).

It was not that Locke did not see some role for usury laws. Not only was he concerned, like Smith later on, about the demands for funds from those mortgaging their estates for consumption purposes, but he believed that a fixed rate of interest could be of value in legal cases as well (pp. 54-5). But it should be, he argued, at the natural, market clearing, rate.

Locke had no difficulty in disposing of a number of subsidiary issues. Pressure for a reduction in the legal maximum rate of interest came in part from those who believed that it would raise the value of land – mechanically applying the value ('number of years purchase') obtained by dividing the annual rental by the maximum rate of interest. Locke analysed the market for land and showed that the price of land depended upon a great many other factors (pp. 32-3, 45). Indeed there was significant regional variation in land prices, due to the unequal geographical distribution of industry – land near to industrial activity had a higher price as the successful entrepreneurs sought to buy estates. The value of land tended to be depressed through social decline – the spendthrifts who sold their estates – whose behaviour he contrasted strongly with what he believed social attitudes to have been in the days of Queen Elizabeth I (pp. 45-6).[1] The price of land was also depressed by the fact that the majority of taxes fell, in the last resort, on land. Low land values were thus not due to the high level of interest, and lowering the interest rate maximum to 4 per cent would not raise the price

---

[1]Locke might not have welcomed the reminded that such prudence probably stemmed from consciousness of the recent acquisition of such estates from church lands seized at the Reformation.

of land.

The distributive effects noted above would also alter land values in England. As the specialist financial classes benefited from a widening of the loan-deposit margin, the price of land would rise in the vicinity of London (p. 45). But altering distribution in this way would certainly not affect national income, which was the ultimate determinate of the value of land. It was low income which produced low land values, and this was due to a restricted money supply (pp. 59-60).[2]

4.2 Locke's Macroeconomic Vision

Central to Locke's understanding of the operation of the low-income developing economy which was 17th century Britain was the idea that the level of national income depended upon the money supply. This was a popular 17th century idea which had been put forward by a number of other writers (Viner, 1937, pp. 36-40). Indeed it was also the idea which was at the back of the minds of those advocating the development of credit institutions, notably the personally interested Nicholas Barbon, especially the land bank enthusiasts (Horsefield, 1960). It was not an absurd idea, and there is a parallel to be found in development economic literature in the 20th century (Meier, 1980, p. 284). Some writers denied the idea completely – Dudley North was one (1691, pp. 525, 530, 539-40) – but they were very much in the minority.

To Locke, the idea was fundamental. 'Trade then is necessary to the producing of Riches, and money necessary to the carrying on of Trade' (p. 12). Note the line of argument; the money supply is viewed not in terms of developing bank credit (despite the emerging role of the goldsmiths) but in terms of specie. The source of specie is trade. Locke emphasises that gold and silver are themselves not riches but constitute the money supply which

---

[2]Locke's market analysis, which was carried out with considerable assurance, has been supported by later research into the determinants of the price of land in the 17th century (Habakkuk, 1952).

determines economic activity.

The money supply determined the level of activity because, in an economy only partially transformed into a full market system, metallic money provided a unit of account, a standard for deferred payments, and a source of liquidity which could be used to command working capital.

> Every Man must have at least so much Money, or so timely Recruits, as may in hand, or in a short distance of time, satisfie his Creditor who supplies him with the necessaries of Life, or of his Trade. For no body has any longer these necessary Supplies, than he has Money or Credit, which is nothing else but an Assurance of Money in some short time. So that it is requisite to Trade that there should be so much Money, as to keep up the Landholders, Labourers and Brokers Credit: And therefore ready Money must be constantly exchang'd for Wares and labour, or follow within a short time after. (p. 20)

Money, in other words, is the lubricant which enables the wheels of the market system to go round.

This leads Locke to calculate the necessary amount of money in the economy in relation to the frequency of receipts and payments, a matter he had raised in his early work in 1668 (Kelly, 1991, Vol. I, p. 172). Petty had made a preliminary approach to this in his *Treatise of Taxes* (1662, pp. 164-5), and had developed the argument in his *Political Arithmetick* (1690, pp. 110-11). Locke's approach was to argue in 1691 that regular payments require one fiftieth of the labourers' annual wages, one quarter of land rent due, and so on. However, the average balance held by labourers, landlords, merchants, and so on, would, on a notional straight line decline from the beginning of a payment period until its end, be only half the period sum, and Locke indeed adjusts the money supply required to one hundredth of the labourers' annual wages, one eighth of rents due, and so on.

This gives the impression of a static approach to the analysis of macroeconomic activity; and it is perfectly true that a static Keynes-type model can be constructed from Locke's writing (Leigh, 1974). But in a developing economy Locke is concerned with increasing the money supply in order to keep the economy growing. By contrast, a country with a falling money supply is classified as 'a decaying country' (p. 14).

A number of writers have been led by this to accuse Locke of confusing money and capital (Viner, 1937, pp. 31-2). A similar point had been made by Locke's contemporary, Barbon. According to Barbon, interest is paid for capital, not for money (Barbon, 1690, p. 20). This criticism rightly attracted the scorn of Keynes, who responded, 'interest means interest on money' (1936, p. 344).

The loan of money enables resources, which can then be used productively, to be captured. Locke makes this quite clear, in drawing a parallel between the rent of land (which is directly productive) and interest on money (which is indirectly productive) (pp. 28-9). Just as ownership of land is unequally distributed, so is access to funds for productive investment. It is the role of interest, as the price of access to those funds, to bring them into the market for loanable funds where they may be used productively. This argument (which was given a radical interpretation by Massie, who seems to have believed that interest existed because money was concentrated in a few hands) foreshadows the work of Cantillon (1730), who analysed the effects of an increase in the money supply as dependent on those hands into which it first flowed.

Locke envisaged two cases which would bring about a high level for the rate of interest, both of them designed to explain the mechanics of determination of the rate of interest. Firstly, he considered the case of debt. He argued, uncontroversially, that a high price would have to be paid for funds in a case where a large number of debts were suddenly called in (pp. 8-9). He does not labour this case, and it seems to be designed merely to show the importance of an elastic supply of funds. He may possibly have had political instability at the back of his mind, given the time at which he wrote. His main emphasis in explaining a high rate of interest, however, was upon a shortage of money, which would make it difficult for the market for loanable funds to have sufficient liquidity.

Thus a high rate of interest could be a result either of a shift in the demand schedule in the market for loanable funds, or in the supply schedule. The more obvious source of an increase in the demand for loanable funds, however, would be an increase in investment opportunities, rather than the sudden calling in of existing loans. 'That which raises natural Interest of Money, is the same that raises the Rent of Land, (i.e.) its aptness to bring in Yearly to him that manages it, a greater Overplus of Income above his Rent, as a Reward to his Labour' (p. 39).

However it is shifts in the supply of loanable funds on which Locke concentrates his attention. It does not follow that a high rate of interest indicated a shortage of such funds, since there was always the possibility of an increased demand for funds at each rate of interest. Indeed Locke was quite prepared to argue that a high market rate of interest could be a symptom of prosperity (p. 56). The modern analysis of a positive change in the money supply as it affects the interest rate (e.g. Mishkin, 1986, p. 123) includes an effect on income (which would have a positive effect on the interest rate), an effect on the price level (the effect on the interest rate should again be positive, as people seek to maintain the real value of the return), and a liquidity effect. It is only the last of these which is liable to lower the interest rate. If we then add to that the possibility that a rise in income, while leading initially to a rise in the demand for loanable funds could, through a reduction of investment opportunities, lower the potential return from the employment of loanable funds, we end up with the possibility that the interest rate may not respond unidirectionally to a change in the supply of money. Both the supply of, and demand for, loanable funds may shift simultaneously.

It is none the less the case that the supply schedule for loanable funds has a positive slope (p. 10). This view was by no means unique to Locke; it was accepted by other writers such as North (1691, pp. 519-20), who was in fact close to Locke on a number of issues.

4.3   The Price Level

However there are two quite serious difficulties with Locke's model as it stands. The first is that there are a number of instances where Locke emphasises the effect on the price level, rather than on the income level ('trade'), of a change in the supply of money. His relentless emphasis on the relative nature of value, as applied to money as well as to commodities (though the value of money is steadier than that of commodities because less is 'consumed', that is, taken into idle balances), leads to the proposition that the price level depends on the money supply (pp. 34, 43-4).

This aspect of Locke's work has probably been over-emphasised in the past. For one thing, Locke was certainly not a pioneer of the quantity theory of money. Bodin's work was well known in England, and Locke was also familiar with the Scholastic literature (Kelly, I, pp. 84, 98) which was the source for Bodin's own treatment of the quantity theory (chapter 5). It is clear from what is known of Locke's education that he was a fluent reader of Latin, the academic language of the Scholastics (Letwin, 1963, pp. 149-50; Vaughn, 1980, pp. 1-2). This familiarity with the existing literature on the quantity theory seems to have been fairly general among 17th century writers. Malaynes was familiar with Bodin's *Response to Malestroit* (1568); see, for instance, Bowley (1973, p. 11).

But if Locke was not a pioneer of the quantity theory, there certainly are points in his *Considerations* where his emphasis is upon the effect of a change of money on the price level rather than upon the income level.

4.4   The Balance of Payments

This leads us to a second difficulty – the balance of payments. Now it seems clear that Locke accepted the Law of One Price for a metallic currency, at least as an equilibrium proposition (pp. 41-2). He does not seem to have got as far as the price-specie-flow mechanism – an omission which, as we shall see, may have been of crucial importance – although he did envisage specie flows as taking place as a result of international differences in interest rates (pp. 43-4). Thus differences in money supplies gave rise to differences in interest rates, which in turn gave rise to flows across the exchanges. The positive or negative effect of an inflow of money on the interest rate thus became crucial. If such an inflow did indeed lower the interest rate, which was certainly one possibility, the money could then flow out again to seek higher interest rates abroad. But if the inflow of money had an effect upon the price level, that also raised the possibility of self-correction, since exports would lose markets, imports would seem more attractive, and money would flow out again across an adverse balance of payments.

However Locke did not himself envisage a direct effect on relative amounts of exports and imports, resulting from an inflow of money. But this means in turn that the idea of a self-correcting balance of payments, which was to prove so central to classical economics from Hume onwards, is absent from Locke's essay. In turn, the idea of a money supply in equilibrium with respect to relative international price levels is absent.

Of course there are other possibilities which Locke may have had in mind, possibilities indeed which are rather more subtle than the mechanical 'water finds its own level' theorem associated with Hume and, later, Ricardo. In particular, a rise in the money supply which led to a rise in income rather than to a rise in the price level could have a positive effect on the balance of payments. This would come about through industrial development leading to a 'vent for surplus' of the kind which later became familiar in the development economics literature (Myint, 1958). There is certainly at least one passage in the *Considerations* which would support such an interpretation (p. 42). In addition, Locke argues elsewhere that exports depend upon the rate of interest; the rate of interest depends upon the money supply; and thus an increased money supply will, through the agency of the rate of interest, increase exports, leading to increased export earnings – and a further inflow of specie (p. 10).

It is then reasonable to conclude that, for Locke, the primary importance of changes in the money supply was in relation to the level of income; and that price-specie-flow considerations do not necessarily damage his model fundamentally.[3] Yet such an acceptance does involve ruling out the possibility that the income increase will be accompanied by price rises at all – and here Hume's account of the process of inflation in his essay on money seems all the more persuasive – or the even more extreme assumption that exports and imports are not price sensitive, which would be inconsistent with Locke's acceptance of the Law of One Price as an equilibrium proposition.

The answer to these puzzles may perhaps lie in the way that Locke received the quantity theory of money from Bodin and the Scholastics. In their writings, the emphasis is upon secular trends – the long-term fall in the value of the precious metals in Europe as they flowed in from the New World. Some of Locke's statements of the relation between the money supply and the price level will bear this interpretation, since changes in the quantity of the precious metals are not linked to the balance of payments. Indeed for Locke it seems reasonable to take the view that he accepted that such changes worked themselves out all over Europe, and that for any one country the silver price of commodities was the international price – as with Adam Smith (Humphrey, 1993, p. 346).

---

[3] Against that, it has to be conceded that Locke's involvement in the recoinage episode of the 1690s runs counter to a recognition of the key importance of a large money supply in determining income, as Vickers has pointed out (1960, pp. 70-71).

4.5 Joseph Massie

Little is known about Massie. However he was clearly a major collector of economic literature, and in the 1930s a catalogue of his collection was published (Shaw, 1937). The vast majority of his work was concerned with economic statistics (Mathias, 1957; Dixon, 1925). He died in 1784.

The work by which Massie is best known, however, is *The Natural Rate of Interest* of 1750. This is a criticism of the proposition that the rate of interest depends upon the money supply. The development of Massie's thesis on the rate of interest is preceded in the tract by 17 quotations from writers holding the view that the rate of interest depends in some way upon the money supply. One of the quotations is from Petty's *Political Arithmetick* (Massie, 1750, p. 6; Petty, 1690, p. 99); all the rest are from Locke.[4] It is thus Locke who is the focus of Massie's critique.

For this, Massie's tract has come to be regarded as an important milestone in the development of economics. He is held to have anticipated Hume's position by two years, and to have laid the foundations for the development of the orthodox position that the rate of profit determines the rate of interest, and that monetary influences are only transitory, with any deviation of the rate of interest from the rate of profit being removed through consequent adjustments in the price level.

On closer examination, however, it becomes doubtful whether Massie is due so much credit. Firstly, he devoted a number of pages to arguing that, since the debt level in 1750 was much greater than in the 1690s, the level of the rate of interest should accordingly be much higher if Locke's theory were to be correct (Massie, 1750, pp. 16, 29, 31). This is doubly mistaken; not only did Locke treat the question of debt in relation to the rate of interest as a marginal special case, but he was writing about a sudden demand to honour

---

[4]The quotations are from pp. 7, 8, 8-9, 10, 13 (2), 24, 27-8, 28, 31, 34-5, 39, 43, 45-6, 56, 65 of the edition of Locke cited in this study. There are thus 16 quotations from Locke.

debt, not positing a relationship between the absolute level of outstanding debt and the rate of interest. Thus Massie's criticism seems to be directed at an argument which Locke never put forward.

Massie also gives a radical twist to Locke's argument that interest arises because of the unequal distribution of funds, arguing that dispersed sums would not constitute a supply of loanable funds because the interest payments would be too small in absolute size to persuade people to lend (Massie, pp. 23-4).[5]

Massie's fundamental argument is that the rate of interest depends not upon the money supply, but upon the rate of profit in the economy. It can fluctuate around the rate of profit, but that is its central value (Massie, pp. 17, 31). Pure interest is apparently the rate of interest charged on loans which are secured on land (Massie, p. 21).

This is, however, established not by reference to data on profit rates (which, as we shall see, would have posed formidable difficulties for Massie), and interest rates, but by reference to data which appeared to undermine the alternative hypothesis that the rate of interest depends on the money supply.

Massie's basic thesis may be summarised as follows. The price of wheat can be used as a price index. Over long periods its relative market value, as against other commodities, is very steady. This was actually an argument which Massie could have taken from Locke himself (Locke, pp. 39-40). At the same time, the price level, as measured by the absolute price of wheat, reflects in turn the money supply. Thirdly, data supplied by Massie, showing a falling price of wheat, must therefore indicate that the money supply had fallen over the same period. Fourthly, the rate of interest, Massie asserted,

---

[5] 'Much Borrowing and Lending among the Inhabitants of a Country, is not the Effect of a Want or Scarcity of Money, but of an unequal Distribution of it; when the Riches of a Country are collected into a few Hands, much borrowing naturally follows, for Affluence of Fortune induces most Men to think of Ease and Pleasure; to procure which, instead of employing their Money themselves, they must let it out to other People for them to make a Profit of, reserving for the Owners a Proportion of the Profits so made' (Massie, pp. 23-4).

had displayed a secular fall, and not risen as, with a falling money supply, it should have done according to the theory that the rate of interest depended on the money supply.

Having satisfied himself that such a theory could not be true, Massie then fell into a simple theoretical error. For he claimed that the rate of interest was determined by the opportunity cost of funds, which depended on the profit rate (Massie, pp. 47-8). But profit opportunity simply determined the demand for funds, not the market clearing rate of interest. Locke understood this perfectly well.

Massie had no data on profit; but he asserted that interest was equal to half gross profit (pp. 49-51), and felt confident that changes in profit rates explained variations in the rate of interest, not only across time but also across space, that is between different countries (Massie, p. 51).

He was certain that in Britain the rate of interest had declined secularly (Massie, pp. 51-2), a decline which he explained by increased competition at home and abroad which had in turn, he believed, depressed the profit rate.

His claim that the rate of interest had declined secularly quite rapidly assumed the status of a stylised fact in subsequent economic literature. Unfortunately, like most other stylised facts in economics, then as now, it was not true.

We can see this from a table which the late Graham Tucker discovered (Tucker, 1960, p. 31) and which had been carefully compiled from the records of a legal firm and published in a pamphlet of 1826. The original data give the number of mortgages at different interest rates in different years; and Tucker simply reproduced the data without interrogating them further.[6] However if a weighted average interest rate is calculated from the data provided in the table, as in table 4.1, it turns out that there is no strong evidence of a decline

---

[6]Indeed he asserted loosely that the table did indeed provide evidence of a decline in interest rates (Tucker, 1960, pp. 31-2).

Table 4.1: Interest Rates 1681-1752

Years	Weighted Mean of Interest Rates	
	Arithmetic Mean	Geometric Mean
1681-1690	5.19	5.18
1691-1710	4.95	4.94
1711-1718	5.12	5.10
1719-1732	4.95	4.95
1733-1742	4.45	4.44
1743-1752	4.47	4.45

Source: *Some Practical Remarks on the Effect of the Usury Laws on the Landed Interests, in a Letter to John Calcraft, Esq. M.P.* (1826). The table from which means are calculated is from Tucker (1960, p. 31).

in interest rates.[7] A half percentage point at most hardly represents the significant decline in interest rates over the years 1681-1752, that is between Locke's era and Massie's own, which Massie seems to have believed to have occurred (pp. 51-6).

Moreover, the interest rate seems to have remained steadily in the vicinity of 5 per cent for long periods. Richard Grassby has noted that charitable trusts were lending at 5.4 per cent between 1480 and 1660, and that merchants in the 1670s were lending at 5 per cent on mortgages (Grassby, 1969, pp. 740-1).

The interest rate assertions by Massie thus do not seem to be well founded. But the price calculations are also defective. Using the Schumpeter-Gilboy price index (Mitchell, 1962, p. 468), and taking 1697 as 100, we find the price level declining between 1690 and 1750 by approximately 5 percentage points. Yet Massie, confident in the accuracy of the price of wheat, as an index of the price level, records a 38 per cent fall between the 1686-1705 average and the 1729-1748 average.

---

[7]In view of the development of the stylised fact noted in the text, it is worth noting that there was no secular decline in interest rates after the date at which Massie published his pamphlet either. The data for the yield on consols (Mitchell, 1962, p. 455) show no evidence of a secular trend in a series running from 1756 onwards.

Table 4.2: Gold and Silver Coinage: Ten Year Annual Averages

Years	Gold (£000)	Silver (£000)	Total Coinage	Cumulative Total
1662-1671	91.23	131.53	222.76	222.76
1672-1681	244.74	196.04	440.78	663.54
1682-1691	334.90	68.97	403.87	1,067.41
1702-1711	100.20	19.25	119.45	1,186.86
1712-1721	776.13	7.27	783.40	1,970.26
1722-1731	341.81	18.53	360.34	2,330.60
1732-1741	297.47	4.36	341.07	2,671.97
1742-1751	287.29	16.63	303.92	2,975.59

Source: Calculated from Mitchell (1962, p. 439). Mitchell's table was compiled by Craig (1953, Appendix I).

Neither the interest rate claims nor the price calculations on which Massie relies are thus in fact reliable. Thirdly, it is evident that Massie's claim that the money supply had declined – and he had no data for this but was simply relying upon his erroneous price calculations and a simple quantity theory – was adrift as well. We do at least have data for gold and silver coinage (Table 4.2). If we take a ten year average of the figures (while ignoring the decade of the 1690s recoinage episode), and assume that, at least averaged over a decade, new coinage had a fairly stable relationship with the existing circulation, we find evidence strongly suggestive of an increasing money supply.[8] This is however hardly surprising; Massie's claim about a declining money supply must have been surprising to contemporaries familiar with the effects of the flow of precious metals from the New World. Indeed Hume, as we shall see, believed the money supply to have risen by 'much more' than four times, and the price level to have adjusted accordingly.

Thus every leg of Massie's critique is inadequate to support his conclusions. Finally, there is the essential meaninglessness of talking of a single

---

[8]Over the 89 years covered by Table 4.2, the cumulative coinage of nearly £3 million was an enormous sum, given Petty's estimate (1690, p. 110) that the total money supply required was only £6 million.

profit rate at all. It is evident from the detailed researches of Richard Grassby
that claims about the level of 'the' profit rate could have little basis in fact.
Profit rates were highly variable and, in terms of the loose accounting procedures of the time, poorly defined. The range for the majority of rates seems
to be about 4–25 per cent, with an overall range of 3–100 per cent (Grassby,
1969, pp. 722-4, 749-50). This is for the 17th century. After 1713, the
records are better. But again there is a very wide dispersion of profit rates.
They ranged from 3 per cent in the Wiltshire clothing trade to 25 per cent
in the Irish trade. As Grassby reports: 'there was no ascertainable rate of
return considered normal for all branches of business for any length of time'
(Grassby, 1969, p. 738).[9]

4.6 David Hume

Massie's attack upon Locke was on an empirical basis. Hume's, by contrast,
though containing some empirical claims, was essentially founded upon a
priori considerations.

Compared with Cantillon (1730), with his subtle consideration of different
channels of circulation, Hume pursues a very simplified approach. We begin
with an empirical statement – that the rate of interest has no direct connection with the supply of precious metals. If anything, comparison across
countries suggested that interest rates were higher in countries rich in gold
and silver. Since this was perfectly possible in terms of Locke's model, it
does not pose any particular problem. In any case, the claim related only to
differences over space, not over time, so it was hardly destructive of Locke's
model (Hume, 1752, p. 47).

---

[9]Mirowski (1982, pp. 182-3) feels able to dismiss the views of economic historians such
as Grassby, Pollard (1972) and Lee (1975) on 17th and 18th century accounting data.
However, what is interesting from the point of view of the present discussion is that the
profit data which he does present, for various sub-periods within the years 1728-1826,
again conflict with the stylised fact that profits were experiencing a secular decline. On
this evidence, at least, they were not.

Hume also asserted that 'An effect always holds proportion with its cause. Prices have risen near four times since the discovery of the INDIES; and it is probable gold and silver have multiplied much more: But interest has not fallen much above half. The rate of interest, therefore, is not derived from the quantity of the precious metals' (Hume, p. 48).

This single paragraph contains a remarkable collection of empirical claims. Firstly, we begin with a claim of proportionate effect for which Hume could have had no basis. Secondly, his statement about prices – for which he gives no authority – is inaccurate, as we have seen above. Thirdly, though we do not have figures for gold and silver, the coinage figures in Table 4.2 would not support Hume, any more than they support Massie, though admittedly Hume is protected by writing about a longer (and undefined) period. Finally, his statement about the rate of interest, as we saw from Table 4.1, is also inaccurate.

Hume's own theory of interest is essentially bound up with his theory of economic development. High interest results from a large demand for borrowing, great profits from commerce, and little supply of loanable funds ('riches' as Hume ambiguously calls them). Hume believed that in the early stages of economic development there were more borrowers, in relation to the supply of 'riches', than at later stages. This was because it was only in later stages that a merchant class, which was not only frugal but a source of loanable funds out of the fruits of that frugality, developed. Once this merchant class had become established, competition between lenders would lower the rate of interest; at the same time, the results of the investments made with the loanable funds would, through the development of competition in the product market and the progressive exhaustion of investment opportunities (this at least is the sense of Hume's allusive discussion), lower the rate of profit (Hume, pp. 49-55).

Hume did accept that changes in the money supply could have a transitory effect upon the rate of interest (pp. 57-8) – and this recognition was to be carried over into the corpus of classical economics, like his fundamental thesis. But such monetary effects were only transitory.

Hume's attack upon the Lockean theory of interest is fundamentally distinct from that of Massie. On the one hand, Massie believed the money supply to have fallen: Hume believed it to have increased more than fourfold. Yet both believed that his own account of the money supply behaviour – neither account being accurate – supported his argument. Secondly, Massie, who was not a theorist, has the simple proposition that the rate of interest is equal to the profit rate, or is at least determined by it. Hume, on the other hand, has a loanable funds theory, with the rate of interest determined by the supply of, and demand for, loans.

Neither critique seems, on its own, convincing. The irony is that it was not Massie's defective empiricism, nor Hume's dubious combination of empirical claims and a priorism, which destroyed the Locke case, as far as Hume's successors were concerned. What really proved damaging were two other essays by Hume, those on money and on the balance of payments. In these two essays, Hume produced a convincing argument that, under a metallic standard, the beneficial effects on economic activity of increasing the money supply could only be transitory. He accepted that, in the short term, an inflow of money would stimulate economic activity (Hume, p. 37). Once the price level had adjusted to the new money supply, however, the balance of payments constraint would ensure that the increase in the money supply would again flow out over the balance of payments, returning the money supply to its original level (Hume, p. 63). Thus, so long as a metallic currency was involved, there was no scope for stimulating economic activity in the long term through seeking to increase the money supply. International equilibrium would be restored. It was indeed precisely an understanding of this – forty-seven years before Hume – which led John Law to advocate a paper currency.

4.7   Conclusions

Locke's analysis of changes in the money supply, and the concomitant effects on economic activity and the rate of interest, was subtle, and contained many insights which, under a different kind of monetary regime, would have provided understanding of the operation of the development of an economy from a low level.[10] But what Locke failed to incorporate into his theoretical framework was a mechanism explaining the operation of the balance of payments under a metallic currency. While he is wrongly credited with being an early – even the first – formulator of the quantity theory, it is ironic that it was precisely price level effects which Locke failed to incorporate into his model, and which led to its virtual obliteration from 1752 onwards, with the publication of Hume's *Political Discourses*. However, the mechanisms which Locke envisaged were still of considerable interest in understanding the operation of a developing monetary economy.

---

[10] At the Revolution of 1688, national income for the United Kingdom (including Ireland) was probably only about £48m, and the population slightly over 9 million.

Part III

19th Century British Controversies

Chapter 5

The Currency and Banking Controversy

This chapter is about the conduct of monetary policy in an economy which is characterised by repeated departures from long-run equilibrium values of the price level and of output. It seeks to demonstrate that the very nature of the response to a departure from equilibrium is of central importance in determining the magnitude ultimately achieved by that departure. This was a matter which was of fundamental concern to those engaged in the Currency and Banking controversy of the mid-19th century which led to – but was by no means extinguished by – the introduction of the Bank Charter Act of 1844 which imposed upon the monetary system a form of monetary response to disturbance which was deliberately designed to act counter-cyclically.

Mark Blaug (1995) identified three interrelated propositions as making up the quantity theory of money. The first is that causality runs from the money supply to the price level. The second is that there is a stable demand for money balances, implying, in turn, a stable velocity of circulation. This does not of course mean that the demand for balances is completely fixed; simply that if it changes, it must do so in a predictable way. It can in fact change not only in response to financial innovation over time but also – as envisaged by Overstone, the key member of the Currency School – in response to changes in publicly available information about the central bank. Overstone envisaged an increase in precautionary balances held by both the non-bank private sector and the commercial banking sector as the reserves of the central bank – the Bank of England – were seen to fall, thus limiting – under the Act of 1844 – the power of the Bank to act as lender of last resort. Thirdly, Mark Blaug identified the determination of a volume of output as being independent of the quantity of money. However, this last certainly does not mean that the level of output is necessarily fixed – though this is certainly the interpretation of the independence of output from the money supply which became the standard one in the second half of the 20th century and which has become ever more standardised as a result of the routine employment of mathematical modelling. As we shall see, in the 19th century, an inbuilt trade cycle, with output varying according to a regular pattern over time, was an accepted idea, and this acceptance (although this is not documented in the present chapter) extended far beyond the Currency School to whose position it was central. Moreover, as we shall see, the economic data for the period clearly suggest, as later research by economic historians has demonstrated, the reasonableness of the belief in a trade cycle.

The 19th century debate has relevance for any world in which there are underlying disturbances in the 'real' part of the economy. For such disturbances raise the question of the proper monetary stance to be employed in the face of varying demands for money. In addition it throws light on the dangers – highlighted by recent 'free banking' reinterpretations of the Currency and Banking controversy – of concentrating on long-run equilibrium values while ignoring short-run disturbances and the need to damp these disturbances if possible. This brings us to the basic theme of the chapter.

The basic theme of this chapter is straightforward. It is that although there are long-run equilibrium values of monetary variables, and of price and income levels, the existence of these in no way justifies ignoring the analysis of the correct response to short-run disturbances which move these variables away from their long-run values. To do so is to ignore the essential question, widely recognised in other contexts, of whether a disturbance from equilibrium results in positive or negative feedback.

To ignore this question is to engage in one of Ricardo's less-recognised vices. The Ricardian Vice made famous by Schumpeter was to turn theory into tautology. As Schumpeter put it:

> The comprehensive vision of the universal interdependence of all the elements of the economic system that haunted Thünen probably never cost Ricardo as much as an hour's sleep. His interest was in the clear-cut result of direct, practical significance. In order to get this he cut that general system to pieces, bundled up as large parts of it as possible, and put them in cold storage – so that as many things as possible should be frozen and 'given.' He then piled one simplifying assumption upon another until, having really settled everything by these assumptions, he was left with only a few aggregative variables between which, given these assumptions, he set up simple one-way relations so that, in the end, the desired results emerged almost as tautologies. (Schumpeter, 1954, pp. 472-3)

However, this was by no means Ricardo's only vice. Ricardo (whose private life was, to the best of my knowledge, blameless) had another vice which may be called the 'Ricardian telescope'. An example of this is the proposition that a tax on wages would be passed on and be paid out of profits. Ricardo's main justification for this belief was that, with wages at subsistence, there was no scope for depressing wages by taxation.[1] But the justification for his belief that the tax would be passed on involved a long process of population adjustment, when wages were pushed below subsistence by taxation, so that only in the long run would a tax be passed on. Yet

---

[1] His alternative mechanism – government spending the proceeds of such a tax entirely on demand for labour – need not detain us in this context.

Ricardo habitually concentrated on the long-run equilibrium position and ignored the process of adjustment. Economists who concentrate only upon the relationship between the long-run equilibrium values of macroeconomic variables are guilty of the vice of employing the Ricardian telescope.

The basic thesis in this chapter is illustrated by reference to classical monetary controversies: but there are much wider lessons, including some applicable to the misnamed 'monetarist' view of the exchange rate mechanism of the European Monetary System (ERM). According to this view the immediate imposition of what are deemed to be long-run equilibrium parities − leaving aside the question of the determination of such parities − is held to justify neglect of the adjustment of the monetary, price, and output variables of the participating economies to these long-run values.

The discussion is organised as follows. Section 5.1 begins with an examination of the meaning of long-run equilibrium for an open economy possessing a currency made up of gold and of notes convertible into gold. Section 5.2 examines the illegitimate use of the concept of long-run equilibrium to deny the validity of the investigation of the stability of adjustment processes. This is followed in section 5.3 by an examination of real cyclical disturbances within the economy, which are endogenous to the system as a whole though exogenous as far as the monetary system is concerned. Given the nature of these disturbances, the next question explored is the proper response to such disturbances on the part of the monetary authorities. This in turn raises the question, examined in section 5.4, of precisely what it is that the monetary authorities are seeking to control − which turns out to be by no means straightforward. It is argued that controlling the wrong monetary aggregate could, and did, produce macroeconomic disaster. In section 5.5 the conclusion is drawn that while long-run values are not irrelevant, the question of positive or negative feedback to equilibrium, once disturbed, is critical. The chapter is complemented by chapter 10, which explores the mathematical aspects of the stability question.

5.1 The Nature of Long-Run Equilibrium

Long-run equilibrium of the price level was determined in the classical literature by two factors – the international price of gold and domestic factor productivity. This was clearly explained by Nassau Senior in his *Three Lectures
on the Cost of Obtaining Money* (1830). In these lectures, Senior explained
that the general price level of a country, covering both goods and factor
services, depended upon the price of gold and the productivity of factors
engaged in exporting. The higher that productivity, the greater the capacity
to produce an inflow of gold through an export surplus. The inflow of gold
would continue until the price level had risen to the point where the balance
of payments was once again in equilibrium. It was this which explained the
high level of wages in England compared with other countries. The fixed
price of gold in terms of domestically issued currency would ensure that, *in
long-run equilibrium*, the money supply was endogenous – it was that money
supply implied by the need for the balance of payments to be in equilibrium
in the long run with given relative factor productivity:

> [L]abour in England is eight times as productive of exportable
> commodities as in Hindostan, and labour in North America is
> one-fourth more productive of exportable commodities than in
> England. (1830, p. 12)

> [T]he wages obtained by the labourers, in return for whose labour
> the precious metals are imported, ... regulate the wages of all
> other labourers in the same country [and] ... the price, or, in other
> words, the value in gold and silver of all those commodities which
> are not the subjects of a monopoly, [depends] ... in a country not
> possessing mines, on the gold and silver which can be obtained by
> exporting the result of a given quantity of labour[,] the current
> rate of profit, and, in each individual case, the amount of the

wages which have been paid, and the time for which they have
been advanced. (1830, pp. 13-14)

Unfortunately a series of misunderstandings about this proposition –
including a disregard of the role of factor productivity – seems to have
arisen. Prominent among these misunderstandings is the idea that because
the money supply is *in the long run* endogenous, short-run exogenously-
induced changes (for instance resulting from a change in banking structure)
can be disregarded. Thus the existence of this long-run equilibrium has been
used to defend the Banking School of the mid-19th century and to argue
that Tooke and Fullarton were correct to be unconcerned about monetary
disturbances, *as long as* the currency was convertible into gold. This argument is also linked to the work of those, especially Gilbart, that the modern
Free Banking School would claim as forerunners, even though Gilbart, in
particular, was only concerned to defend free competitive issue and certainly
considered that the Bank of England could bring about a monetary crisis –
as indeed White (1984, pp. 73-4) makes clear.

These misunderstandings have their origin in a model originally put forward by Thompson (1974). This model is re-expounded by Glasner (1985,
1989) to produce an account of classical monetary theory which is hard to
recognise.[2] If we were to assume – which the classical writers, correctly,
did not – that the Law of One Price holds *at all times*, like many modern
monetary models of the balance of payments, it then becomes possible to
contend not merely that the Banking School were always right, but even
that the Wicksellian case (with the bank lending rate below the marginal
rate of profit leading to an upward spiral of inflation) is impossible – indeed
it even becomes possible to claim that Say's *Identity* is valid in a *monetary*

---

[2]The model used by Glasner (1985, 1989) is simply one of a money market clearing,
with demand for money a function of the price level and the net interest cost of balances,
the price level in turn being determined by the price of gold which is unlikely to be affected
by the domestic economy. There is no goods market.

economy. Most remarkable of all, it makes possible the assertion that the Currency School (as well as Hume and the Bullionists) were wrong in using a quantity theory approach, because the quantity theory could not operate in a world in which the price level of a country was determined by world prices. It should hardly be necessary to emphasise that long-run determination of the price level by the exchange rate of the domestic currency with gold is entirely compatible with monetary disturbances which move the economy away from long-run equilibrium and which are validly analysed by a model in which changes in the money supply affect the price level. It is of course not necessary to deny that output changes can also take place; I have argued elsewhere that Joplin's model can be well represented by a model of the neo-Keynesian type, though one rather more complex than that to be found in the textbooks; see O'Brien (1993) and chapter 9 below.

Although some of these misunderstandings undoubtedly have their origin in enthusiasts for free banking who wish to find historical predecessors, another source of misunderstanding is the simplification employed in modern (especially textbook) models of the monetary approach to the balance of payments. Here, typically, we find written

$$P_h = SP_f \tag{5.1}$$

where P_h is the home price level, P_f is the foreign price level and S is the spot exchange rate – in this context, the price of gold.

This is coupled with the assumption that because S is fixed under convertibility $\bar{Q} = \frac{P_h}{SP_f}$ where $\bar{Q}$ is the constant real exchange rate. Such models thus typically assume purchasing power parity and a constant real exchange rate. This enables the home price level to be treated as given and fixed. Given S (the price of gold), P_f (exogenous) *and* a constant real exchange rate $\bar{Q}$, P_h is indeed determined tautologically. It thus becomes possible to argue that banking competition will accommodate the money supply to this fixed price level.

But this is a good deal too simple for a world in which policy decisions have to be taken, and the classical economists understood this very well. Although Ricardo's reputation as a monetary theorist stands considerably higher, perhaps, than it deserves, he did put this essential matter very well:

> Gold and silver having been chosen for the general medium of circulation, they are, by the competition of commerce, distributed in such proportions amongst the different countries of the world, as to accommodate themselves to the natural traffic which would take place if no such metals existed, and the trade between countries were purely a trade of barter. (1817, p. 137)

This of course is a statement of long-run equilibrium. Note that it does not rule out short-run deviations from that equilibrium. As Ricardo put it in *The High Price of Bullion*:

> It is only after a comparison of the value in their markets and in our own, of gold and other commodities, and because gold is cheaper in the London market than in theirs, that foreigners prefer gold in exchange for their corn. If we diminish the quantity of currency, we give an additional value to it: this will induce them to alter their election, and prefer the commodities. (1810, p. 62)

It is particularly noteworthy that Adam Smith, who is credited by the advocates of free banking with the above propositions, actually wrote quite explicitly that different countries would have different price levels – and was criticised by Ricardo for this because Smith extended the argument to cover corn, which Ricardo believed would indeed have a single uniform price internationally, based on the cost of production in its cheapest source, in the event of free trade being adopted. For Smith wrote:

Gold and silver, like all other commodities, naturally seek the market where the best price is given for them, and the best price is commonly given for every thing in the country which can best afford it. Labour, it must be remembered, is the ultimate price which is paid for every thing, and in countries where labour is equally well rewarded, the money price of labour will be in proportion to that of the subsistence of the labourer. But gold and silver will naturally exchange for a greater quantity of subsistence in a rich than in a poor country, in a country which abounds with subsistence, than in one which is but indifferently supplied with it. If the two countries are at a great distance, the difference may be very great; because though the metals naturally fly from the worse to the better market, yet it may be difficult to transport them in such quantities as to bring their price nearly to a level in both. If the countries are near, the difference will be smaller, and may sometimes be scarce perceptible; because in this case the transportation will be easy. China is a much richer country than any part of Europe, and the difference between the price of subsistence in China and in Europe is very great. Rice in China is much cheaper than wheat is any where in Europe. England is a much richer country than Scotland; but the difference between the money-price of corn in those two countries is much smaller, and is but just perceptible. (1776, book I, chapter xi, part e, para. 34)

Moreover, Smith took explicit account of a point which was later to be central to Senior's *Three Lectures* – differences in real wages:

The difference between the money price of labour in China and in Europe, is still greater than that between the money price of subsistence; because the real recompence of labour is higher in

Europe, than in China, the greater part of Europe being in an improving state, while China seems to be standing still. The money price of labour is lower in Scotland than in England because the real recompence of labour is much lower; Scotland, though advancing to greater wealth, advances much more slowly than England. The frequency of emigration from Scotland, and the rarity of it from England, sufficiently prove that the demand for labour is very different in the two countries. The proportion between the real recompence of labour in different countries, it must be remembered, is naturally regulated, not by their actual wealth or poverty, but by their advancing, stationary, or declining condition. (1776, book I, chapter xi, part e, para. 35)

It is true, as Jacob Viner has noted, that Ricardo's stress upon a uniform price of corn internationally, in the presence of free trade, 'bears a superficial relationship to Cassel's so-called purchasing-parity theory' (1937, p. 126n); but, as Viner points out, Ricardo is talking about *particular prices of identical transportable commodities*' which, indeed, 'makes this part of his reasoning a truism if transportation costs and tariffs are abstracted from' (ibid.). It does not imply general purchasing power parity. Viner's critique of purchasing power parity (1937, pp. 379-87) is a penetrating one; and without rehearsing his objections here, it is clear that he quite rightly objected to attributing what he believed to be an erroneous theory to the classical writers. As Viner wrote:

It is easy to conceive ... of changes in cost or demand conditions or both, in one or the other countries, or both, which so changed the relative demands of the two countries for each other's products in terms of their own as to bring about an enduring and substantial relative change in their levels of prices, including the prices of domestic commodities and services, even under the gold standard. (1937, p. 381)

A simple diagrammatic analysis can be used to demonstrate this point although – in classical style – only two commodities are involved and these will be used to represent the general price level in each of the two countries specialising in them. In Figure 5.1 the opportunity costs for wine and cloth for England and Portugal are shown and in Figure 5.2 these are translated into relative prices, in the style of Ricardo's own analysis. In Figure 5.3 the related reciprocal demand curves demonstrate the equilibrium terms of trade and these are shown in Figure 5.4, where the national price lines have moved to intersect. The relative price is given by the slope of the line PW_1EC_1. An increased English demand for wine in Figure 5.3 then shifts the terms of trade from OT_1 to OT_2, and this is reflected in Figure 5.5, where the relative prices of wine and cloth, reflecting the exports of Portugal and England respectively, have changed so that wine (representing Portugal's price level) has risen in value compared with cloth (representing England's price level). The relative price is now given by the slope of the line PW_2EC_2. The change from OT_1 to OT_2 (and from PW_1EC_1 to PW_2EC_2) is *a change in the real exchange rate* for which the resuscitated Banking School model makes no provision.

If the reader finds this point being laboured rather excessively, it is only because such a conclusion, which would have been commonplace to a previous generation, is denied in the free-banking inspired literature. As representative of this we have the propositions that:

1. 'The price level in any country was fixed by the internationally determined value of the metal' (Glasner, 1989, p. 261);

2. 'With the value of precious metals unchanged, the price level, under a metallic standard, would not change either' (Glasner, p. 263);

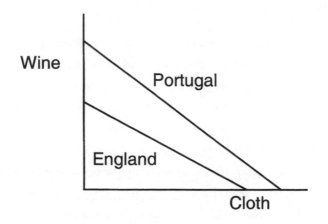

Figure 5.1: Opportunity Costs of Wine and Cloth

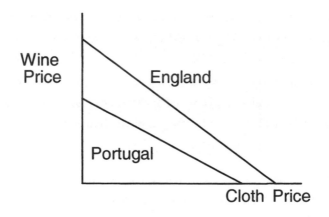

Figure 5.2: Relative Prices of Wine and Cloth

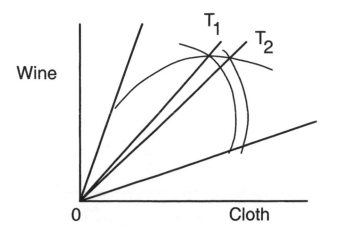

Figure 5.3: Terms of Trade Before and After a Demand Shift

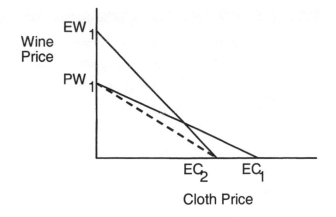

Figure 5.4: Real Exchange Rate

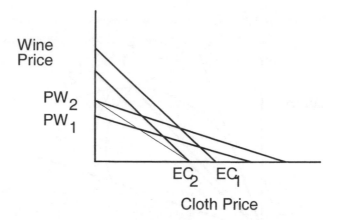

Figure 5.5: Real Exchange Rate After Demand Shift

3. Adam Smith rejected the price-specie-flow mechanism 'because it in-
   correctly applied the quantity theory to determine the price level of a
   country with a metallic currency. A national price level depends on
   the international value of the metal used as money, not the quantity of
   money in the country' (Glasner, 1989, p. 264);

and so on. Indeed it does seem that the free-banking re-interpretation
of classical monetary theory is based upon the proposition that, under all
normal circumstances, a constant real exchange will exist – and Senior is
chided 'for failing to see that national price levels could not vary under a
gold standard' (Glasner, 1985, p. 288).

From this it is clear that the combined confusion of assuming purchasing power parity and instantaneous adjustment to long-run equilibrium, in
defence of the free banking school, has produced some distinctly curious results. Against the charge of concentration on long-run equilibrium, Glasner
attempts to invoke Samuelson's (1980) model in which 'prices for all goods are
perfectly arbitraged across markets' (p. 265) which is, of course, something
which would never occur during an adjustment period, if it ever occurred

at all. In fact, as a recent paper examining the operation of the 19th century gold standard has shown, prices (of goods in terms of gold) were not equalised (Moosa, 1993).[3]

5.2 The Need for Monetary Control

The core part of the position advanced in this chapter is that if there are endogenous disturbances, inherent in the normal progress of economic activity through time, we *must* have a theory of monetary control.

The Currency School recognised this very well. Indeed Overstone was one of the very first authors to put forward the idea of an endogenous trade cycle. His description is well known. In his first published work, *Reflections Suggested by a Perusal of Mr. J. Horsley Palmer's Pamphlet on the Causes and Consequences of the Pressure on the Money Market* (1837), Overstone wrote:

> The history of what we are in the habit of calling the 'state of trade' is an instructive lesson. We find it subject to various conditions which are periodically returning; it revolves apparently in an established cycle. First we find it in a state of quiescence,

---

[3]Nor – despite persistent misconceptions to the contrary – is it necessary for price *equalisation* to exist, for the gold standard mechanism to correct the balance of payments. Indeed, as the quotation from Viner in the text would indicate, one would not expect purchasing power parity – merely the adjustment of relative price levels to the point at which reciprocal demand would bring payments into balance. But the adjustment mechanism is all that is required for the present argument; it is, as noted by Samuelson (1980), put forward by Viner and Haberler. Unfortunately, Samuelson simply dismisses their argument and assumes price equality in order to put forward a version of the modern 'monetary' theory of the balance of payments. It should hardly be necessary to emphasise that one set of assumptions can not invalidate an alternative set of assumptions. However, even Samuelson's model (1980, p. 150) does not require complete purchasing power parity *at all times*, and he contrives to allow for changes in the real exchange rate. These occur (1980, p. 149) because as relative money supplies (rather than price levels) are adjusted in two countries, via the balance of payments, the country increasing outlay may spend more on the good in which the other country has a comparative advantage, while the country reducing outlay may cut down on its consumption of the exports of the other country.

> – next improvement, – growing confidence, – prosperity, – ex-
> citement, – overtrading, – convulsion, – pressure, – stagnation, –
> distress, – ending again in quiescence. (1837, p. 31)

The existence of this pattern of underlying disturbance necessitated the
development of a theory of monetary control. In his *Second Letter to J.B.
Smith* (1840), Overstone wrote:

> Speaking practically, I am inclined to think that fluctuations in
> prices will in most cases be found to originate in some predis-
> posing circumstances; and that fluctuations in the circulation act
> 'as a subordinate agent', increasing or diminishing the force of
> those predisposing circumstances, and accelerating or retarding
> the rapidity of their action. (1840b, p. 204)

Prices would themselves change without monetary causes; but the monetary causes could magnify or diminish the inherent fluctuations:

> Prosperity will generate excess, over-trading and over-production
> will cause a fall of prices, accompanied by temporary depression
> and despondency; this fall of prices will, in turn, check produc-
> tion, increase consumption, augment the exports, cause the pre-
> cious metals to return to the country, the quantity of money will
> be thus increased, prices will again rise, and the country will in
> the end find itself very far removed from the verge of utter bank-
> ruptcy. Such is the 'constant rotation of the unwearied wheel that
> Nature rides upon'. (letter of 1862, quoted in O'Brien, 1971, p.
> 64)

Monetary control, as envisaged by Overstone, involved damping the endogenous cycle through counter-cyclical monetary movements. This was indeed the 'currency' principle, as contrasted with the 'banking' principle, ac-

cording to which the money supply expanded and contracted with the supposed 'needs of trade'. The key flaw in the latter position was that the 'needs of trade' were not independent of the price level, and that price level could change, not only because of the price level changes inherent in the inbuilt cycle but also because of monetary changes if these were allowed to magnify the price effects of the cycle. This is why it is crucially important to avoid the fallacy that the price level was fixed by long-run equilibrium considerations.

The control mechanisms envisaged by Overstone were of three kinds. Firstly, and most importantly, there was control of the high powered monetary base (as Overstone envisaged it) in the form of Bank of England notes and thus (it was hoped) control of the total means of payment. Secondly, there was a role for the rate of interest, which could not only be used to signify to the market the need to alter precautionary balances but which could also reduce demand for discounts at the Bank, thus reducing the high powered money base. Thirdly, there was the device which I have called elsewhere the 'information-velocity-of-circulation' mechanism (O'Brien, 1975, pp. 156-7; O'Brien, 1971, p. 129). This was the provision that weekly publication of the state of the Bank of England reserves would indicate whether it was necessary to increase precautionary balances and thus contract aggregate demand. A falling reserve would indeed indicate that this was the case.

Overstone's vision of an endogenous trade cycle was highly influential. Indeed it was followed by Marshall (Laidler, 1990, p. 59; O'Brien, 1990, pp. 136, 147), who had a marked personal copy of Overstone's *Tracts*. But this is hardly surprising; there was a very good basis for such a belief. Although attempts to find an 18th century cycle do not seem to have been successful (Klein, 1992) the evidence from 19th century data seems clear enough. There are indeed major studies of 19th century economic fluctuations which appear to follow a cyclical pattern. According to J.R.T. Hughes, whose study covers the years 1848-60, 'The cycle itself was an important variable among the several determinants of the course of British economic expansion during the

1850's' (1960, pp. 27-8). He identifies significant price fluctuations involved in this process. Thus, for instance, in 1848 'Most prices were down sharply from 1847, e.g. pig iron prices averaged some 40 per cent. lower than in 1847 and English wool prices were down by roughly 30 per cent.' Data suggestive of cyclical movements in an earlier period (1833-1842) are also to be found in Matthews (1954, especially pp. 202-224). The most comprehensive study is that of Gayer, Rostow and Schwartz (1953), covering the years 1790-1850. This, like the later Hughes study, contains material on significant price fluctuations, and also notes significant changes in unemployment (a phenomenon of which some 19th century economists, especially Joplin, were only too well aware).

This evidence is interesting not only as a key assumption of Overstone's analysis, at a time when – the studies of Tooke and Newmarch (1838-57) apart – the macroeconomic evidence was limited, but also as a salutary warning against reliance upon models of long-run equilibrium in macroeconomic matters.

5.3 Macroeconomic Management of Disturbances

Given the nature of the macroeconomic disturbances, cyclical in nature with both price and output changing, the question arises of the proper response of a monetary authority that wishes to dampen macroeconomic fluctuations. If we consider the classical literature we find some clear divisions. The two most important of these are (i) the nature of the relevant monetary aggregate and (ii) the kind of feedback required for the control mechanism. Since it is the latter which is of the greater theoretical interest, let us deal with that first. In this context there is a vital distinction, *whatever* the monetary aggregate, between two approaches – the Currency approach and the Banking approach already mentioned.

The matter was explained clearly by George Warde Norman – a Bank Director for more than 50 years and also a critic of the conduct of the Bank in the 1830s – in his *Letter to Charles Wood* (1841). Norman explained that the principles upon which a banker would supply notes were different from the principles upon which a metallic currency would operate – the *currency* principle:

> When the prices of goods rise or when there is a struggle in progress against an impending fall of prices, the customers of a banker usually call upon him for increased assistance, which it is difficult for him to refuse, but if at the same time interest rises, the prospect of enlarging his profit is an additional inducement for him to enlarge his advances, and to aid his banking resources by an augmentation of his circulation. Now a rise in prices frequently precedes an unfavourable state of the exchanges, and a struggle against a fall of prices, and an advance in the rate of interest, are its ordinary concomitants. Thus we see that the first stages of an export of treasure are generally characterised by circumstances, which tend to cause an augmentation in the amount of bank-notes, while with a metallic currency they would necessarily be accompanied by a reduction in the circulation .... Thus, then, we see that upon our present system there is and must be a strong tendency in our circulation, which is regulated upon banking in opposition to currency principles, to increase and decrease precisely at those periods when it ought naturally to decrease and increase. (1841, pp. 29-31)

Thus the question is whether monetary control would be pro-cyclical or anti-cyclical. Pro-cyclical monetary control would amplify the fluctuations in prices (and indeed in output, since the classical economists did not rigidly assume output to be at all times fixed at full employment) inherent in the economic system by accommodating the 'needs of trade'. By contrast, the anti-cyclical policy would seek to damp those fluctuations by operating counter-cyclically. In the upswing, as the balance of payments weakened and then went into deficit, the rate of growth of the money supply would be at first slowed and then reversed; in the downswing, the opposite would apply. Thus the amplitude of fluctuations would be reversed.

In the pro-cyclical case, the economy will *eventually* be forced into conformity with long-run equilibrium values – but wide fluctuations from those long-run equilibrium values will be inherent in the case because of *positive* feedback from disturbances to the money supply. By contrast, in the anti-cyclical case, departure from long-run values will be minimised because the feedback from disturbance to the money supply will be *negative*.

The understanding of the distinction between these two cases hinges on a clear, and perfectly legitimate, application of the quantity theory of money to explain the price implications. At the same time this is only a first approximation, because it is recognised that the economic dislocation resulting from the fact that goods markets adjust more slowly than financial markets will result in *real* dislocation. Another way of looking at the distinction between the Currency and Banking principles is to view it as a distinction between rules and discretion. This is because at some point the reality of long-run equilibrium values will force even the adherents of the Banking principle into discretionary action. This was indeed recognised by the leading member of the Banking School, Thomas Tooke, who proposed that the Bank of England should hold a gold reserve of between £10 million and £15 million and that it should avoid taking contractionary action on a discretionary basis, only pursuing monetary contraction if the reserve, starting at £15 million, fell below £10 million (1840, pp. 187, 252-8; 1844, pp. 107-120). The Currency School sought to link the money supply *automatically* to the balance of payments while the Banking School relied on discretion to avert the catastrophe of a sustained departure from long-run equilibrium values, resulting in the suspension of convertibility. But in neither case – and this is highly relevant, given that the modern advocates of free banking cite the members of the Banking School as their forerunners – does the existence of a long-run equilibrium remove the necessity for some kind of theory of monetary control to ensure that convertibility – which is essentially a guarantee of eventual conformity with that long-run equilibrium – is maintained.

Some of those associated with the free banking literature apparently believe – like the Bullionists during the era of inconvertibility, whose belief was to be falsified by the experiences of the 1820s and 1830s – that the incentive structure associated with convertibility would be sufficient to prevent overissue, and indeed to ensure the maintenance of convertibility itself.[4] But, as practical bankers, both Norman and Overstone understood clearly enough the incentives and profit opportunities facing an issuing banker. Any attempt by the Bank of England to tighten the money supply would, at least in the first instance, generate incentives for other issuers to undermine this tightening:

> When the central issuer contracts his issue, the effect is felt, principally, perhaps, but not exclusively, in the circle which immediately surrounds that centre; a scarcity of money and a pressure upon trade is felt throughout the country. The local issuer, in the first instance, meets this, not by a corresponding contraction, but by an increase of his issues. He is induced to resort to

---

[4]The Thompson model itself is of a strange world in which, in a naive short-run optimisation framework with zero profits earned by perfectly competitive bankers, *holders* of money are paid 'competitive interest' *by* bankers. Since this has no corresponding element in the world inhabited by Tooke, Fullarton, *et al.*, Thompson then feels free to argue that (*long run*) appreciation of the gold into which bank notes were convertible constituted such an implied interest (1974, pp. 441-2n). But the appreciation of gold during the period that he cites (though he uses the dates 1775-1850, this is hardly admissable since it includes a long period of *inconvertible* paper currency in the years 1797 to 1819-21, and only the years 1821-50 can really be considered) was nowhere near the competitive rate of interest (the implied rate of interest is approximately 0.5 per cent, whereas market rates were typically between 2.8 and 5 per cent). Moreover the argument involves neglect of the fact that, as subsequently established by Jevons, gold *fell* significantly in value after 1850.

this course by several considerations; first, such increase of his issues is a ready relief to himself, under the tightness of money, (to use the common expression,) which the action of the central issuer has produced; second, it enables him to extend his accommodation to his customers, at a time when it is most wanted, and the tender of it is most valued; third, it affords him some probability that he may be enabled to occupy permanently with his issue, that portion of the circulation, at least in his immediate neighbourhood, which has hitherto been filled by the notes of the central issuer. These are not mere theoretic suppositions; we have little doubt that these motives are constantly in action, and exerting a practical influence over the conduct of the country issuers. They explain that phenomenon, the constant occurrence of which is proved by the published returns, viz. an increase of country issues, immediately following the commencement of the drain of bullion, and the first contraction of the central issuer. (Overstone, 1840a, p. 99)

Having dealt with the correct means of control, let us now look at the matter of the relevant aggregate.

5.4   The Monetary Aggregate

The position of the Currency School on monetary control was clear cut. What was to be controlled was bank notes. The position may be summarised as follows. The Bank of England, through its note issue, supplied the high powered money base for the monetary system; and thus control of the Bank of England note issue provided strategic control of the total means of payment. But the Bank of England was by no means the sole issuer of bank notes. The Currency School believed that ultimately the country banks would have to submit to the leverage of the monetary base but that they were capable, because they issued according to the Banking Principle, of an inappropriate pro-cyclical monetary stance which would only be overcome in the long run. It was thus necessary to limit their issue by direct action – and limits were thus imposed, in the Bank Act of 1844, on the issues of the country banks. Overstone put the matter like this:

> When, however, the central issuer, by a steady prosecution of his system of contraction, has produced, not only the numerical re-duction of his notes, but the more important moral results which are evidenced by the shock given to confidence and credit; ... then the country issuer, in common with all parties engaged in monied or commercial operations, submits to this influence; and in pro-portion that his first steps had been in the wrong direction, so his subsequent retreat is sudden and rapid. .... the country banks of issue first resist, then suffer, and, in the end, submit. (1840a, pp. 99-101)

In taking this position the Currency School had advanced significantly beyond the point taken by the majority of the Bullionists in an earlier con-troversy when they argued that differences in the price level between 'Lon-don' and the 'Country' would be sufficient to ensure that the country bank issues were controlled by those of the Bank of England. In fact however the Currency School were much too optimistic. Testing the hypothesis that the country bank note issue, whatever the lag structure involved, was dependent upon either the Bank of England note issue, or even upon total liabilities of the Bank, results in resounding falsification.[5] There seems a very strong case for accepting the view of Thomas Joplin that the Currency School were

---

[5]I have estimated equations with a whole variety of lags, seeking to explain both levels of, and changes in, the country bank note issue, by reference to Bank of England notes, Bank of England deposits and Bank of England total liabilities. Without exception, the coefficients on the explanatory variables are insignificant, once the form of estimation used incorporates a correction for the serial correlation which dogs OLS estimation; see chapter 6 below.

directing their attention entirely to the wrong note issue. Joplin argued convincingly (O'Brien, 1993) that the note issue of the country banks was what was relevant for the vast majority of transactions in goods and services; that failure to control the note issue of the country banks was at the root of the monetary control failures of the 1830s; and that reductions in the note issue of the Bank of England, when the Bank was losing gold as a result of a balance of payments deficit, simply produced a liquidity crisis in the London money market (because the notes of the Bank were a reserve asset in that market) without affecting the price level of goods and services which depended upon the country bank note issue.

Of course, this still left open the matter of bank deposits. Torrens (within the Currency School – Torrens, 1837; pp. 6-19; 1844, pp. 9-22) and Joplin and Pennington (both outside it – Joplin, 1841; O'Brien, 1993, p. 115; Sayers, 1963, pp. xiv-xv) expounded the concept of a deposit multiplier, and Torrens was inclined to accept that deposits were, to all intents and purposes, money (though Overstone intervened forcefully to prevent him from endorsing publicly the proposition that deposits *were* money – O'Brien, 1971, 2, pp. 713-17). But reserve ratios were not fixed, so that even control of *all* note issue would not control the total means of payment, including deposits. The Currency School members were uncomfortably aware of this but felt that, since deposits were uncontrollable, the best they could achieve was monetary base control.

Overstone, it is true, argued emphatically that, because deposits could not be used in 'final settlement' of an account (in contrast to coins or bank notes) they were not money, and the implication of his argument is that because deposits ultimately rested upon means of 'final settlement' it was really only necessary to control those means. George Warde Norman – at once both more subtle and more unsure – addressed the problem directly in his 1841 *Letter to Charles Wood*, the sub-title of which is *On Money and the Means of Economizing the Use of It*. Norman argued that both deposits and bills of exchange were devices for 'economizing' on money but were not themselves money. Payments were made in commercial society by the use of such 'expedients' which included the off-setting of claims so as to leave only net balances, and transfers of credit. Deposits were transfers of credit; bills of exchange were partly in this category but also involved clearing arrangements for the off-setting of debts. Norman's view was that both deposits and bills were part of a credit superstructure which could be controlled through the high-powered money base.

Such a belief may not have been well founded. Earlier calculations by the Yorkshire banker William Leatham (1840), and later calculations by Newmarch (1851), using data from stamp duty returns, indicated that such control, if it existed at all, was extremely imperfect. Norman however insisted that the logic of the case must be that there was control through the high powered money base because it was the high powered money base which provided the means of 'final settlement' – bank deposits were of only limited acceptability because the payee had himself to possess a bank account. Moreover deposits could only be available on demand to a limited extent if the stability of the system were not to be endangered. Thus bank deposits could not have an influence on the price level independent of the high powered money base. But even if – perhaps through variable reserve ratios – there was a degree of independence, Norman did not believe that this constituted any case for ignoring the need to reform control of that base itself.

The Currency School were thus perfectly clear about what it was that they sought to control, and about their reasons for wishing to do so. When we encounter the Banking School literature, however, we enter a much more cloudy domain. There is no doubt that the members of this School believed that to concentrate solely upon control of the note issue was wrong. They attached importance to means of payment other than notes, especially deposits, and they were very alive to the importance of financial innovation – indeed to the problem of what is now called 'disintermediation'. But beyond that there are issues in the Banking School literature which are simply unre-solved. There seems to be a willingness on the part of some Banking School writers – John Stuart Mill is the leading example – to broaden the concept of means of payment to the point where it stretches to an almost Radcliffean vagueness. J.S. Mill's concept of 'purchasing power' included virtually every form of *credit* available (1844; 1848, bk 3, chs 11-12).

There was also some considerable divide between members of the Banking School about whether there was any need for control of the money supply and indeed whether causality ran from the money supply to the price level or vice versa. On the one hand it is true that most members of the Banking School invoked the long-run fixity of the price level, resulting from the fixed exchange rate with gold *and* the convertibility of the note issue into gold, to argue that over-issue was impossible; and it is also true that the members of the School believed that the note issue was demand-determined. But on the other hand there were important differences and critical inconsistencies. Tooke, as noted above, believed that the Bank should maintain its bullion level at a minimum of around £10 million; this would not only enable the Bank to cushion the monetary system from payments imbalances which (it was hoped) were temporary, but ensure that the Bank followed a cautious policy with respect to its issues. Yet if the note issue were demand-determined there was no need to try to impose such caution. Moreover Tooke poured scorn upon the views of Gilbart and others who, while accepting that the note issue was demand-determined, also accepted that a low rate of interest could stimulate speculative demand (1844, ch. 13). Tooke also attempted to use the 'dual circulation hypothesis' (Tooke, 1844, ch. 7; O'Brien, 1993) but in an untenable form because by 'circulation of capital' Tooke actually meant wholesale transactions in commodities, and here the price level of goods was of critical importance in determining the note issue required.[6]

---

[6]The 'dual circulation hypothesis', which originated with Smith, was central to Joplin's model. It involved the proposition that one set of prices depended on one particular source

But again and again in what Tooke wrote there is a basic hole in the argument which can only be filled – and here at least it is possible to agree with the free-banking revisionist interpretation of the history of monetary thought – by assuming that not only was the price level fixed *in the long run* by the price of gold but fixed also *in the short run* in the same way. Otherwise the price level in Tooke's writings is simply indeterminate – for on the rare occasions when he addressed directly the determination of the price level he maintained that it depended upon aggregate supply and aggregate demand; but aggregate supply depended upon cost of production while aggregate demand depended upon the total of money incomes, and these were one and the same thing (1840, p. 276; 1844, ch. 12 and p. 123). The acute Robert Torrens saw the difficulty (Torrens, 1852); but in his writings Tooke repeatedly attempted to avoid the whole issue of the determination of the price level.

5.5 Conclusions

In matters of macroeconomic management, long-run equilibrium values are certainly not irrelevant. The history of exchange rates is littered with examples of governments attempting to choose prices for their currency which were not long-run equilibrium ones. Examples of this stretch from 1819-21, with a price of gold of £3.17s. $10\frac{1}{2}$d., to 1990-92 and DM 2.95. But given that a long-run equilibrium value has been chosen – or even that, in accord with the mis-named 'monetarist' view of European monetary union, participating economies have been forced into the Procrustean bed of what was initially an unrealistic rate – the question of positive or negative feedback to equilibrium, once disturbed, was, and is, critical. Such very basic questions as the direction of causality involved in the relationship between the money supply and

---

of note issue. Thus the country bank note issue determined the price level of transactions in goods and services. The Bank of England note issue was used for financial transactions. See Tooke (1844, p. 71) and for a discussion of Smith's hypothesis see Zallio (1990).

the price level or, more generally, the level of money income, have to be faced at both a theoretical and an empirical level. It is simply not satisfactory to apply the Ricardian telescope, focus on conditions of long-run equilibrium, and ignore the nature and amplitude of disturbances around that long-run equilibrium.

Chapter 6

Monetary Base Control

The 1844 Bank Charter Act, introduced after a testing, and at times acrimonious, debate over the theory of monetary control, set out to impose monetary base control on the British economy. The aim was to protect convertibility of the note issue into gold, and to produce macroeconomic stability, via control of the Bank of England note issue which was seen as the high powered monetary base of the financial system. The Bank of England note issue (and any issues of the Scots and Irish banks above a permitted level) were linked directly to gold flows across the exchanges, and thus to the balance of payments, while the issues of the English and Welsh country banks were constrained within a fixed low limit.

This chapter explores the impact of the Act, by contrasting results obtained from data between 1832 and 1844 with those obtained from data covering 1844-57. In the first period it is apparent that it was the country bank note issue, together with some small contribution from bills of exchange (though these were for the most part themselves dependent on the country bank note issue) which controlled the level of prices. The country bank note issue in turn was not controlled by the Bank of England note issue, nor by its liabilities more widely defined. For the second period this was also true. The price level continued to depend on the country bank note issue and, to a much lesser extent, bills of exchange, and the metal holdings of the Scots and Irish banks were not influenced by the issues of the Bank of England. However the note issues of the Bank in the second period do seem to have exercised some limited influence on the price level and on the issues of bills of exchange. But for the most part the hopes of the Currency School with regard to monetary base control were not realised; and a wide range of measures of macroeconomic variability indicate that – with the important exception of prices – greater stability was not achieved after 1844.

The chapter is organised as follows. The monetary background and the theoretical issues in the debate over monetary control are outlined in sections 6.1, 6.2 and 6.3. The approach to testing these issues is set out in section 6.4, and section 6.5 contains the results of tests for the era before the 1844 Act. Section 6.6 contains the corresponding tests for the era after 1844. Matters of causality, and price data, are dealt with in Appendices.

6.1   The Monetary Background

After the best part of two decades of controversy, the Bank Charter Act of 1844 set out to impose monetary base control on the British economy. Prior to the Act, the money supply – still predominantly bank notes – had come from two main sources, the Bank of England and the note-issuing country banks.

It was on the note issue of the Bank that the controversy had focused, for the most part. The Bank professed, under the Palmer Rule, to be guided by the exchanges in regulating its issues of notes. The Palmer Rule was essentially a balance sheet rule; it was that, when the exchanges were 'full' (that is, just on the point of becoming unfavourable), the Bank should aim at having one third of its assets in gold and two thirds in securities – commercial bills and government debt. On the liabilities side were notes issued by the Bank, and its deposits. When the exchanges turned against Britain and gold flowed out, the securities were supposed to be kept constant on the asset side of the balance sheet, while the combined liabilities of notes and deposits contracted to reflect the loss of gold on the asset side.

As its critics, especially Overstone (1837), pointed out, there were so many special circumstances to be taken account of that the Bank hardly ever managed to follow this Rule. In exercising its discretion, the Bank departed so far from the Rule that this constituted a prima facie case in favour of clearer and rigorously enforced rules rather than discretion.

More fundamentally, the critics pointed out that the balance sheet approach was flawed; for by allowing a gold drain to be reflected in total bank liabilities, it made no provision for ensuring that the note issue – seen as the high powered money base – would be contracted. A drain of gold might thus fall on the Bank's deposits – indeed it was likely to do so, because depositors would demand gold to settle international balances – so that the Bank might be drained of gold without the note issue being corrected to the level which – and this is the crux – *was compatible with international equilibrium.*

The critics of the Bank thus had, at the heart of their argument, two basic postulates: firstly, that the note issue of the Bank constituted a high powered money base which controlled all other means of payment, and, secondly, one derived from what Robbins (1958, pp. 99-100) has called the Ricardian definition of excess – the idea that if gold was flowing out then, *by definition*, the money supply was excessive. Since total means of payment were controlled ultimately by the high powered money base, this meant that the Bank of England note issue was excessive.

However, as noted above, there was, in addition to the note issue of the Bank, the note issue of the country banks; and this was by no means negligible. The note issue of the country banks as a whole, including the Bank of Ireland, during the 1830s was approximately half the total note issue of the United Kingdom. For England and Wales, the Bank note issue was slightly more than 60 per cent of the total for most of the period. Thomas Joplin argued that it was the country bank note issue which was critical in determining the price level – and thus the state of the balance of payments. The evidence now available supports Joplin (O'Brien, 1993), but he was ignored and his views brushed aside by the economic establishment, which took the position that the Bank of England note issue provided the high powered money base. It was true, the Currency School conceded, that the country banks could resist a Bank of England contraction of its note issue, and that very power to resist was itself damaging because it involved the prolongation of a balance of payments disequilibrium. Thus the loss of gold overseas continued for longer than would have been the case had the country banks responded rapidly to the Bank's own contraction, and the reduction in the Bank's gold reserve was the greater. But ultimately the country banks had to conform to policy as dictated by the supplier of the monetary base. As Overstone put it:

> The country issues, no doubt, are based upon those of the central issuer, and must ultimately conform to them; but, previously to that result, a struggle ensues [following contraction], by which the monetary system, generally, is exposed to confusion and danger, and the corrective measures of the central issuer are rendered more stringent and severe than they would otherwise have been. (Overstone, 1840a, p. 101)

The problems associated with this resistance on the part of the country banks clearly required attention; but it was a secondary issue compared with the primary need to control the Bank of England note issue which lay at the base of the monetary system. It was this which the 1844 Act set out to achieve.

6.2   The Bank Charter Act of 1844

6.2.1   The Debate

The Charter of the Bank was renewed in 1833 for a period of twenty-one years; but the government could change it after ten years and a further year's notice (Gregory, 1929, 1, p. 22; 3&4 Will. 4, c. 98, para. 5). Thus, as 1844 approached, the question of the form which renewal should take became of considerable public interest. The Currency School – Overstone, Norman, Torrens – argued that the renewal of the Charter should be the occasion for significant legal change. Their proposals encountered fierce resistance, most notably in the Select Committee on Banks of Issue in 1840-1841. Indeed Overstone, the leading member of the Currency School, felt thoroughly mauled by his treatment at the hands of the Committee. He turned for help to Henry Warburton, who was a member of the Committee, and Warburton's advice to him was that he should persevere, despite the treatment which he was receiving from Joseph Hume and Matthias Attwood (Warburton to Overstone, 23 July 1840, in O'Brien, 1971, pp. 280-1). But Overstone was not mollified.

> I must however add that it is my fixed determination in case any
> further questions are put to me by Mr Attwood or Mr Hume to
> decline giving any but a *written* answer to them. The questions
> emanating from those gentlemen appear to me calculated ... to
> entrap a witness in an unguarded admission or expression, and
> to reduce the proceedings of the Comee to a mere arena for the
> display of logical dexterity and quickness. During the last two
> days of the examination I confess that I felt myself rather in the
> situation of a Roman Gladiator drawn forth for the exhibition of
> cruel but unprofitable sport, than in that of a gentleman brought
> before a Comee of Parliament for the purpose of contributing

his humble share towards the effectual investigation of a very
important but at the same time a difficult and abstruse subject.
(Overstone to Warburton, 25 July 1840; O'Brien, 1971, p. 283)

Overstone thus attempted to insist that he would deal only in writing
with questions from the two of whom he complained. But he was ultimately
persuaded by Charles Wood and Warburton to undergo further examination,
and indeed his last appearance before the Committee on 31 July 1840 (qq.
3465-614) was almost entirely monopolised by Hume.

It is perhaps worth emphasising this in view of the belief which seems to
have developed that the 1844 Act had an easy passage. It is true – although
the precise political sequence is still unclear – that Peel succeeded in piloting
it through Parliament without too much difficulty. But a major battle had
already been fought away from the floor of the House. At all events the Act
passed into law essentially embodying the proposals of the Currency School.

6.2.2   Provisions of the Act

Under the Act, rules were substituted for Bank of England discretion, at least
as far as the note issue was concerned. (The Bank was, within three years,
to find other areas for the exercise of discretion, notably in the level at which
it set its discount rate, with disastrous effects.) Beyond a 'fiduciary' issue of
£14 million, which was to be matched on the asset side of the balance sheet
by securities, note issues had all to be backed by gold. Thus a loss of gold
by the Bank *automatically* required a contraction of the note issue. To bring
this about, and to ensure that a 'drain' did not fall on deposits, the Bank
was separated into Departments of Issue and Banking. The proposal for this
originated with Norman, the Currency School's representative in the Bank
itself, and with the ever-agile and resourceful Robert Torrens. Under this
provision of the Act, the depositors who required gold would obtain notes
from the Banking Department, and then present these notes at the Issue

Department, in exchange for gold. Thus the note issue had to fall as gold flowed out.

The Currency School vision was one of an almost hydraulically smooth macroeconomic system. It envisaged that the Act would produce a remarkable contrast with the years up to 1844. In that era, the Bank of England had ultimately controlled the money supply, but only after disastrous lags which allowed fluctuations – originating in the real sector (O'Brien, 1995 and chapter 5 above) – to be magnified. In accordance with this belief, they expected that after 1844 the early contraction required of the Bank would result in a much reduced amplitude of economic fluctuation. The price level would be controlled by Bank of England note issue variation directed by gold flows; and other means of payment, since they depended upon the monetary base, would simply increase the leverage of the gold flows in producing equilibrium.

Others of course were less sanguine. The Banking School warned that, far from smoothing things, the contraction forced on the Bank by the Act would lead to damaging fluctuations in Bank Rate (its discount rate), as the Bank sought to reduce its discounting. Thomas Joplin warned that liquidity crises would occur in the London money market – as indeed they did, in 1847 and in 1857, though by that time Joplin was dead.

The problem of the country banks was solved – for England and Wales alone – by imposing ceilings on their issues, calculated on the basis of an average of previous issues. There was a stringent penalty for exceeding these. The ceilings themselves were, as Joplin and others pointed out, artificially low (1844, pp. 2, 93-4), and this, combined with a provision that lapsed issues (where a country bank ceased to issue) would be taken over by the Bank, but only to the extent of two thirds of the previous level, ensured that the country bank note issue for England and Wales was effectively neutered.[1]

---

[1] The penalty was £1 fine for every £1 excess issue, by paragraph 17 of the 1844 Act (7 and 8 Vict. c. 32). The two thirds provision is in paragraph 5 of the Act. The maximum which each bank was to be allowed to issue was the average of its circulation for the twelve weeks ended 27 April 1844 (paras 13, 14). The Act is reprinted in Gregory (1929,

The country banks were simply concerned with the ceiling, and took very good care to make this the first priority in regulating their issues. They were no longer free to respond to what they perceived as the 'needs of trade' even though they, like their Banking School advocates, especially Tooke and Fullarton, saw themselves doing this. Instead they concentrated on maintaining a safety margin between their issues and the upper limits imposed. This was exactly what the Currency School desired – its members believed that the country banks would, in this way, be prevented from thwarting a monetary contraction imposed by the Bank following gold loss.

However, Peel knew full well that to try to impose such a ceiling on the Scots notes was not practical. There was already one episode in recent political memory when an attempt to tamper with Scots note issues – abolition of the Scottish one pound notes – had proved explosive (Feaveryear, 1963, pp. 241-2; Clapham, 1944, II, pp. 106, 186-7). Instead, therefore, of capping the Scots bank note issues with an upper limit, they were allowed (as were the Irish banks) to issue freely above a level based upon their previous issues, where such extra issues were backed by specie. They were not, however, allowed to issue extra notes on the basis of their holding of Bank of England notes. Hubbard, before the 1857 Committee, was later asked to comment on this limitation (*Parliamentary Papers*, 1857, part 1, qq. 2486-90; see also qq. 2494, 2722-27). But it was perfectly sensible in terms of the logical structure of the Act: an inflow of gold and silver did not, under its provisions, produce a multiple issue – Bank of England notes, with Scots notes on top of these – but could, if it were received by the Scots banks, give rise directly to an increase in their issues.

I, 129-147); see also Clapham (1944, II, 183-4).

6.3 Wider Considerations

6.3.1 Other Means of Payment

There were, as contemporaries recognised, a number of other questions which were rather left to one side by the Act. In particular, there was the matter of other means of payment than bank notes. With the growth of joint stock banking, engineered by Joplin, deposits were of increasing importance, as cheques drawn on deposits became an important means of payment.

This was a matter which much exercised the Currency School. Torrens even leant towards the view that bank deposits were money. This is apparent from his discussion of the matter in his *Letter to Lord Melbourne* (Torrens, 1837). Twenty years later he was still flirting with this idea, only to find himself sharply rebuked by Overstone for his '*alarming heretical tendency*':

> Col: Torrens maintains that Deposits are money!! – If you pub-
> lish this to the world – you let loose upon us the Floodgates of
> Confusion – it will be the Deluge of Monetary science. Tooke will
> be in the third Heaven – he will be more violent, more inconsis-
> tent and more abusive than ever – . He will strut about with your
> authority – like Ulysses wielding the arms of Achilles. (Overstone
> to Torrens, 21 January 1857, in O'Brien, 1971, p. 713)

The general Currency School position may be summarised as a belief that deposits were part of an inverted credit pyramid, with the high powered money (Bank of England notes) at its base. In the words of Norman (1841) they were 'economising expedients', which reduced the necessary size of the note issue but were ultimately controlled by the notes issued.

There was also the question of bills of exchange as means of payment. This matter had been raised by the Yorkshire banker William Leatham, who made a first attempt at collecting data (Leatham, 1840). It was however Tooke's associate William Newmarch (1851) who did the main work in collecting data on the basis of stamp duty returns. The Banking School believed that bills of exchange were an important, and independent, means of payment, in contrast to the Currency School belief that they were part of an inverted credit pyramid controlled by the Bank notes at its base.

There are no satisfactory data on bank deposits with which to test the pyramid hypothesis. However the data set on bills of exchange collected by Newmarch was extensive, and this will be used below to explore the issue of base control.

6.3.2   The Nature of the Monetary Base

So far, in accordance with Currency School thinking, it has been assumed that the monetary base itself consisted of Bank of England *notes*, but there was a wider problem, and one which was largely avoided. This was the question of whether Bank of England total liabilities (or at least total *private* liabilities, thus excluding government deposits) provided a better base for control of the monetary system. The view of the Currency School was clear: the Palmer Rule was defective precisely because it focused on (private) liabilities of the Bank, rather than just on notes. If the Currency School were wrong, however, and the private liabilities were crucial as a whole, then the 1844 Act was flawed in a serious way. This is thus an important question and it is explored on the basis of the available data below.

6.3.3   Causes of Gold Loss

A further question – one of which the Currency School could hardly be unaware (though some modern critics have implied that they were) since it had figured in monetary controversy since the 1800s – was that a loss of gold might not be due to the balance of payments but to an 'internal drain'. In addition, even if the drain were external, this might not be due to a disequilibrium relative international price level. But, as Overstone explained, to attempt to distinguish the causes of a loss of gold, and thus to return to discretion rather than rules, when there could be no clear evidence about the causes of a particular drain, could only lead to a situation in which gold continued to flow out. There was no basis on which to distinguish different sources of metal loss, and it was better to check the drain early by contraction, for only in that way could monetary disruption be contained. At the basis of this, one can detect the Ricardian definition of excess already referred to; but the argument was articulated with considerable clarity and rhetorical force by Overstone:

> There is an old Eastern proverb which says, you may stop with a bodkin a fountain, which if suffered to flow will sweep away whole cities in its course. An early and timely contraction, upon the very first indication of excess in the circulation, is the application of the bodkin to the fountain; commercial convulsion and ruin in consequence of delay, is the stream sweeping away whole cities in its course. (Overstone, 1837, p. 23)

This leads us to the question of causality. An issue, raised by both the Banking School and by their latter-day disciples in the 'free banking' literature, was the direction of causality. The Currency School, like the vast majority of economists before and since, assumed that causality ran from the money supply to the price level. However, the Banking School argued, like their latter-day successors, that causality ran in the opposite direction. This is an issue on which the data are sufficiently good to allow us to conduct some tentative tests.

6.4 The Issues Tested

To examine the impact of the legislation, we begin by looking at the picture provided by the data during the era in which the Currency School programme became fully articulated, and examining how far their basic assumptions about the mechanics of the monetary system were based on fact. They did not, of course, have all the data now available; but they were highly intelligent individuals, well versed in the day-to-day experience of banking, so it would be foolish to discount their views lightly. The evidence obtained from the data is examined in the next section. The central issue of control of the note issue is discussed in the first subsection below. The influences on *changes* in the price level are examined in the second. The absolute *level* of prices is the subject of the next subsection, and the control of bills of exchange is discussed in the last one.

The emphasis is on estimating linear relationships between changes in dependent and independent variables, in line with the Currency School model which implies proportionality. Since the emphasis is on monetary control, it is reasonable to concentrate on changes, although some attention is also paid to the absolute level of prices because of its role in the theory of international equilibrium. (The question of stationarity of the variables is dealt with in App. III. to O'Brien, 1996.)

6.5   Era I: The Data 1833-44

6.5.1   Control of the Note Issue

The Currency School hypothesis concerning note issue control can be examined using data from 1833 to 1844. Tables 6.1 and 6.2 show that the equation relating changes in the country bank notes to changes in Bank notes is insignificant. Despite the apparently significant t value on the unlagged value of changes in the Bank of England note issue, the F value for the equation is insignificant. These results confirm those obtained in O'Brien (1993), suggesting that the Bank of England's control of the money supply was far less than the Currency School believed. Even lags of four quarters do not pick up any clear indication of control, by the Bank, of the country bank note issue

Table 6.1: Control of the Country Bank Note Issue 1833/4-1844: Part A

Variables	Dep. var: ΔCBN Coefficient	t	Dep. var: ΔUKN Coefficient	t
INPT	0.1331	0.6872	1.4225	4.0963#
ΔBEN	0.2144	2.0077*	0.2576	1.5135
ΔBEN$_{-1}$	0.0785	0.7149	0.1519	0.8652
ΔBEN$_{-2}$	-0.1051	-0.8203	0.0068	0.0359
ΔBEN$_{-3}$	-0.1288	-1.0429	-0.1187	-0.6247
ΔBEN$_{-4}$	-0.1366	-1.1064	-0.0856	-0.4870
Q_1	0.0260	0.0838	-1.7578	-3.1580#
Q_2	-0.4034	-2.1093*	-1.8580	-4.5127#
Q_3	-0.4120	-1.3950	-2.1462	-3.9775#
R^2	0.1239		0.5209	
DW	1.9936		2.0858	
F(df)	1.4478(12,26)		6.0730(9,33)#	
n	43		43	
Period	1833Q4-1844Q2		1833Q4-1844Q2	
Method	AR(4)		AR(1)	

Significance levels: $+ = 10\%$, $^* = 5\%$, $\# = 1\%$, one-tailed except on Q_i and INPT, intercept; ΔCBN, first differences of country bank note issue for England and Wales; ΔUKN, first differences of country bank note issue for England and Wales, Scotland and Ireland (including Bank of Ireland); ΔBEN, first differences of Bank of England note issue; ΔPRIVL first differences of private liabilities of the Bank of England (note issue plus private deposits). Explanatory variables lagged up to four quarters. Q_i are quarterly dummies.

for England and Wales. Nor is there any support for the beliefs underlying the Palmer Rule: Tables 6.1 and 6.2 also show that the private liabilities of the Bank, taken as a whole, did not control the country bank note issue for England and Wales either.

During this period the note issue from the country banks in England and Wales, and that for the United Kingdom as a whole, moved in parallel as Figure 6.1 indicates. This is in sharp contrast to the era following the Act (Figure 6.2), when the issues of the country banks in England and Wales

Table 6.2: Control of the Country Bank Note Issue 1833/4-1844: Part B

Variables	Dep. var: ΔCBN Coefficient	t	Dep. var: ΔUKN Coefficient	t
INPT	0.0630	0.5261	1.1457	4.6921[#]
ΔPRIVL	0.0659	1.2330	0.0676	0.8764
ΔPRIVL$_{-1}$	0.0665	1.1110	0.1670	1.9022*
ΔPRIVL$_{-2}$	-0.1039	-1.6687	-0.0587	-0.6519
ΔPRIVL$_{-3}$	-0.0842	-1.4442	-0.0742	-0.8166
ΔPRIVL$_{-4}$	-0.0449	-0.8030	-0.0957	-1.1762
Q_1	0.0960	0.6077	-1.3308	-4.1381[#]
Q_2	-0.3885	-2.4847*	-1.7801	-5.6683[#]
Q_3	-0.2460	-1.6338	-1.6623	-5.5253[#]
R^2	0.1838		0.5526	
DW	2.0549		2.0227	
F(df)	1.8106(10,26)		6.4886(9,31)[#]	
n	41		41	
Period	1834Q2-1844Q2		1834Q2-1844Q2	
Method	AR(4)		AR(1)	

were subject to a ceiling while those of the Scots and Irish banks were free to vary according to holdings of precious metals. The wider UK dimension was not included in an earlier study of Joplin (O'Brien, 1993), but the parallelism evident from Figure 6.1 makes it unsurprising that, when we look at the UK data, the negative results obtained for Bank control of the country banks in England and Wales are again reflected in the lack of control of the UK issues. This is true whether we regard the monetary base as Bank of England notes or as Bank of England private liabilities (Tables 6.1 and 6.2, columns 4-5). The only glimmer of hope is a tiny coefficient (17 decimal pence in the pound), significant at 5 per cent, for Bank of England private liability control with a one quarter lag.

6.5.2   Changes in the Price Level

With regard to the effect on the price level of Bank of England notes and country bank notes, the picture obtained in O'Brien (1993) is confirmed. Ta-

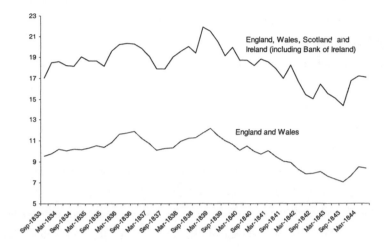

Figure 6.1: Country Bank Notes (£m), 1833-44

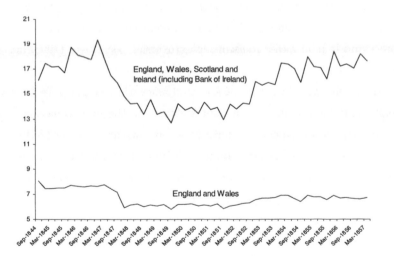

Figure 6.2: Country Bank Notes (£m), 1844-57

bles 6.3 and 6.4 show that there are no individually significant coefficients in the relation between changes in the price level, as measured by the magnificent Gayer-Rostow-Schwartz price index, and changes in the note issues of the Bank. The only coefficient with a large absolute t value has the wrong sign. There is however, as Joplin had argued, a significant relationship between changes in prices and changes in the country bank note issue for England and Wales (this reflects the result reported in O'Brien (1993)). This is also true of the relationship between prices and the country bank note issue for the UK as a whole (for details see O'Brien, 1996). Both the unlagged and the three quarters lagged changes are large and significant.

But at the same time those changes in the country bank note issues do *not* reflect Bank of England control (Tables 6.1 and 6.2). The country banks may well have responded to the balance of payments in other ways, as Joplin argued (O'Brien, 1993, pp. 104-108), but they did not do so in response to the Bank's own reaction to gold loss.

These results seem to be robust; in particular, dropping the most insignificant lagged values produced no real change in the overall picture. The procedure is in any case somewhat controversial; see Mayer (1995, pp. 99-105).

The question of whether bills of exchange affected the price level was explored by adding data for bills of exchange to the price equations. This issue is central to the differences between the Currency School concentration on notes and the rather vague Banking School insistence on the importance of 'credit' in relation to means of payment. Indeed, as noted above, the data utilised here were compiled by Newmarch, one of the Banking School leaders.

Adding changes in bills of exchange to changes in Bank of England notes produces little illumination – the value of $\bar{R}^2$ is less than 0.24 and there are no significant coefficients on changes in Bank notes – and the equation is not reported here. Thus, even allowing for the effect of bills of exchange, variations in the Bank of England notes did not explain price changes. It is

Table 6.3: Price Level Changes - Note Issues 1833/4-1844: Part A

| | Dep. var: ΔGRSP | | | Dep. var: ΔGRSP | |
Variables	Coefficient	t	Variables	Coefficient	t
INPT	-2.1079	-0.8781	INPT	-0.3133	-0.2726
ΔBEN	-0.0812	-0.0830	ΔCBN	4.2225	2.4452*
ΔBEN$_{-1}$	0.6305	0.6550	ΔCBN$_{-1}$	0.7190	0.3361
ΔBEN$_{-2}$	-3.2983	-2.6540	ΔCBN$_{-2}$	1.0330	0.4818
ΔBEN$_{-3}$	1.0652	1.0285	ΔCBN$_{-3}$	5.0298	2.3141*
ΔBEN$_{-4}$	-0.3399	-0.3025	ΔCBN$_{-4}$	0.0390	0.0220
Q_1	5.4185	1.2287	Q_1	1.6009	0.8209
Q_2	-1.5289	-1.0033	Q_2	3.1530	2.1377*
Q_3	4.6248	1.0724	Q_3	0.2166	0.1088
R^2	0.2468		R^2	0.4128	
DW	2.0943		DW	2.1662	
F(df)	2.3105(10,30)*		F(df)	3.3899(10,24)*	
n	45		n	39	
Period	1833Q2-1844Q2		Period	1834Q4-1844Q2	
Method	AR(4)		Method	AR(4)	

For variable definitions see Table 6.1

Significance levels: $+$ = 10%, $*$ = 5%, $\#$ = 1%, one-tailed except INPT
and Q_i. Since the alternative hypothesis tested is that of a positive
effect on prices, 'significant' negative coefficients on explanatory
variables (as distinct from quarterly dummies) are not signalled.
ΔGRSP, first differences of the Gayer-Rostow-Schwartz wholesale
price index; INPT, ΔBEN, ΔCBN, Q_i defined for Table 6.1; ΔBEXT, first
differences of total bills of exchange (the Newmarch series). Explanatory
variables are lagged up to four quarters.

Table 6.4: Price Level Changes - Note Issues 1833/4-1844: Part B

Variables	Dep. var: ΔGRSP	
	Coefficient	t
INPT	2.2449	1.1599
ΔCBN	2.8500	1.5824
ΔCBN$_{-1}$	0.5061	0.2365
ΔCBN$_{-2}$	-3.1891	-1.3236
ΔCBN$_{-3}$	6.2845	2.3091*
ΔCBN$_{-4}$	0.5641	0.2136
ΔBEXT	0.6327	2.5452$^{\#}$
ΔBEXT$_{-1}$	-0.0698	-0.2980
ΔBEXT$_{-2}$	-0.1778	-0.7238
ΔBEXT$_{-3}$	0.1286	0.7239
ΔBEXT$_{-4}$	0.0348	0.2481
Q_1	-3.0743	-0.8215
Q_2	1.7594	1.1305
Q_3	-5.5838	-1.3871
R^2	0.4777	
DW	1.9302	
F(df)	3.0734(15,19)*	
n	39	
Period	1834Q4-1844Q2	
Method	AR(4)	
For variable definition see Table 6.3		

also the case that an equation with both contemporaneous and lagged values of changes in country bank notes *and* Bank notes – not reproduced here – has significant and correctly signed coefficients only on the country bank note changes.

In contrast to the case of Bank of England notes, adding changes in bills of exchange to the equation featuring changes in country bank notes – the result reported in Tables 6.3 and 6.4, cols 7-9 – produces an equation with an $\bar{R}^2$ virtually twice that for the Bank of England case, significant at 5 per cent, and with a significant coefficient on the three quarter lag on the country bank issues. There is a significant, though small, additional effect from contemporary changes in bills of exchange. The impact effect on prices of changes in the country bank note issue, reported in cols. 4-6, can be restored by dropping insignificant lags from the equation in cols 7-9; but in view of reservations about this procedure referred to above, the result is not reported here.

The result for changes in country bank notes for England and Wales is confirmed by the relation between changes in prices and changes in the whole UK country note issue (though this result is not reported here). This still holds when changes in bills of exchange are added as explanatory variables to the equation. Again, the coefficient on the three quarter lag on changes in the UK note issue is significant and positive (and, consistently with Tables 6.3 and 6.4, so is that on the one quarter lag), and again there is a small impact effect of changes in bills of exchange on prices as well as a small additional effect from the three quarter lag on such changes.

In summary, the price equations are dominated by the country bank note issue, with some small additional effect from bills of exchange.[2] Whether the bills of exchange themselves are subject to some control is an issue which will be addressed below.

---

[2] There is however some colinearity between ΔCBN and ΔBEXT, as is clear from Table 6.8.

6.5.3   The Price Level

While the source of *changes* in the note issue is of key importance in considering issues of monetary control, it is not only *changes* in prices which are of concern in relation to the price level. In this context, the determination of the absolute *level* of prices is also of interest, because of the implication for equilibrium in the international distribution of the precious metals, on which the Currency School placed so much emphasis. While several lagged values of level variables could not be used as explanatory variables in the same equation, because of high colinearity (around 0.9), which occurred both in raw data and in logs (which could otherwise have been used to pick up successive proportional changes), there are two alternative methods of exploring relationships in levels with varying lag lengths. One procedure, adopted in O'Brien (1993), uses a series of bivariate regressions between a dependent variable and a particular lagged value of an explanatory variable. Although open to the obvious objection of mis-specification, this problem may be quantitatively less severe than the effects of colinearity. An alternative, and perhaps more appealing, approach is to use the Koyck procedure, which allows lagged values of explanatory variables to be expressed as a one period lag on the dependent variable. This procedure can also be extended to two explanatory variables (Johnston, 1984, pp. 346-8), so that it is possible to explore the relationship not only of note issues but of bills of exchange to the price level.

The approach adopted here was to use the Koyck procedure, with both one and two explanatory variables, and then to provide supporting evidence via the bivariate regressions. The Koyck equations are reported in Table 6.5. It is apparent that the results are consistent with those from the equations dealing with *changes* in levels. The equation relating the price index to the country bank note issue for England and Wales (Table 6.5, cols 1-3) is significant, and indicates that country bank notes provided a good explanation of the price level. The coefficient on the lagged dependent variable, indicating the influence of past values of the country note issue on the price level, is positive and significant, while that on the unlagged value of the country note issue is also positive and significant. The same is true of an equation relating the price level to the UK note issue (not reported here). By contrast, and consistently with the results obtained for price level changes, the Bank of England note issue seems to provide little information about the price level (Table 6.5, cols 4-6). The problem here is that, while the coefficient on the lagged dependent variable is both positive (as required by the Koyck procedure)[3] and significant, the coefficient on the unlagged Bank of England note issue is negative. This implies that not merely the contemporaneous values of the Bank of England note issue, but those of past issues, have a *negative* effect on the price level.[4]

By utilising the Koyck procedure for inclusion of two (lagged) explanatory variables it was possible to explore the determination of the price level in relation to note issues and bills of exchange at the same time. As Table 6.5 (cols 7-9) shows, the results obtained were consistent with those obtained previously. For England and Wales, there is a significant relationship between country bank note issues and the price level (as Joplin had maintained), even when allowance is made for the influence of bills of exchange. The same is true if we use data for UK note issue. The Bank of England note issue does not seem to have influenced the price level: the regression is not reported here. This is consistent with Joplin's claims that the Bank of England very largely supplied the financial circulation, while the country bank notes were used for transactions in goods except in Lancashire (Ashton and Sayers, 1953, pp. 45, 48; Matthews, 1954, p. 177).

---

[3]Given $Y_t = \mu + \beta X_t + \alpha\beta X_{t-1} + \alpha^2\beta X_{t-2} + ... + u_t$, a negative value for α would change the sign of $\alpha^i\beta$ in successive terms, whatever the sign of β, the coefficient on X_t; and by standard manipulation the above equation can be transformed to $Y_t = \mu^* + \alpha U_{t-1} + \beta X_t$.

[4]This can be seen by referring to the first equation in the previous note. Since α is positive, the coefficients on $X_{t-1}, ..., X_{t-n}$ must have negative values.

Table 6.5: Price Levels, Note Issues and Bills 1832/3-1844

| | Dep. var: GRSP | | | Dep. var: GRSP | |
Variables	Coefficient	t	Variables	Coefficient	t
INPT	-0.3163	-0.0491	INPT	18.0282	0.8637
$GRSP_{-1}$	0.8392	13.0364#	$GRSP_{-1}$	0.8439	7.5953#
CBN	1.5379	3.0528#	BEN	-0.2094	-0.2663
Q_1	1.0478	0.5989	Q_1	1.4184	0.6561
Q_2	1.9588	1.1214	Q_2	2.0533	1.4470
Q_3	0.1041	0.0596	Q_3	0.5099	0.2207
R^2	0.8511		R^2	0.831	
h	-1.3763		LM(1)	0.1115	
F(df)	50.1624(5,38)#		F(df)	38.7061(6,40)#	
n	44		n	49	
Period	1833Q3-1844Q2		Period	1832Q2-1844Q2	
Method	OLS		Method	AR(2)	

| | Dep. var: GRSP | |
Variables	Coefficient	t
INPT	-9.4840	-1.5607
$GRSP_{-1}$	0.3122	2.0049+
$GRSP_{-2}$	0.2594	1.9574+
CBN	4.2367	2.7840#
CBN_{-1}	-2.8462	-1.7601+
BEXT	0.3601	3.1244#
$BEXT_{-1}$	0.2052	1.7272+
Q_1	0.4008	0.2567
Q_2	3.3882	2.2287*
Q_3	0.1177	0.0664
R^2	0.9001	
LM(1)	3.6833	
F(df)	43.0552(9,33)+	
n	43	
Period	1833Q4-1844Q2	
Method	OLS	

Significance levels: $+ = 10\%$, $* = 5\%$, $\# = 1\%$, LM(1) is reported for equations 2 and 3 as h was undefined (negative value under square root). Two-tail significance levels are reported although, as indicated in note 5, the signs of some of the coefficients in the third equation are strictly incorrect under the Koyck procedure.

For variable definitions see Tables 6.1 and 6.2.

However, the sign of the coefficient on $GRSP_{-2}$ conflicts with that required by the Koyck procedure, as does the sign of the coefficient on $BEXT_{-1}$,[5] so the results in Table 6.5 are weakened.

As noted above, an alternative to the Koyck procedure is a series of bivariate regressions. Although not tabulated here, these tests were conducted, and they confirm the general picture already obtained. The country bank note issues significantly influenced the price level up to a lag of three quarters, with the strongest results associated with lags of zero, one, and three quarters. The same general picture emerged from consideration of the relationship between the price level and the UK note issue. By contrast, in such bivariate regressions no lag (up to four quarters) on the Bank of England note issue indicated a significant relationship with the price level.

6.5.4 Bills of Exchange

The inclusion of both levels of, and changes in, bills of exchange, in the preceding equations, and the finding that bills of exchange did appear to exert some minor influence on the price index, raises the question of the control of those bills themselves. The Currency School, as noted above, believed that they were controlled as part of the upper structure of an inverted credit pyramid, while the Banking School maintained that they were money substi-

---

[5]Given:

$$Y_t = \mu + \beta X_t + \alpha_1 \beta X_{t-1} + \alpha_1^2 \beta X_{t-2} + \dots$$
$$+ \gamma Z_t + \alpha_2 \gamma Z_{t-1} + \alpha_2^2 \gamma Z_{t-2} + U_t,$$

which by standard manipulation (Johnston, 1984, p. 347) reduces to:

$$Y_t = \mu^* + (\alpha_1 + \alpha_2) Y_{t-1} - \alpha_1 \alpha_2 Y_{t-2}$$
$$+ \beta X_t - \alpha_2 \beta X_{t-1} + \gamma Z_t - \alpha_1 \gamma Z_{t-1} + V_t,$$

and given that, to avoid alternating signs in the first equation (and to be able to define a mean lag) α_1 and α_2 have both to be positive, the following restrictions on signs emerge: the coefficient on Y_{t-1} should be positive; the coefficient on Y_{t-2} should be negative; if the coefficient on X_t is positive that on X_{t-1} should be negative (and vice versa); if the coefficient on Z_t is positive, that on Z_{t-1} should be negative (and vice versa).

tutes freely created whenever monetary contraction by the Bank made this necessary.

Data are available for large, medium, and small bills of exchange total values. The overall total and the first two categories are very closely correlated, so there seems no point in running separate regressions. The behaviour of small bills of exchange is however different (and it proved much more difficult to obtain a satisfactory equation).

From Table 6.6 it is apparent that the main controlling influence on total bills of exchange issues was the country bank note issue during this era. This is true whether we consider the influence of the country bank note issue for England and Wales (as reported in the table) or the related figures for the United Kingdom as a whole. Thus, though the total issues of bills of exchange were subject to some control, that control was not on the basis of Bank of England notes *either directly or indirectly* (since, as established earlier, the Bank of England note issue did not control the country bank issue). Changes in interest rates, or at least in the Bank's discount rate, did not influence changes in total bills of exchange, but a two quarter lag on changes in the English and Welsh country bank notes results in a coefficient which is large (the units of measurement are the same on both sides of the equation) and significant at 1 per cent. Similar results emerge if we consider changes in the whole United Kingdom country bank note issue, and if we take account of total Bank of England private liabilities rather than merely Bank notes.

But if the news is not good for the Currency School, it is no better for the Banking School. For the idea that the total of bills of exchange could be shown to be dependent on the price level is at variance with the regression results reported in Table 6.6 (cols 4-6). However, direct tests of causality, reported in Appendix 6.1, do provide some support for the Banking School; Granger, Sargent and Sims tests of causality all support the notion that price changes resulted in changes in the total value of bills of exchange issued.

But, for the most part, neither the Currency School nor the Banking

Table 6.6: Total Bills of Exchange and Note Issues, 1834-1844

Variables	Dep. Var: ΔBEXT coefficient	t	Variables	Dep. Var: ΔBEXT coefficient	t
INPT	-4.6582	-1.4679	INPT	-3.5288	-1.9231$^+$
ΔBR	1.3473	0.8016	ΔGRSP	0.3215	1.6193
ΔBR$_{-1}$	0.8081	0.3903	ΔGRSP$_{-1}$	0.3311	1.5546
ΔBR$_{-2}$	0.5457	0.2321	ΔGRSP$_{-2}$	0.2038	0.9308
ΔBR$_{-3}$	1.5085	0.7691	ΔGRSP$_{-3}$	-0.2712	-1.2783
ΔBR$_{-4}$	-0.2196	-0.1445	ΔGRSP$_{-4}$	-0.1255	-0.6364
ΔCBN	0.7627	0.5088	Q_1	6.8366	2.1663*
ΔCBN$_{-1}$	2.9400	1.5237	Q_2	-0.4766	-0.2046
ΔCBN$_{-2}$	5.9458	3.1569$^\#$	Q_3	8.6935	2.7828$^\#$
ΔCBN$_{-3}$	-1.5648	-0.7737	R^2	0.4729	
ΔCBN$_{-4}$	-2.7077	-1.3979	DW	2.0909	
ΔBEN	0.0356	0.0341	F(df)	4.9469(10,34)$^\#$	
ΔBEN$_{-1}$	-0.2678	-0.2495	n	45	
ΔBEN$_{-2}$	-1.7727	-1.5562	Period	1833Q2-1844Q2	
ΔBEN$_{-3}$	0.8869	0.7613	Method	AR(2)	
ΔBEN$_{-4}$	0.2749	0.2644			
Q_1	10.3530	1.7668$^+$			
Q_2	-2.4865	-1.1966			
Q_3	13.3121	2.2697*			
R^2	0.8218				
DW	1.7023				
F(df)	8.8421(20,14)$^\#$				
n	39				
Period	1834Q4-1844Q2				
Method	AR(4)				

Significance levels: $+ = 10\%$, $* = 5\%$, $\# = 1\%$.
ΔBR, first differences of Bank of England discount rate ('Bank Rate');
ΔCBN, ΔBEN, Q_i are defined in Table 6.1; ΔBEXT, ΔGRSP are
defined in Table 6.2. Explanatory variables lagged up to four quarters.

School can take much comfort from this study of the data for the years leading up to the 1844 Bank Charter Act. The only person who could, posthumously, take comfort from this is Thomas Joplin, who argued consistently that the key variable in the monetary system was the country bank note issue. Details of his model are given in O'Brien (1993) and chapter 9 below.

Both the Currency and Banking Schools made clear predictions about the way in which the system would operate once the 1844 Act provisions were in operation. Unfortunately, as we shall see, the data for the years 1844-1856 provide little more support for either School.

6.6   Era II: 1844-57

The era after 1844 saw significant changes in the balance of the note issue from different sources, compared with the period before 1844, and these are outlined in the next subsection. The control of that note issue is explored in the second subsection. Influences on price changes are examined in the third subsection using a special new index, the construction of which is explored in Appendix 6.2. This index is also used to examine influences on the absolute price level in the next subsection. The control of bills of exchange is the subject of the next one. Finally, the question of whether, as promised by the Currency School, the Act produced greater macroeconomic stability is explored.

6.6.1   The Change in the Composition of the Country Bank Note Issue

The contrast in treatment of the country banks in England and Wales and of those in Scotland and Ireland was bound to produce a change in the balance of the note circulation. As Figures 6.1 and 6.2 show, the note issue from the country banks in England and Wales diminished in importance while that of the 'Celtic fringe' increased.

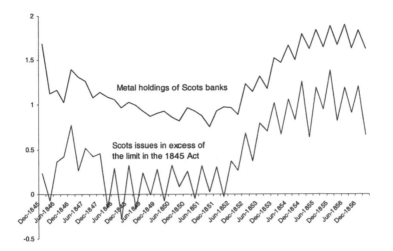

Figure 6.3: Scots Metal Holdings and Extra Note Issues (£m), 1845-57

The institutional arrangements, as already noted, allowed the Scots and Irish banks to issue extra notes above the limits set for them in the 1845 Act, which paralleled the 1844 Act for England and Wales. The limits were based on their average circulation prior to the Act. They could exceed the limits where there was metal (bullion or coin) to back the notes. Of course they were not compelled to do this: and, as Figures 6.3 and 6.4 show, the relationship between the precious metal holdings and the note issues was far from perfect, especially in the case of Ireland.

By contrast, the note issuing activities of the country banks in England and Wales were, as the Currency School had intended, largely neutered by the 1844 Act. Before the Act, Joplin had warned that this would happen. He pointed out that the Act set limits on the country bank note issues which were too low, because it made no allowance for their till-money which they had previously been able to supply freely. In addition, the provision that the Bank could take over only two thirds of the lapsed issues of country banks

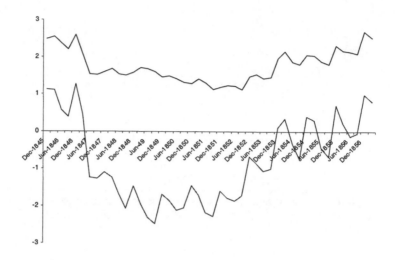

Figure 6.4: Irish Metal Holdings and Extra Note Issues (£m), 1845-57

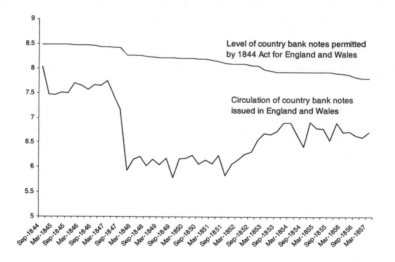

Figure 6.5: Country Bank Issues (£m), 1845-57 (England and Wales)

rested on a fiction about the circulation of gold in the country bank areas (O'Brien, 1993, pp. 77-8). Moreover, as J.W. Gilbart was later to argue, the Act had forced the country banks to keep well below even the levels of issues permitted to them under the Act (Gilbart, 1854, pp. 310-11). Gilbart, as a practical banker, was aware that the balance of profit (from inadvertently exceeding the limit) and (statutory) penalty for so doing, ensured that the country banks felt it prudent to have a significant safety margin below the limit. Indeed as Figure 6.5 shows, the country bank note issues for England and Wales were effectively hemmed in. There was also, as is apparent from Figure 6.5, the catastrophic effect of the October 1847 crisis on the country bank note issues – they had not recovered their March 1847 level ten years later.

6.6.2   Control of the Note Issue

A plot of Bank of England note issue, country bank note issue for England and Wales, and total country bank note issue including Scotland and Ireland, appears to indicate that the Act had indeed produced monetary base control of the UK country note issue, albeit at the cost of neutering the English and Welsh issues. But this is an illusion. The Bank of England note issue and the issues of the banks in Scotland and Ireland were simply responding to the same changes in the balance of payments which produced gold inflows and outflows. Indeed the Scottish and Irish banks were, as already noted, not allowed to expand their note issues on the basis of Bank of England notes. The view of some witnesses before the 1857 Committee was that they were unduly restricted;[6] but, as indicated above, the position of the Act on this matter was entirely logical, given its own terms.

---

[6]See *Parliamentary Papers* (1857). The Bank witnesses favoured the restriction; Hubbard did so circumspectly (qq. 2486-90, 2722-7) while Norman did so directly (qq. 3545-6). J.S. Mill, while reluctant to be drawn on the details of the legislation, disapproved of the Act of 1845 as he did of that of 1844. Most of the Scots banks themselves did not favour the limit (1857, Appendix, pp. 328-62).

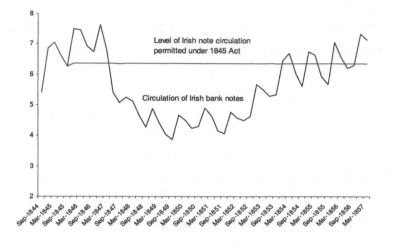

Figure 6.6: Actual and Permitted Irish Note Circulation (£m), 1845-57

As Table 6.7 shows, the Scots banks increased their issues in response to additional metal holdings, though not completely. However, at nearly 90p in the pound the effect is direct and unlagged. The Irish banks actually increased their note issues more than in proportion to changes in their metal holdings, with a coefficient on unlagged changes of 1.37. However, this simply reflects the fact that their issues were for long below the level permitted by the 1845 Act, as Figure 6.6 shows.

Since the country banks in England and Wales now regulated their issues with regard to the upper limits placed upon them by law, it is hardly surprising that they were still, as they had been (though for different reasons) during the years 1832-1844, little influenced by the note issues of the Bank of England. A regression of changes in country bank note issues on changes in the circulation of Bank of England notes (after 1844 it is, for the first time, possible to distinguish between notes in the hands of the public and those still within the Bank) is significant only at 10 per cent, with an $\bar{R}^2$ of

Table 6.7: Scots and Irish Additional Note Issues, 1847-1857

Variables	Dep. var: ΔSX Coefficient	t	Variables	Dep. var: ΔIX coefficient	t
INPT	0.3372	4.0851$^\#$	INPT	0.6217	6.9750$^\#$
ΔMETS	0.8974	2.3154*	ΔMETI	1.3703	6.9469$^\#$
ΔMETS$_{-1}$	0.3693	0.9919	ΔMETI$_{-1}$	0.5804	3.0491$^\#$
ΔMETS$_{-2}$	-0.2368	-0.6263	ΔMETI$_{-2}$	-0.1352	-0.6696
ΔMETS$_{-3}$	0.1049	0.2826	ΔMETI$_{-3}$	0.3181	1.5816
ΔMETS$_{-4}$	-0.1924	-0.7084	ΔMETI$_{-4}$	-0.2809	-1.3351
Q_1	-0.853	-6.7473$^\#$	Q_1	-0.9494	-7.6173$^\#$
Q_2	0.1068	0.8372	Q_2	-0.9352	-6.4043$^\#$
Q_3	-0.5112	-3.8908$^\#$	Q_3	-0.6327	-4.9767$^\#$
R^2	0.8496		R^2	0.8838	
DW	1.9977		DW	1.8306	
F(df)	29.2371(8,32)$^\#$		F(df)	39.0208(8,32)$^\#$	
n	41		n	41	
Period	1847Q1-1857Q1		Period	1847Q1-1857Q1	
Method	OLS		Method	OLS	

Significance levels: * $= 5\%$, $\# = 1\%$.
ΔSX, first differences of the series of Scottish note issues in excess of
the level permitted under the 1844 Act; ΔIX, the corresponding data for
Irish note issues; ΔMETS, first differences of metal holdings (variously
classified as bullion and coin in the Appendices to the 1857 Committee
on Bank Acts) of Scottish banks; ΔMETI, the corresponding figures for
Irish banks. The Q_i are quarterly dummies. Explanatory variables lagged
up to four quarters. Under the 1845 Act the permitted level of Scots
note issues without metal backing was £3.0872m. The corresponding
level for Ireland was £6.3545m. The data source is App. 17 of the 1857
Committee on Bank Acts.

Table 6.8: Control of the Country Bank Note Issue, 1845/6-1856

Variables	Dep. var: ΔCBN		Dep. var: ΔUKN	
	Coefficient	t	Coefficient	t
INPT	0.0018	0.0218	1.2763	6.5495#
ΔBENP	-0.0512	-0.8563	0.0133	-0.0996
ΔBENP$_{-1}$	0.1367	2.2674*	0.2863	2.1191*
ΔBENP$_{-2}$	0.0635	1.0610	0.1061	0.7915
ΔBENP$_{-3}$	0.0966	1.5914	0.1849	1.3577
ΔBENP$_{-4}$	-0.0478	-0.7884	0.0368	0.2707
Q_1	0.0403	0.3302	-1.8735	-6.8594#
Q_2	0.0208	0.1647	-1.3702	-4.7880#
Q_3	-0.1507	-1.2527	-1.8438	-6.7591#
R^2	0.1439		0.6718	
DW	2.4044		2.1089	
F(df)	1.9248(8,36)+		12.0022(8,35)#	
n	45		44	
Period	1845Q4-1856Q4		1846Q1-1856Q4	
Method	OLS		OLS	

Significance levels: $+ = 10\%$, $* = 5\%$, $\# = 1\%$, one-tailed except INPT and Q_i.
For ΔCBN, ΔUKN and Q_i, see Table 6.1. ΔBENP, first differences of series of Bank of England notes excluding Banking Department reserve. Explanatory variables are lagged up to four quarters.

0.1439. As Table 6.8 shows, the most that can be claimed for control of the issues of the country banks in England and Wales is under 14p in the pound with a one quarter lag, for variations in Bank of England notes. It is 4p in the pound with a two quarter lag when changes in all of the Bank's private liabilities are considered. The results look slightly stronger when changes in the whole UK country note issue are considered; but this is due to a degree of correlation between variations in the Bank notes and other liabilities and the note issue of the Scots and Irish banks, the misleading nature of which has already been indicated.

But if the country bank note issue in England and Wales was not controlled by the issues of the Bank of England, and if the Scottish and Irish issues responded *independently* of the Bank of England to bullion flows, the Act had resoundingly failed to achieve its objective of monetary base control.

There remains however the possibility that changes in the specie holdings of the Scottish and Irish banks might themselves be related to changes in the Bank of England note issue. Thus even if the price data (which, for reasons to be discussed below, are not really satisfactory for the period 1844-56) failed to reveal Bank of England control, it might be that specie flows to the Scots and Irish banks might reveal such control. However as Table 6.9 reveals, the data do not support this view. There appears to be a tiny association (3p in the £) between changes in Scots specie holding and changes in Bank of England notes in the hands of the public, significant at 10 per cent. But the sign is wrong – an increase in the Bank issue should weaken the balance of payments and cause metal outflow. Although the regression is significant at 1 per cent, this is not due to the lagged effects of changes in the Bank of England circulation. In the case of the Irish banks the same is true (Table 6.9, cols 4-5). Little more support for the Currency School emerges when we attempt to explain changes in Scots and Irish specie holdings by changes in the total private liabilities of the Bank, and the results are not reported here. An indirect test of the influence of the Bank of England's liabilities on the price level thus fails to provide support for the basic assumptions underpinning the Act. However, the issue can also be tested directly using price indices, although there are difficulties with this approach, as we shall see.

6.6.3 Changes in the Price Level

The major problem encountered in investigating control of prices during the period 1844-56 is a data one. The remarkable Gayer-Rostow-Schwartz series (hereafter GRSP) stops at 1850, and economic historians do not seem to have attempted anything so ambitious since (Feinstein, 1995). But 1844

Table 6.9: Scots and Irish Bullion and Coin, 1846-1856

	Dep. var: ΔMETS		Dep. var: ΔMETI	
Variables	Coefficient	t	Coefficient	t
INPT	0.2308	2.5791*	0.2550	4.0677#
ΔBENP	0.0306	1.6996	0.0283	0.6574
ΔBENP$_{-1}$	-0.0003	-0.0156	0.0471	1.0826
ΔBENP$_{-2}$	0.0132	0.6839	0.0104	0.2408
ΔBENP$_{-3}$	0.0117	0.6783	-0.0356	-0.8133
ΔBENP$_{-4}$	0.0158	0.9108	0.0117	0.2681
Q_1	-0.3413	-1.9374+	-0.2280	-2.5940*
Q_2	-0.1603	-6.4369#	-0.4134	-4.4891#
Q_3	-0.3899	-2.2155*	-0.3560	-4.0558
R^2	0.7965		0.3517	
DW	1.9507		1.8466	
F(df)	16.6599(10,30)#		3.9156(8.35)#	
n	44		44	
Period	1846Q1-1856Q4		1846Q1-1856Q4	
Method	AR(3)		OLS	

Significance levels: $+ = 10\%$, $* = 5\%$, $\# = 1\%$. The coefficient on ΔBENP in equation 1 is not reported because the sign is wrong (see text).

For ΔBENP, see Table 6.8; for ΔMETS, ΔMETI, see Table 6.7. Explanatory variables are lagged up to four quarters.

quarter three[7] to 1850 quarter four provides only 22 observations, which greatly increases the vulnerability of statistical investigation to any of the standard problems encountered in economic (especially time series) data. The GRSP index also contains elements, notably iron, which cause it at one point to be distorted; in 1847 it goes from 109 to 130 and back again. Given the availability of this major source, it seemed sensible to run preliminary tests using it. However the results of such tests were insufficiently clear to be worth reporting; in particular several of the equations exhibited the unusual combination of an insignificant $R^2(F)$ and significant t values on a few of the explanatory variables.[8]

Before proceeding further it seemed sensible to attempt to remedy the shortage of data points for the GRSP index. Accordingly, a new index was constructed, using data supplied by J.G. Hubbard to the 1857 Committee on Bank Acts. This provided another 12 data points. Details of the construction of this index are supplied in Appendix 6.2. Using this new index, an interesting result emerged, although it is hardly one that would have been welcome to the Currency School. As Table 6.10 shows, the only strong relationship is that between changes in the new index and changes in the note issue of the country banks in England and Wales – an issue which, it has already been established, was not controlled by the issues of the Bank of England. There is some relationship between changes in the new index and changes in Bank of England notes in circulation (cols 1-3). The same is true of changes in total Bank of England private liabilities, and in UK country bank notes as a whole, though these results are not reported here. But the coefficients, where

---

[7]The Act is dated 19 July 1844 and the banking system was fully prepared for its provisions by the time they passed into law.

[8]The situation where there are 'significant' t values but R^2 is not significant is rare. It is one of the six cases identified by Geary and Leser (1968). See also Maddala (1977, pp. 122-4). Since the R^2 is itself not significant, the most sensible conclusion seems to be that apparently significant t values involve a Type I error. I am indebted to John Ashworth for discussion on this point.

significant, are much smaller than those in the English and Welsh country bank note case, and for changes in Bank of England notes (cols 1-3) the $\bar{R}^2$ is only 0.36, significant at 10 per cent. In support of the view that in Era II the Bank was beginning to influence the price level, it is noteworthy that – in contrast to Era I – an equation (not shown here) relating changes in the price index to contemporaneous and lagged values of changes in country bank notes *and* Bank notes did contain significant and correctly signed coefficients on both sets of explanatory variables. The contribution of bills of exchange is once again small; the only significant (positive) coefficients are on changes lagged by two, three and four quarters, and they are of small size.

All this relates to the relationship between changes in the levels of different variables. However, as with the data for 1832-1844, it seemed reasonable to investigate the determination of the absolute price level, given the importance of that level for international equilibrium.

6.6.4   The Price Level

The Koyck procedure was again employed to investigate the determinants of the price level. The equations in Table 6.10 are significant, and the signs on the variables in the first two equations are as required by the Koyck procedure (see notes 4 and 5). The clearest relationship is between the country bank note issue for England and Wales and the newly constructed price index (cols. 1-3), a result which is consistent with that obtained using first differences. The relationship between that index and the UK country note issue is also clear, though it is not reported here.

There also appears to be some relation between the absolute level of this price index and that of the note issue of the Bank in the hands of the public (cols 4-6). Thus, allowing the Bank to take over some of the country circulation may have allowed it to play a bigger role even though it is, relative to that of the country banks, still small. There is thus some support for the

Table 6.10: Price Level Changes - Note Issues and Bills, 1845-1853

Variables	Dep. var: ΔPHUB Coefficient	t	Variables	Dep. var: ΔPHUB Coefficient	t
INPT	8.2108	2.0795$^+$	INPT	-4.4931	-1.7050
ΔBENP	2.4641	2.2505*	ΔCBN	7.6241	2.7375$^\#$
ΔBENP$_{-1}$	0.8489	0.7151	ΔCBN$_{-1}$	4.8914	1.4480$^+$
ΔBENP$_{-2}$	3.2596	2.6341$^\#$	ΔCBN$_{-2}$	8.9304	2.5823$^\#$
ΔBENP$_{-3}$	-0.7041	-0.5898	ΔCBN$_{-3}$	2.4742	0.6330
ΔBENP$_{-4}$	1.8401	1.3626$^+$	ΔCBN$_{-4}$	9.9507	3.5575$^\#$
ΔBEXT	0.2413	0.8777	ΔBEXT	0.1282	0.3805
ΔBEXT$_{-1}$	-0.2973	-0.9138	ΔBEXT$_{-1}$	-0.4639	-2.0246
ΔBEXT$_{-2}$	0.7959	2.4160*	ΔBEXT$_{-2}$	-0.7579	-3.2467
ΔBEXT$_{-3}$	-0.7704	-2.3572	ΔBEXT$_{-3}$	0.5641	1.6155$^+$
ΔBEXT$_{-4}$	0.4338	1.4939$^+$	ΔBEXT$_{-4}$	-0.6976	-1.8705
Q_1	-13.9371	-1.9950$^+$	Q_1	9.6830	2.4685*
Q_2	-3.4530	-1.4811	Q_2	-1.3998	-0.8706
Q_3	-16.4075	-2.3633*	Q_3	14.9202	3.2041$^\#$
R^2	0.3600		R^2	0.6793	
DW	2.2307		DW	2.1522	
F(df)	2.2052(14,16)$^+$		F(df)	4.4894(17,11)$^\#$	
n	33		n	33	
Period	1845Q4-1853Q4		Period	1845Q4-1853Q4	
Method	AR(2)		Method	AR(4)	

Significance levels: $+ = 10\%$, $* = 5\%$, $\# = 1\%$, on one-tailed tests on all variables except INPT and Q_i.
ΔPHUB is first differences of the price index series calculated by applying Gayer-Rostow-Schwartz weights to the price data supplied to the 1857 Committee on Bank Acts by J.G Hubbard (Appendix 32, pp. 290-1) details of which are given in the appendix to this chapter. For ΔBENP, see Table 6.8; for ΔCBN, and Q_i, see Table 6.1; for ΔBEXT, see Table 6.3. Explanatory variables are lagged up to four quarters.

Currency School in this result; and this is consistent with the result for first differences of the variables reported in Table 6.11.

If we extend the investigation of levels to employ the two variable Koyck procedure, including bills of exchange in the price equation, we do find that the country bank note issue affects the price index, even allowing for the presence of bills of exchange. The signs on the coefficients of the equation including UK note issues and bills of exchange (cols 7-9) are all as required, with the exception of the (insignificant) coefficient on lagged bills of exchange. An equation relating the price index to the Bank of England notes, and bills, was, as for Era I, unsatisfactory, with an incorrect sign on the two-quarter lagged dependent variable. Perhaps the most interesting aspect of this is the fact that, once we allow for bills of exchange, the influence of the note circulation of the Bank of England loses most of the importance indicated in cols 4-6 of Table 6.11.

6.6.5   Bills of Exchange

This last point raises the question of the control of the supply of bills of exchange in the second period, 1844-56. The results obtained are consistent with those obtained for the first period.

As Tables 6.12 shows, increases in interest rates at first *increase* the total value of bills of exchange in the equations (which also allow for changes in country bank notes and in both total Bank liabilities and Bank notes), indicating the kind of resistance to credit tightening to which Overstone had referred. However, coefficients on lagged values of interest rate increases tend to be negative, which is again consistent with Overstone's view. The country bank note issue changes have a large and significant positive effect, implying support for the Currency School view that bills of exchange were part of the credit superstructure, rather than substituting for notes as the Banking School argued. This effect seems to have been reinforced by changes

Table 6.11: Price Levels, Note Issues and Bills, 1844/5-1853

Variables	Dep. var: PHUB Coefficient	t	Variables	Dep. var: PHUB Coefficient	t
INPT	-0.4108	-0.0411	INPT	1.0409	0.0897
$PHUB_{-1}$	0.5578	$4.0181^{\#}$	$PHUB_{-1}$	0.7126	$5.2939^{\#}$
CBN	5.4161	$3.0064^{\#}$	BENP	1.1045	2.3727^{*}
Q_1	1.0134	0.4442	Q_1	1.4049	1.0496
Q_2	-1.5679	-1.4281	Q_2	-1.6709	-2.3840^{*}
Q_3	1.1056	0.4940	Q_3	0.8522	0.6251
R^2	0.7894		R^2	0.8344	
h	1.1596		h	-0.7584	
F(df)	$22.2369(6,28)^{\#}$		F(df)	$24.0371(7,25)^{\#}$	
n	37		n	37	
Period	1844Q4-1853Q4		Period	1844Q4-1853Q4	
Method	AR(2)		Method	AR(4)	

Variables	Dep. var: PHUB Coefficient	t
INPT	40.4089	$2.8019^{\#}$
$PHUB_{-1}$	0.2355	0.6866
$PHUB_{-2}$	-0.3044	-0.8900
UKN	1.8792	1.9089^{+}
UKN_{-1}	-0.1153	-0.1175
BEXT	0.0454	0.2687
$BEXT_{-1}$	0.1692	0.8230
Q_1	4.6800	1.4965
Q_2	0.5274	0.3834
Q_3	4.4320	1.3544
R^2	0.8907	
LM(2)	5.7857	
F(df)	$17.9264\ (13,\ 14)^{\#}$	
n	32	
Period	1846Q1-1853Q4	
Method	AR(4)	

Significance levels: $+ = 10\%$, $* = 5\%$, $\# = 1\%$, one-tailed on PHUB, CBN, UKN, BENP and BEXT explanatory variables, otherwise two-tailed. For PHUB, see Table 6.10; for INPT, CBN, UKN, Q_i, see Table 6.1: for BENP, see Table 6.8. Following the standard Koyck procedure, PHUB is subject to a one period lag as an explanatory variable, in columns 1-6 and to a one and two period lag in columns 7-9.

in the Bank's note circulation (lagged one quarter). The picture is less clear cut when we consider UK country issues rather than those for England and Wales (this result is not reported here), though again changes in these seem to have a significant controlling effect quite rapidly.

In contrast to the corresponding equation for Era I (Table 6.6), there is evidence, in Table 6.13, of some small feedback from changes in the price index (though lagged one quarter) to changes in the total value of bills of exchange. This result, which would bring at least some comfort to the Banking School, is consistent with the results of causality tests discussed in Appendix 6.1.

6.6.6   Macroeconomic Variability

The Currency School confidently expected that the 1844 Act would stabilise macroeconomic activity. There would be reduced fluctuations in the level of the Bank's bullion holding because 'drains' would not go on for so long, being checked early in their course. Changes in the level of bullion would themselves occur in a steadier manner, rather than experiencing the sort of acceleration which might occur with a continuing 'drain', as an internal demand for gold was added to an external one.

Since bullion fluctuations were to be reduced, fluctuations in the price level would also be reduced as part and parcel of an early correction of balance of payments disequilibrium, the price level depending on the money supply, linked by the Act to the bullion level and thus to the balance of payments.

Price changes would be steady and not erratic, as part of the equilibrating process of achieving a balance of payments equilibrium and a price level which was appropriate for this.

Interest rates should also be more stable; the Bank would have to act early when faced with a 'drain' and would thus be unable to delay things to

Table 6.12: Total Bills of Exchange and Note Issues, 1845-1853: Part A

Variables	Dep. var: ΔBEXT Coefficient	t	Variables	Dep. var: ΔBEXT Coefficient	t
INPT	-4.9899	-5.0068	INPT	-4.222	-2.9868
ΔBR	3.1658	2.3523*	ΔBR	2.8011	1.8400+
ΔBR$_{-1}$	-0.0954	-0.0698	ΔBR$_{-1}$	-0.1602	-0.1053
ΔBR$_{-2}$	0.2186	0.1696	ΔBR$_{-2}$	-0.7191	-0.4934
ΔBR$_{-3}$	-0.2796	-0.2117	ΔBR$_{-3}$	-0.2781	-0.1880
ΔBR$_{-4}$	-0.5702	-0.4742	ΔBR$_{-4}$	0.0662	0.0523
ΔCBN	7.3726	3.2760#	ΔCBN	8.8924	4.3205#
ΔCBN$_{-1}$	1.4987	0.4909	ΔCBN$_{-1}$	1.4272	0.4206
ΔCBN$_{-2}$	1.8239	0.6304	ΔCBN$_{-2}$	0.7715	0.2185
ΔCBN$_{-3}$	0.8103	0.2793	ΔCBN$_{-3}$	2.3653	0.7006
ΔCBN$_{-4}$	-0.5573	-0.2415	ΔCBN$_{-4}$	1.0315	0.3776
ΔBENP	-0.3758	-0.4008	ΔPRIVLP	-0.0419	-0.1321
ΔBENP$_{-1}$	1.9766	2.2418*	ΔPRIVLP$_{-1}$	0.2912	0.9070
ΔBENP$_{-2}$	-0.0390	-0.0455	ΔPRIVLP$_{-2}$	-0.3646	-0.8546
ΔBENP$_{-3}$	0.0076	0.0076	ΔPRIVLP$_{-3}$	0.0317	0.0879
ΔBENP$_{-4}$	-0.0620	0.0555	ΔPRIVLP$_{-4}$	0.2968	0.8228
Q_1	9.9209	6.3350#	Q_1	6.9982	3.1284#
Q_2	2.8961	1.8708*	Q_2	2.3322	1.0266
Q_3	8.6860	5.5062#	Q_3	10.159	4.9820#
R^2	0.7970		R^2	0.7730	
DW	2.1136		DW	2.2948	
F(df)	7.9790 (18, 14)#		F(df)	7.0525(18, 14)#	
n	33		n	33	
Period	1845Q4-1853Q4		Period	1845Q4-1853Q4	
Method	OLS		Method	OLS	

Significance levels: $+ = 10\%$, $* = 5\%$, $\# = 1\%$, two-tailed on all variables. For ΔBEXT and ΔBR, see Table 6.6; for ΔCBN, ΔUKN, Q_i, see Table 6.1; for ΔBENP, see Table 6.8; for ΔPHUB, see Table 6.10; ΔPRIVLP, first differences of series for private deposits at Bank of England plus Bank notes in the hands of the public. Explanatory variables are lagged up to four quarters.

Table 6.13: Total Bills of Exchange and Note Issues, 1845-1853: Part B

Variables	Dep. var: ΔBEXT Coefficient	t
INPT	-4.9600	-6.8049[#]
ΔPHUB	0.0052	0.0437
ΔPHUB$_{-1}$	0.3441	2.8124[#]
ΔPHUB$_{-2}$	0.1276	1.0387
ΔPHUB$_{-3}$	0.0324	0.3065
ΔPHUB$_{-4}$	-0.1127	-0.9702
Q_1	9.1619	8.5515[#]
Q_2	2.4825	2.2485*
Q_3	9.8893	8.7130[#]
R^2	0.8259	
DW	2.0584	
F(df)	16.1820 (10, 22)[#]	
n	33	
Period	1845Q4-1853Q4	
Method	OLS	

For INPT and Q_2 see Table 6.1.
for PHUB see Table 6.10

the point where a panic raising of the rate of discount was required. This in turn implied that changes in Bank Rate would be orderly and smooth.

Unfortunately, in comparing the two periods 1832-44 and 1844-56 we find that virtually none of these hopes was realised (Table 6.14). It is true that the variance in the bullion level of the Bank is lower in the second period; but this decrease is not significant. The variance of quarterly changes in the bullion level actually increases in the second period, and the increase is significant at 5 per cent. Prices, as judged by the variance of the GRSP index, were actually less stable in period 2, although the increase in variance is not significant at 5 per cent. But not only is the variance of quarterly changes in that index higher in the second period but the difference is significant at 1 per cent. This may reflect, however, the economic turbulence of the late 1840s, with the railway boom and the financial crisis of 1847-8 – the GRSP index stops at 1850. Indeed this adverse result is sensitive to the index used; if we use the index constructed from the data supplied by Hubbard (PHUB), which runs to 1853, we do indeed find that the variability of prices has fallen, and by a statistically significant extent. The variability of price changes has also fallen, though the difference is not significant. The construction of the Hubbard index is discussed in Appendix 6.2.

However, despite the hopes of the Currency School, there was no greater smoothness in the issues of the Bank. The variance of total Bank of England note issues increased in the second period, and the increase is significant at 1 per cent. The variability of the quarterly changes in the total of that note issue also increased, and again the increase is significant at 1 per cent.

The Currency School attached more importance to Bank notes in the hands of the public than to the total issues of the Bank. Even here, though the variability *seems* to have increased (we cannot be sure, as notes outside the Bank are not shown separately in the data up to 1844, so that we have to compare variability in the public circulation of Bank notes after 1844 with variability of all Bank of England notes before 1844), the increase is not

Table 6.14: Macroeconomic Variability, 1833-1844 and 1844-1857

Variable	Standard deviation		F	df
	ERA I	ERA II		
BEBULL	3.2103	3.0847	1.0831	44, 50
ΔBULL	1.2590	1.6235	0.6014*	44, 50
GRSP	10.0904	13.1254	0.5910	50, 26
ΔGRSP	4.3461	7.5964	0.3273#	50, 26
PHUB	10.1853	7.1532	2.0274*	42, 38
ΔPHUB	4.8668	4.1812	1.3548	42, 38
BR	0.8839	1.2090	0.5345*	50, 50
ΔBR	0.4694	0.6873	0.4664#	50, 50
BEN	1.1987	2.8348	0.1788#	49, 49
ΔBEN	0.9593	1.7131	0.3136#	49, 49
BENP*	1.1987	1.3615	0.7751	49, 49
ΔBENP*	0.9593	0.6812	1.9829#	49, 49
UKN	1.6976	1.8484	0.8435	43, 45
ΔUKN	0.9600	0.9765	0.9665	43, 45

Significance levels: * = 5%, # = 1%.
BEBULL is the bullion holding of the Bank of England; for
GRSP, see Table 6.3; for BR, see Table 6.6; for BENP,
see Table 6.8 (the asterisk indicates that there is no
distinction before 1844 between Bank notes in the hands
of the public and those held by the Bank itself); for UKN,
see Table 6.1.

significant. However, with the same caveat, we do indeed find variability in the quarterly changes in such notes to have decreased after 1844, and this decrease is significant at 1 per cent so that the Currency School could take some comfort from that.

The Banking School had warned that separation of the Bank into a Department of Issue and a Department of Banking would lead to wide fluctuations in the rate of interest after 1844, as the Banking Department varied Bank Rate to protect its reserve, in a situation in which it was not free to do so by adding to the issue of its own notes (for example, Tooke, 1844, pp. 109, 124, 164). This prediction of the Banking School with regard to Bank Rate is borne out; the variance of Bank Rate was higher in the second period, and the difference is significant at 5 per cent. It is also true that the variance of quarterly changes in the Rate is higher in the second period, and this is significant at 1 per cent. However, though the Banking School writers were correct about the variability of Bank Rate, its average level was no higher – perhaps as a result of attempts by the Bank to increase its market share of discounts, especially up to 1847, the average of Bank Rate was lower after 1844. The geometric mean for 1832-44 is 3.8729, while for 1844-56 it is 3.4663, and a t-test which allows for a statistically significant difference in the variance (as established above) indicates that this difference in means is significant at 5 per cent on a one-tailed test.

It may well be the case that the hopes of the Currency School were disappointed because they were targeting the wrong money supply, as Joplin had argued. However, the 1844 Act was no more successful in reducing the amplitude of the country bank note issues than it was of the Bank of England issues. The variance of UK country note issues actually increased during the second period, although the increase is not significant at 5 per cent. The variance of the quarterly changes also increased, although again this was not significant. There would be no reassurance for the Currency School in this.

6.7   Conclusions

Despite the imperfections of some of the data, notably those for prices, it seems clear that, notwithstanding the magnificent coherence of the Currency School vision, the Act of 1844 did not succeed in its aims of introducing monetary base control for the British economy, and of stabilising the price level and the monetary aggregates. In the period up to 1844 there is considerable support for the view, put forward by Thomas Joplin, that the country bank note issue was the most important part of the money supply. It was the country bank note issue for England and Wales which had the dominant influence on the price level, with some small additional contribution from bills of exchange. The bills themselves were however significantly influenced, though not completely controlled, by the country bank note issues. But the Act failed to bring that country note issue under the control of the Bank – rather it was the imposition of statutory limits which was important.

The country banks in Scotland and Ireland had greater freedom to vary their issues, on the basis of metal holdings; but those metal holdings themselves did not respond significantly to changes in the Bank of England's notes, or indeed of its more widely defined private liabilities. The price level however continued, as in the first period, to depend principally on the country bank note issue. There was, again, some small additional influence exerted by bills of exchange. The country bank note issue itself was still uncontrolled by the Bank. There are, after 1844, some tentative signs that the Bank was beginning to influence the price level directly, however. Without data on bank deposits it is impossible to say exactly how the system was working after 1844 and whether, indeed, bank deposits were themselves subject to some control both through Bank Rate and through variations in the Bank's private liabilities.

The hopes of the Currency School for monetary control were, then, for the most part, not realised. Most of their hopes for greater economic stability were unrealised as well. Only with regard to prices is there evidence which the Currency School could find reassuring. But there is little evidence to support the Banking School's positions either. Moreover, the Currency School could claim, for their part, that after 1844, and in stark contrast to events before that date, convertibility of the note issue into gold was never in doubt. Essentially what happened is that the Currency School had developed a model which was appropriate, if at all, for a different financial system, in which large scale joint stock banking (as pioneered by Joplin) did not operate. The results of this study would certainly indicate that both this model and that of the Banking School were inadequate.

Appendix 6.1. The Question of Causality

Both members of the Banking School, and the latter-day enthusiasts for their work to be found among the apostles of free banking, have questioned a basic assumption made by the Currency School – that causality ran from the money supply to the price level. However, employment of standard causality tests, associated respectively with Granger, Sargent and Sims, indicates no support for the Banking School position and indeed provides some support for the Currency School on this key matter. The results are summarised in Table 6.15. It is clear that there is support from the tests for the proposition that changes in the country bank note issue for England and Wales caused changes in prices. Almost all of the test statistics are significant at 10 per cent or better, and those on the Sims test are significant at 1 per cent. Because of the difficulties over price data for the second period referred to above, these tests were confined to the data for the first period.

By contrast, changes in prices did not cause changes in the country bank note issues. Only one of the available statistics, the Sims LM test, which is significant at 10 per cent, provides any support for this view. When causality tests are applied to changes in bills of exchange and changes in prices, the results, unlike those for country bank notes and prices, conflict to some extent with the results obtained above. While some weak effect of bills of exchange on prices, when these were added to the price equations, was reported above, this is not supported by the causality tests. In contrast, the causality tests conflict with the failure of regression analysis to find any statistically significant coefficients on the price changes, when changes in bills of exchange are regressed on (lagged) changes in prices (table 6.6, cols 4-6), using data for 1832-44. However, according to such tests, causality runs from (changes in) country bank note issues to (changes in) total values of bills of exchange, and not the other way round – the country issues do not seem to have expanded in response to increased usage of bills of exchange.

Table 6.15: Causality Tests, 1833-44

Hypothesis	Granger	TEST Sargent	Sims
ΔCBN causes	LM 8.9958$^+$	LM 9.2028$^+$	LM 21.7595$^\#$
ΔGRSP	LR 10.2267*	LMF 2.0847	LMF 7.8062$^\#$
	F (4, 27) 2.0238		
ΔGRSP causes	LM 0.1590	LM 6.5992	LM 8.2625$^+$
ΔCBN	LR 0.1240	LMF 1.3748	LMF 1.4678
	F (4, 27) 1.3748		
ΔBEXT causes	LM 1.4069	LM 1.4069	LM 3.7958
ΔGRSP	LR 1.4294	LMF 0.2663	LMF 0.6002
	F (4, 33) 0.2663		
ΔGRSP causes	LM 9.6784*	LM 11.2085*	LM 11.9257*
ΔBEXT	LR 10.8976*	LMF 2.7301*	LMF 2.5636
	F (4, 33) 2.2606$^+$		
ΔCBN causes	LM 24.1308$^\#$	LM 28.4961$^\#$	LM 23.3492$^\#$
ΔBEXT	LR 37.6065$^\#$	LMF 18.3122	LMF 9.5194$^\#$
	F (4, 27) 10.9544$^\#$		
ΔBEXT causes	LM 0.9045	LM 0.9046	LM 4.0316
ΔCBN	LR 0.9152	LMF 0.1603	LMF 0.6184
	F (4, 27) 0.1603		

Significance levels: $+$ = 10%, * = 5%, $\#$ = 1%. The LM figure is the Lagrange Multiplier statistic (χ^2); LMF is the F distribution version of this; LR is the Likelihood Ratio statistic.

For ΔCBN, see Table 6.1. For ΔGRSP and ΔBEXT, see Table 6.3.

Apendix 6.2. Price Data

As mentioned in the body of the chapter, the remarkable Gayer-Rostow-Schwartz index runs only to 1850. This results in too few observations for the period 1844-57, especially when lags of up to four quarters are employed, for standard techniques of statistical inference to be reliable. A partial remedy for this was provided by the index PHUB used in the text, which provides another twelve observations, extending to Q4 of 1853.

The data for this index were supplied by J.G. Hubbard to the 1857 Committee on Bank Acts, and are reproduced in its appendix (II, appendix 32, pp. 290-1). Hubbard's data contained quarterly observations for the years 1834 to 1853 for prices of fifteen commodities. After dropping overlapping items (e.g. cotton yarn and cotton cloth) the prices of the remaining eleven commodities were used to construct a geometric mean of price relatives for 1844 Q3 to 1853 Q4 of the form following Gayer, Rostow and Schwartz (1953, vol. 1, pp. 480)

$$M = \left[\left(\frac{p_1}{b_1} \right)^{w_1} \left(\frac{p_2}{b_2} \right)^{w_2} \cdots \left(\frac{p_n}{b_n} \right)^{w_n} \right]^{1/\Sigma w} \tag{6.1}$$

where M is the weighted geometric average of the price relative, p_i and b_i represent the price of commodity i in current and base year respectively, and w_i is the weight in the index for commodity i. The weights used are those employed in the Gayer-Rostow-Schwartz study (1953, vol. 1, p. 484).

Chapter 7

The Lender of Last Resort Concept

The idea that a fractional reserve banking system needs a lender of last resort is so deeply embedded in the mentality of most economists (with the possible exception of members of the Free Banking School) that it seems to many to be unquestionable.[1] Yet this was not always so. Even in the two most highly developed economies in the 19th century, those of Britain and the United States, the idea underwent a long struggle for recognition. It developed slowly, in the teeth of considerable resistance, with the debate being shaped to a considerable extent by the pressure of events.

This chapter traces the development of the idea in Britain, where it is widely recognised to have originated in the 1790s, and to have been artic-

---

[1] The Free Banking School finds common ground with Walter Bagehot in his statement that one single centralised reserve for the monetary system was not a natural state of affairs, but one resulting from the legal restrictions on the development of English banking and, in particular, from the Bank of England's privileges (Bagehot, 1873, pp. 66-71; White, 1984, pp. 43-4, 57, 145-6). However Bagehot's remarks have to be seen in the context of the time and, in particular, in the light of the emphatic endorsement of the privileges of the Bank by the Currency School which, ironically, argued for decentralised reserves to avoid reliance on the Bank. Bagehot (1873, p. 69) himself was quite clear that there was no going back: 'I do not suggest that we should return to a natural or many-reserve system of banking. I should only incur useless ridicule if I did suggest it'. As David Laidler (1991, pp. 184-7) has shown, it was left to Edgeworth, in a little-known paper, to establish a decisive case for centralisation of reserves, based upon a probability distribution of demands on the reserve, and economies of scale in reserve holding.

ulated by Francis Baring and Henry Thornton (section 7.1). The Bank of England was reluctant to accept such a role; but the financial crisis of 1825 witnessed a dramatic volte face on the part of the Bank which, literally overnight, changed its policy, from one of resistance to requests for assistance to that of lending freely (section 7.2). A key question, largely ignored in the literature, is the origin of that remarkable change (section 7.3).

Following the events of 1825, the role of the Bank as lender of last resort was examined during the course of the Select Committee hearings of 1832 on the renewal of the Bank Charter (section 7.4). In the subsequent debate during the 1830s, Thomas Joplin played a significant role (section 7.5). During the debate the Currency School strongly, and for theoretically cogent reasons, opposed the idea that the Bank should have a last-resort role, and was successful in seeing the logic of its opposition embodied in the 1844 Bank Charter Act (section 7.6).[2] But the credibility of the Act was damaged by a crisis only three years later, a crisis, moreover, in which the question of the availability of last-resort facilities played a central role (section 7.7). An even more severe crisis of a similar type was to follow in 1857 (section 7.8). The experience of the Act in operation had pinpointed a central flaw in the application of the Currency School model in the context of an economy like Britain where there was only one, centrally held, reserve for the whole financial system. In these circumstances the Bank, the holder of that reserve, was forced, despite strong resistance from some of its own Directors, to accept its position as lender of last resort (section 7.9).

Bagehot's Lombard Street (1873), widely associated in later literature with the formulation of the last-resort doctrine, in truth rationalised and analysed (albeit with outstanding ability) the outcome of an eighty year process of development of an initial idea. It is the history of that process

---

[2] As explained in section 7.6, the principle of metallic fluctuation of the note issue to control the cycle, which was a core theoretical concept for the Currency School, was theoretically inconsistent with the provision of last resort facilities.

which is explored in this chapter.

7.1 The 1790s: Baring and Thornton

The lender of last resort concept developed in Britain over a period extending from the 1790s to the 1870s. While it is true that the Bank of England extended assistance to banks in the 18th century (Baring, 1797, p. 14), it was really only in the 1790s, as war with France threatened financial stability, that the concept of the Bank as indeed the 'last resort' chrystallised. As so often with the genuinely important ideas in economics, it was the pressure of events that brought about the recognition.

Credit for the initial formulation of the idea goes to two writers, Sir Francis Baring and Henry Thornton. It was Baring who published first. He identified a failure of the Bank to recognise its unique position as having precipitated the financial crisis of 1793, in which the liquidity of the system was saved only by direct government intervention and the issue of exchequer bills (Baring, 1797, p. 22; Horner, 1802, p. 135). The Bank, he argued, had rationed discounts so severely that it had precipitated a panic; and it should not have done this because 'there is no resource on their refusal, for they are the *dernier resort*' (1797, p. 22). The Bank should be prepared to act as the last-resort lender to the country banks 'almost to their last guinea' (1797, p. 25). In stressing that the Bank was the *dernier resort* (1797, p. 47), Baring was thus well aware, as Horner was later to emphasise, that it was necessary to save the country banks to save the London ones (Horner, 1802, p. 134).

Baring's role, though recognised in the essays by T.M. Humphrey (1987, 1989, 1997; Humphrey and Keleher, 1984), is generally seen as being much less significant than that of Henry Thornton, who is rightly given pride of place. Indeed since Hayek appended to the 1939 reprint of Thornton's *Paper Credit* (1802) the parliamentary evidence which Thornton gave in 1797, after the suspension of specie payments by the Bank, it is easy for all to see that

Thornton clearly stated the role of the Bank at the heart of the monetary system, in the same year as Baring's pamphlet was published (Thornton, 1802, pp. 277-310).

Humphrey has pointed out that it was Thornton who first made the crucial point that providing last-resort facilities was perfectly consistent with monetary control; last-resort lending dealt with temporary, minor, and self-reversing deviations from the optimal path for the money supply, while denial of last-resort facilities would eventually result in monetary collapse, and major deviations (Thornton, 1802, pp. 186-8; Humphrey, 1987, pp. 571-2). Such major deviations would cause damage to the real economy, interfere with exports, and thus add an external drain of gold to the internal one involved in a financial panic (Thornton, 1802, pp. 122-4; Humphrey, 1993, pp. 12-13).

The provision of last-resort facilities was a commitment to the system, not to individual banks; Thornton saw that there was no need to support the insolvent, and there was a risk of moral hazard if relief were to be given indiscriminately (1802, p. 188). But the system as a whole had to be supported, and the Bank, which was universally expected to provide cash, faced great difficulties if it attempted to contract its note issues (1802, pp. 287, 304-5).

One single national bank was best for the last-resort role and, as the bank in that position, the Bank of England had an interest in the maintenance of public credit. It was not safe itself unless it kept the commercial world safe, and if it attempted to restrict the supply of its notes it would simply bring on itself a demand for gold (1802, pp. 127, 288). A cumulative bank run would spread from the country banks, which held Bank of England notes, rather than gold coin, as their own reserve, resulting in a drain on the Bank 'that we may naturally suppose that it does not very cheerfully endure' (1802, p. 181).

The Bullion Committee of 1810, of whose report Thornton was one of the authors, endorsed this general position, holding that in the event of an internal drain the note issue of the Bank should be increased, the notes of the country banks being discredited (Cannan, ed., 1810, pp. 57, 59-60).

Thornton's views did not of course find universal acceptance among his contemporaries. David Ricardo and other 'rigid Bullionists' (O'Brien, 1975, pp. 147-53) adhered to what became known as the Ricardian definition of excess – if gold were valued above its par value and the exchanges were depressed, then by definition the currency was excessive and should be contracted, come what may in the way of commercial distress. But Thornton himself had made a much more fundamental and subtle contribution to the understanding both of the operation of the monetary system and to its correct management.

Thus by 1810 the major foundations of the concept of lender of last resort had apparently been laid and (possibly with some mention of the Banking School in the 1840s) most accounts of subsequent developments focus on Walter Bagehot. Thornton had established that the Bank was the holder of the final reserve. It was thus different from a normal commercial bank; this meant that it had both the power and duty to lend in a crisis. It should hold a large buffer reserve and distinguish between internal and external drains, lending freely in the former case. Bagehot then revived and restated many of the points made by Thornton, but added the following: the emergency lending should be at a high rate of interest, indeed a penalty rate, and the availability of last resort facilities should be preannounced. The first of these provisions would encourage the return to the Bank of funds which would otherwise increase the money supply unacceptably, and the preannouncement would reduce the likelihood of panic. Like Thornton, Bagehot also held that the Bank should lend to anyone who had good security – carefully defined as what would be good security in normal as distinct from panic conditions – and that it had no duty to uphold those who did not have such security

(Humphrey, 1993; Bagehot, 1873, pp. 173, 196-9).[3]

While this is an accurate and informative treatment of the issues, the full history of the development of the ideas turns out to involve significant progress in the sixty-three years between the Bullion Report and Bagehot's *Lombard Street*, and to include a role, at a crucial juncture, for Bagehot's maternal uncle and one-time employer, Vincent Stuckey.

7.2   The Crisis of 1825

In 1825 London was hit by a major financial crisis.[4] The immediate cause was a reluctance on the part of the Bank to lend on the security of government debt; monetary tightness had already brought commercial bills into discredit. The Bank seems to have thought that the government should and would intervene, initially to suspend specie payments (Fetter, 1965, p. 116) and later, as in 1793, by issuing exchequer bills which would become an acceptable form of commercial security (Clapham, 1944, II, p. 108; Morgan, 1943, p. 8). But the government, apparently fearful of the effect on the rate at which it would have to fund public debt, declined to co-operate. By 13th December 1825, a day on which the lending by the Bank was significantly lower than on previous days, the whole financial system seemed poised on the edge of an abyss. But, the next day, the Bank abruptly reversed its policy, and lent freely, not only on government securities but on a wide range of collateral – even goods – as revealed by the testimony of one of the Bank Directors, Jeremiah Harman, before a subsequent parliamentary hearing (1832 Committee, q. 2217).[5] Not only was the change of policy

---

[3]I am indebted to Tom Humphrey for the point that appraising collateral at pre-panic prices is a rough and ready test of normal solvency that thus avoided lengthy inquiries.

[4]An excellent account of the crisis is to be found in Fetter (1965, pp. 111-20); see also Clapham (1944, II, pp. 98-100).

[5]Details of the Parliamentary Papers containing the reports of the proceedings of the various committees referred to in this chapter will be found in the bibliography under the heading 'Parliamentary Papers'.

dramatic; it involved last-resort lending on a scale hitherto undreamt of, and it marked the emergence of the Bank as unquestionably the *dernier resort* (to borrow Baring's phrase) of the financial system (Hawtrey, 1932, p. 122; Fetter, 1965, p. 116). The central question, from the point of view of the present discussion, is who was responsible for this dramatic development.

7.3   Thomas Joplin and Vincent Stuckey

On the evening of 13 December 1825, as the Bank's reluctance to support financial institutions was becoming starkly apparent, Thomas Joplin, the maverick pioneer of joint stock banking, and much else besides (O'Brien, 1993), published in the *Courier*, a newspaper which was believed to have some links to government (Joplin, 1839, p. 47n), an article urging the Bank to alter course dramatically. (The article is reprinted in Joplin, 1832, pp. 221-4 and Joplin, 1835, pp. 22-5.)

Joplin's case was this. The Bank had precipitated a liquidity shortage by its previous policy of monetary tightness. This had resulted in a completely abnormal increase in precautionary balances outside the Bank. The Bank should respond to this by increasing its note issue to offset the loss of circulation. This could be done with complete safety because increases in the money supply only affected the price level and the exchanges after a long lag, and the extra notes could easily be withdrawn from circulation once the crisis had passed and long before prices were affected (Joplin, 1828, pp. 175-6; 1832, pp. 196-206, 209-17, 221-35, 252; 1833, pp. 80-2; 1835, pp. 23-5, 31-2; 1839, pp. 46-7n; 1841, pp. 44-5n; 1844, pp. 55-6).

The following morning the Bank opened its doors and proceeded to offer financial assistance on a hitherto undreamed of scale, as already noted. In many subsequent publications Joplin claimed credit for the dramatic change of policy, which had saved the financial system. But Joplin was an outsider, a rough man from the timber trade of the North East of England, and the City did not want to acknowledge his claims. He was unsuccessful in his attempt to give evidence before the 1832 Committee on the Bank Charter, and his subsequent call for a public inquiry was ignored (Joplin, 1832, p. 252; 1835; O'Brien, 1993, p. 21).

However another figure, one more acceptable to the City, was to intervene the next morning, and has been accorded more credit than Joplin for the change in the behaviour of the Bank. For on the morning of 14 December – thus roughly twelve hours after Joplin's article had become public – the banker Vincent Stuckey wrote to the Bank pressing the case for a reversal of policy; and it is apparently the case that the letter was received well before the Bank opened its doors (Gregory, 1936, II, p. 149; Clapham, 1944, II, p. 99). In the letter Stuckey made the point, according to the evidence which he later gave to the 1832 Committee (q. 1195), that Joplin had made the previous night; the emergency additions to the money supply would not affect the price level. Stuckey was thus allowed to describe his role in the crisis, and his intervention was also referred to in other evidence (1832 Committee, q. 5012, Richards).

In terms of the development of the lender of last resort concept, however, in the more than half-century between Thornton and Bagehot, there is one incidental fact that relates rather dramatically to all this; Vincent Stuckey (who lived for a further twenty years after the crisis) was Bagehot's maternal uncle, and both Bagehot's father and Bagehot himself worked for the bank of Stuckey and Bagehot (Buchan, 1959, pp. 18-20, 73-5). Bagehot himself, though he makes no reference to his uncle in *Lombard Street*, was undoubtedly deeply impressed by the events of the 1825 crisis (Bagehot, 1873, pp. 179, 199-203), and in the book he quotes from the 1832 evidence of Jeremiah Harman referred to above (Bagehot, 1873, pp. 51-2).[6]

---

[6]That Bagehot's father in law was the famous (or, to the Currency School, notorious) James Wilson, founder of the *Economist*, and a leading light in the Banking School, may also have a bearing on the development of Bagehot's views, although it is argued below that the Banking School did not develop the case for a lender of last resort.

It seems reasonable to infer from all this that Stuckey's intervention owed not a little to Joplin's article; that Joplin's article produced the dramatic intervention by the Bank; and that thus Bagehot's classic statement of the role of the lender of last resort stems from the intervention of the outsider Thomas Joplin.

Joplin was not a man to let go of the initiative, once he had seized it, and he followed his initial article with three more on 14, 15 and 16 December, all of them in the *Courier* (reprinted in Joplin, 1832, pp. 224-7, 227-30, 230-2; 1835, pp. 26-8, 28-31), in which he hammered home the point that additions to the money supply in crisis had nothing to do with optimal management of the money supply in relation to the exchanges.

The case for Joplin is further strengthened by the fact that, up to and including 13 December, other newspapers had supported the Bank in its reluctance to extend help to the City (Joplin, 1832, pp. 196-217). His claim is dismissed by Clapham in his history of the Bank (Clapham, 1944, II, p. 99n), yet the figures of Bank assistance listed by Clapham provide strong support for Joplin. On Tuesday 13 December, with the financial storm raging, the Bank reduced its discounts from £1.265m on the previous day to £0.542m. After Joplin's intervention the figures were £1.049m and £2.054m on 14 and 15 December, and, as the worst of the storm abated and it was apparent that the Bank would lend freely, £0.379m and £0.688m on 16 and 17 December (Clapham, 1944, II, p. 99).

7.4 The 1832 Hearings

When Parliament set up a Committee, at the height of the Reform Bill agitation in 1832, to consider the renewal of the charter of the Bank, the lessons learned from the crisis of 1825 were given an airing. The testimony of several witnesses is particularly interesting.

Vincent Stuckey told the Committee that if note issues by the Bank were regulated by the exchanges – by which he meant contraction in the event of an adverse exchange – there would be no panics (1832 Committee, q. 1201). But given that a panic had occurred, and the drain was internal rather than external, the Bank *must* act as lender of last resort (qq. 1195-6). In such circumstances it would be right to expand the note issue, even were the exchanges unfavourable – though in the crisis of 1825 they had turned before the worst of the panic (qq. 1198-1200). But Bank notes themselves would be enough; he himself had stocked up with both notes and guineas in 1825, but found the guineas were unnecessary and he was able to return them to the Bank (q. 1193).

George Grote made the point that the Bank was necessarily lender of last resort because it was the one institution which would discount bills on demand, rather than requiring that the person with the bill were a customer. As Grote said, in financial exigencies, a person might find that the bank with which he had a special connection was unable to help, and no one else would be prepared to offer assistance; the Bank was thus the last resort (q. 4773). The central position of the Bank was further emphasised by George Carr Glynn, who said that he and the other private bankers kept their reserves with the Bank (q. 2870). From within the Bank, Horsley Palmer also held that the Bank must be the last-resort lender; in times of pressure, its only discretion lay in the discount rate charged (q. 477).[7]

Palmer's acceptance of the Bank's role as lender-of-last-resort was not shared by all his fellow Directors. George Warde Norman opposed the idea. He accepted that the Bank could sell off government debt, in order to give itself more scope for increasing discounts when the need arose (qq. 2452-8), even though, as other witnesses (notably Grote, q. 4771) had indicated, there might be no *net* effect on liquidity in the market, rather than merely a

---

[7]In this, the Bank was hampered by the Usury Laws, which limited the rate to 5 per cent. This restriction, against which both Palmer and George Warde Norman protested, was removed in 1833.

portfolio adjustment.[8] Frustrated by the effect of the Usury Laws, Norman believed that the Bank should be able to charge a high rate for such extended discounts (qq. 2429-32) and, in a remarkable anticipation of the doctrine of high marginal valuation of relief (Humphrey and Keleher, 1984, pp. 300-1), he justified this on the grounds that such relief would thus be obtained by those most able to bear it (q. 2437).

The participation of Thomas Tooke in these hearings is also of interest in the context of the development of the last-resort doctrine. From the opposition of the Banking School to the Bank Charter Act of 1844, it has sometimes been assumed that the School were pioneers of the last-resort doctrine. This, it is evident, was not the case. Tooke in 1832 was doubtful about the idea of having a lender of last resort (q. 3861), and believed that if the note issues of the Bank were properly regulated with reference to the exchanges, there would be no panics and thus no need for last-resort facilities (q. 3862). Nor did he consider panics to be catastrophic; he went so far as to deny that monetary contraction would affect the real economy (qq. 3863-5). By 1847 he was to change his mind on that (*Parliamentary Papers*, 1847-8a Commons Committee, qq. 5419-21); but there is some sign that he was not at one with Newmarch on the issue of last resort facilities, even after 1844. A passage in volume 5 of the *History of Prices* which stressed the unique role of the Bank as the supporter of credit in times of pressures, does indeed, to judge from an answer to a later inquiry, seem to have come from the pen of Newmarch; and Tooke has a footnote that distances himself from the passage without actually disowning it, accepting that, at least in the circumstances then prevailing, the Bank had actually been at fault in acting as lender of last resort in the 'American' crisis of 1836-7 (Tooke and Newmarch, 1838-1857, V, pp.

---

[8]The Palmer Rule, under which the Bank operated at this time, involved keeping securities constant and allowing variations in gold on the asset side of the balance sheet to be matched by variations in the combined liabilities of notes and deposits. Thus, if increased discounts were to be made, the Bank would have to reduce other securities – normally government debt.

543-5; Newmarch evidence, 1857 committee, q. 1364).

Nonetheless the Banking School (which, as Neil Skaggs (1995) has shown, derived much of their theoretical structure from Thornton himself), in their criticisms of the Act of 1844, did pinpoint the key problem that would be caused by the separation of the affairs of the Bank into two separate Departments of Issue and Banking. It would seriously limit the power of the Bank to support commercial credit (Tooke, 1844; Fullarton, 1845, pp. 196, 209-10, 239). Tooke indicated that a financial crisis was likely to result from the separation of departments, and it duly did so in 1847 (Tooke, 1844, pp. 107-9). John Stuart Mill (1848, pp. 652, 662-4) too, endorsing the critique of Tooke and Fullarton, stressed the importance of supporting credit during commercial panics, a case that rested in part on his perception of the possibility of an excess demand for money in times of commercial pressure (1829-30/1844, pp. 275-77).

But when all is said and done, the Banking School did not develop the insights into the last resort role bequeathed them by Thornton. Not only did their criticisms of the 1844 Act go no further than Joplin twenty years earlier – and Fullarton (1845, p. 106) advances, without acknowledgment, Joplin's 1825 argument that emergency lending would not circulate (see also O'Brien, 1993, pp. 17-18) – but they stopped short of Joplin's clear and dramatic conclusion that the Bank must *go on* lending in a crisis, come what may.

7.5   Joplin in the 1830s

Joplin, as already noted, was excluded from the 1832 hearings. But, convinced that the Bank had not learned its lesson in 1825 (1833, pp. 55-62, 80-2), he repeatedly restated the last-resort doctrine, re-using material from 1825. In so doing, he helped to develop further the doctrine, and thus provides a link between Thornton and Bagehot.

The nature of a panic, according to Joplin, was a large increase in the demand for balances (1832, pp. 219, 227-30; 1833, pp. 55-62; 1835, pp. 21-2, 27-8). This in turn represented an untypical dominance of the precautionary motive for holding funds over the transactions motive. In ordinary circumstances, Joplin argued, the demand for money was to use in transactions; but in panic the demand was for money to hold (1835, p. 21).

It followed from this that an increase in the money supply had, as Joplin had argued in his crucial article of 1825, no implications for the price level and the balance of payments when the increase was in response to panic (1828, pp. 175-6; 1832, pp. 24-30; 1835, pp. 24-5; 1841, pp. 42-3; 1844, pp. 56-7). The increase did not go into circulation but into idle balances. Given the amount of normal circulation which had already gone into idle balances as a panic got under way, it was essential that the lender of last resort replaced it with increased issues; for a collapse of the money supply would have serious implications, in terms of loss of output, for the real economy.

Perhaps most strikingly of all, in terms of the ideas with which Bagehot was later credited, Joplin argued that extraordinary note issues of this kind would automatically return to the Bank once the panic was over, and that a penalty rate of discount should be charged to ensure that this happened (1832, pp. 24-30; 1835, p. 21). Moreover, again anticipating Bagehot, Joplin stressed that the availability of last resort facilities should be posted in advance (1832, pp. 220, 230-4; 1844, pp. 56-7).[9]

---

[9]Both Joplin and Bagehot, unlike members of the Currency School, seem to have been untroubled by the potential moral hazard involved in a pre-announced commitment to last-resort facilities. In contrast to those who favour 'constructive ambiguity' concerning the availability of such facilities, which arguably increases the likelihood of panic as a trade-off for reducing moral hazard, their preference for a lack of ambiguity was clear cut. But the pre-announcement of a penalty rate could itself be expected to limit moral hazard to some extent.

7.6   The Bank Charter Debates

During the 1830s, the Bank faced periods of pressure, notably in 1836-7 and 1839, when it found itself called upon to provide assistance to the money market (Wood, 1939, p. 103; Clapham, 1944, II, pp. 152-70). In this it was given some help by the removal of the Usury Laws restrictions already referred to, and also by the grant of the status of legal tender to Bank notes, from 1833 (Hawtrey, 1932, pp. 122, 127). But both these measures had the effect of pushing the Bank further into the centre of the arena, and not all of its Directors agreed with this, let alone its critics outside the Bank.

Overstone wrote caustically to Norman that the Bank should design new notes with Horsley Palmer as Atlas upholding the financial world (O'Brien, 1971, I, p. 225), and within the Bank, as is apparent from his testimony before the 1840 Committee on Banks of Issue, Norman was opposing the last-resort role (qq. 1771-6). Both Overstone and Norman acknowledged before that committee that the Bank had indeed fulfilled the last resort role; and both objected to it (Overstone, qq. 2765-76, 2780-3; Norman, qq. 2271, 2294, 2306-19).[10] Norman indeed was to repeat his objections before another committee seventeen years later (Parliamentary Papers, 1857, qq. 3389-3430), and the Currency School, as represented by Overstone and Norman, believed that if the note issue were regulated by the principle of 'metallic fluctuation', that is varied in amount directly as a purely metallic currency in an open economy would vary, the likelihood of panic was remote (1840, qq. 1771-6).

But there was a key issue involved here. The aims of metallic fluctuation were to stabilise the cycle (O'Brien, 1995, and chapter 6 above) and to ensure convertibility of the note issue into gold; and, as Joplin was quick to observe, the very principle of metallic fluctuation was inconsistent with the

---

[10]Prior to the granting of his peerage in 1850, Overstone was Samuel Jones Loyd, and it is as Loyd that his name appears in reports of committee proceedings up to 1850.

provision of last-resort facilities which required the note issue to be governed by discretion rather than by rules (Joplin, 1832, pp. 150-1; 1839, p. 53). Norman indeed said quite explicitly that convertibility should override any last-resort considerations (1840, qq. 1771-6). Nor should there be any discretion; all 'drains' from the Bank should be treated in the same way, whether the demand for funds was internal or external, and the note issue should be contracted (1840, qq. 1745-64).

Norman was prepared to concede, as he had been in 1832, that the Bank might reduce its holding of government debt, in exchange for increased discounts; but, unlike the author of the Palmer Rule himself (1840 Committee, q. 1417), Norman did not want that Rule treated with discretion but believed that the total value of securities on the assset side of the balance sheet should remain fixed.

The Currency School position was perfectly consistent with their theoretical model of the operation of an open eonomy with a convertible paper currency. Last-resort facilities would undermine stabilisation. In addition they posed problems of moral-hazard; their existence encouraged inappropriate risk taking and inadequate liquidity on the part of financial institutions (Norman, 1840 Committee, qq. 1767-70).

7.7 The 1844 Act and Last-Resort

With the Bank Charter Act of 1844, the Currency School prescription of rules rather than discretion, and metallic fluctuation of the money supply (or at least of the Bank of England note issue, which was not necessarily the same thing, as Joplin consistently argued) were imposed upon the Bank. It was quite clear that the Bank could not, consistently with the Act, create last-resort facilities, and that behaviour of the kind in which it had engaged in the 1830s was ruled out within the terms of the Act. The stage was set for disaster.

The 1844 Act was based upon a model of the economy adjusting with hydraulic smoothness. Awareness of a fall in the reserve of the Bank, made public by the weekly publication of its account, provided for under the Act, would result in market paticipants increasing their own liquidity and thus reinforcing any contractionary action on the part of the Bank. The Act's framers never seem to have envisaged that its very provisions could engender a liquidity panic, resulting from the knowledge that the Bank could not, under the Act, provide unlimited last resort assistance. In the autumn of 1847, just such a panic occurred.

The Bank was reluctant to support the financial system. It raised its discount rate to ration discounts, but hesitated to increase their amount (King, 1936, p. 146). In the end, the government had to intervene and to suspend the limits of the Act. The panic then ended, without the limits having actually to be breached. In the ensuing hearings, before committees of both Lords and Commons, the Bank endorsed the official position. Its spokesmen opposed the idea that the Bank should be lender of last resort (Morris, Commons Committee, 1848, q. 2642; Morris and Prescott, qq. 3223-7; Cotton, qq. 4566-7[11]), insisted that internal and external drains should be treated the same (Morris, Lords Committee, q. 294), and, while recognising that government might have again to intervene in an emergency, took the view that there should be no pre-announcement of such a possibility (Lords Committee, Morris, q. 148; Cotton, qq. 3189, 3286; Norman, q. 2798; Commons Committee: Morris and Prescott qq. 2720-4). Morris and Prescott, for the Bank, were prepared to concede that the Act might have hastened the crisis, but not that it had caused it (Lords Committee, q. 7; Commons, q. 2823; see also Cotton, qq. 4135-6); and this was a view which found support outside the Bank (Lords Committee: Gurney, qq. 1167, 1191,

---

[11]These and other citations in this section pertain to the 1848 Committees; the transcripts of the Lords Committee is in Parliamentary Papers 1847-8b, and that of the Commons Committee in 1847-8a.

1201, 1221; Kennedy, q. 3356; Anderson, q. 3570; Kinnear, q. 3657). Indeed Morris and Prescott believed that the panic would have subsided without the government letter (Commons Committee, qq. 3234-7, 3803) - though at what cost they did not speculate.

The Currency School outside the Bank took the same line. In particular, Overstone went so far as to deny that the 1844 Act had anything to do with the 1847 crisis (Lords Committee, q. 1352; Commons, qq. 5279-81), and he strongly opposed the introduction of a formal 'relaxing power' (to suspend the Act in a panic), on the grounds that this would interfere with the smooth stabilising adjustment of liquidity positions referred to earlier (Lords Committee, qq. 1493, 1554, 1568, 1573, 1576; see also O'Brien, 1971, I, p. 125).

Others, however, were more critical. From the Bank itself, Palmer regarded the events of 1847, culminating in the suspension of the Act, as a repudiation of the Act itself, which he opposed precisely because it removed the Bank's power to provide last-resort facilities (Lords Committee, qq. 791, 825, 828, 878; Commons, qq. 2132-4). A number of witnesses before the committees blamed the Act for causing the crisis (Lords Committee: Glyn, q. 1906; Wright, q. 2909; Commons: Palmer, qq. 2055, 2235, 2083), and several agreed that the events had effectively destroyed the Act, an outcome that they welcomed (e.g. Lords Committee: Brown, q. 2356; Tooke, q. 3068).

There was considerable support for the introduction of a formal relaxing power, though those supporting it did not tackle directly the theoretical objections of the Currency School to such a provision (Lords Committee: Gurney, qq. 1201, 1221; Kennedy, qq. 3357-9; Anderson, q. 3573; Lister, q. 2605).

7.8   The Second Crisis: 1857

The supporters of the Act managed to defend it effectively in 1848, and the Act remained unaltered. But its critics were not satisfied, and the debate continued into the 1850s, with Overstone and Torrens both agile in defence of the status quo (Overstone, 1857, pp. 309-[57]; Torrens, 1848, 1857). But in 1857 the critics managed to secure the appointment of another committee, and the issues were again under review. Overstone, for the Currency School, continued to maintain that the Act had not caused the 1847 crisis (1857 Committee, qq. 4084-9). Moreover he was able to argue that the crises of 1825, 1836-7, and 1839 had involved a threat to convertibility of the Bank's notes into gold; this had never been in question after 1844 (1857 Committee, qq. 3793-6). The limits on the discretion of the Bank put in place in 1844 were necessary for this to be so; there should be no pre-announcement of a 'relaxing power' which would make last-resort facilities possible again (Overstone, 1857, pp. 313-5, [353]-[355]; O'Brien, 1971 I, p. 128) .

From within the Bank, Overstone received support. John Gellibrand Hubbard too opposed pre-announcement of a relaxing power (1857 Committee, qq. 2384-6), and indeed made it clear that the Bank did not accept that it *was* the lender of last resort. He was certainly opposed to such an idea, and stressed the moral hazard argument already noted (1857 Committee, qq. 2380-1). Norman denied that the 1844 Act in any way hampered properly controlled relief, based on the Bank's limited resources, as distinct from an open-ended last-resort commitment (1857 Committee, q. 2979).

But outside the Bank there was much less willingness to take such an uncompromising position. John Stuart Mill, while stressing that borrowers should be solvent, maintained that the Bank indeed had to act as last-resort lender (1857 Committee, q. 2031); and from the house of Overend and Gurney, already a little suspect and to fail in spectacular circumstances nine years later, David Barclay Chapman stressed that in a crisis the Bank must be prepared to discount freely, if discreetly, and its willingness should be public knowledge (1857 Committee, qq. 4904, 4907, 4963, 5190-2, 5230).

But then in the autumn of 1857 came a second liquidity panic. The Act was again suspended; and this time its limits had to be breached before the panic subsided (Clapham, 1944, II, p. 234). Nevertheless, Joplin, who had died in April 1847, would have been pleased to see that, as he predicted, the excess issues quickly returned to the Bank. Thenceforth the Currency School, and its adherents within the Bank, had to accept that in an emergency the Act would be suspended; this was now the general expectation, and whether a 'relaxing power' were made formal or not was academic (O'Brien, 1971, I, p. 137). The parliamentary committee which reported on the crisis accepted that the Bank must act as lender of last resort (Parliamentary Papers, 1857-8, p. viii).

7.9 The Aftermath: the Overend and Gurney Crisis

In the period immediately following the 1857 crisis, the Bank made one last effort to preserve the status quo. Sheffield Neave, then governor, told the 1857-8 committee charged with enquiring into the disaster that the Bank would no longer lend to the discount houses (1857-8 Committee, qq. 396-9, 405-6, 688, 700, 709-11; King, 1936, pp. 196-200). This was strictly in accordance with Currency School thinking; it was designed to force the bill brokers to keep their own reserves. However, as Bagehot was later to point out, it was a futile move since the reserves would have been held at the Bank itself which would thus be forced to support the system as before (Bagehot, 1873, pp. 26-30, 35-6, 42, 57-62, 68-71, 163-96). The move had the added aim of trying to prevent the brokers from holding money at call, which, the Bank believed, led the brokers into unwise use of the funds, in order to meet the interest paid on them (1857-8 Committee, Neave, q. 1102).

But in the end there was no way of avoiding the fact that the whole financial system did depend upon the Bank. When Overend and Gurney failed in 1866, the Bank, while declining to assist Overends, on the grounds (quite correct) that the firm was insolvent by normal criteria, did act as lender of last resort on a large scale to the rest of the financial system (Clapham, 1944, II, pp. 264-9).

7.10   Conclusions

By the time that Bagehot published his justly celebrated *Lombard Street* in 1873, the position of the Bank as lender of last resort was widely recognised, despite pockets of resistance from within the Bank itself, notably Thomson Hankey (Hankey, 1867, pp. iv-ix, xi, 29-30; Bagehot, 1873, pp. 169-71). The ideas which Bagehot put forward in his classic study had evolved during the course of British monetary experience over the almost three quarters of a century since Thornton's work. In the development of those ideas, the crisis of 1825, in which Bagehot's maternal uncle played an important part, was certainly of great significance; and the writer who has the greatest claim both to have resolved that crisis and then to have developed the key ideas in Bagehot's own work, which built on that of Thornton, was Thomas Joplin, who emerges as the unsung hero of the history of the lender of last resort concept.

Part IV

Macroeconomic Models

Chapter 8

Bagehot and Stabilisation

Bagehot's *Lombard Street* is widely recognised as an important document in the history of monetary literature. In particular, his exposition of the essential role of the Bank of England as lender of last resort has been widely appreciated (Humphrey, 1987, 1989, 1997; Humphrey and Keleher, 1984). What is perhaps less well known is that Bagehot changed the emphasis in monetary control from the money supply to the price of credit.

A focus on the quantity of high-powered money was necessarily involved in the Bank's regulation of its note issue under the regime imposed by the 1844 Bank Charter Act. With the Bank divided into a Banking Department and an Issue Department, the latter was responsible for varying the Bank of England note issue directly in response to gold flows, as indicating the balance of payments. Control of the Bank's note issue, seen as the high-powered monetary base, would, in turn, control the total money supply and thus the price level, maintaining balance of payments equilibrium. The Bank thus initially felt free to employ the Banking Department as an aggressive competitor in the discount market, offering low discount rates and allowing its Banking Department reserve to fall to low levels. But following the crisis of October 1847, when the 1844 Act was temporarily suspended, the Bank became more cautious; and, after a further crisis and suspension of the Act in 1857, the Bank was forced to accept that it could not stand aloof from

the money market, but must protect its own position by the active use of its
discount rate – Bank Rate. It was the implications of this which Bagehot
explored.

To do this he developed a remarkably sophisticated economic model with,
at its core, a trade cycle springing from cyclical harvest variation. The real
business cycle which Bagehot developed as the core mechanism of his model of
the economy was a remarkable contribution. The idea of an endogenous cycle
was not new; in particular Overstone had put it forward during the debates
leading to the 1844 Act (Overstone, 1837) and had made it the centrepiece
of the distinction between Currency (anticyclical) and Banking (procyclical)
control of the money supply (O'Brien, 1995). But Bagehot went far beyond
merely assuming the existence of a cycle. He provided a mechanism to explain
fluctuations in national income as a whole, driven by harvest variation. The
nature of the demand for corn allowed these variations to affect the remainder
of the economy via a multiplier-type mechanism which Bagehot formulated.[1]

Working through this model, Bagehot argued that use of Bank Rate as
an active tool to protect the reserve in the Banking Department of the Bank
would stabilise the economy. If, on the other hand, the Bank simply followed
variations in the market rate of interest, as it had tended to do in the years
immediately after 1844, there would be substantial price fluctuations imposed
on the income cycle, the reserve of the Bank would come under threat when
the artificial prosperity of rapidly rising prices was checked, and a threat of
this sort raised the possibility of a financial panic.

The role of the Bank as Lender of Last Resort was indeed vitally necessary
to preserve the fragile confidence of a fractional reserve financial system when
panic threatened.[2] For there was, as Bagehot vividly explained, really only

---

[1] All that remained was to explain the harvest variations, which Jevons was to attempt
to do on the basis of sunspots (O'Brien, 1997a, I, pp. 221–274).

[2] That the Bank was indeed regarded in this way is evident from the testimony given
before the Parliamentary Committees, notably that of 1857 (Parliamentary Papers, 1857,
X, Parts 1, 2). The figures for loans and especially discounts by the Bank, *after* it had

one reserve in the financial system – that held by the Bank. But the Bank *could* only fulfil this role if it had a sufficient reserve – the 1844 Act did not permit it to print extra notes in a crisis, and such a course could only be followed after governmental suspension of the Act, which in practice required a prior panic. Successful stabilisation of the system was thus of overriding importance, and Bagehot's aim was to show how this could be done, using Bank Rate.

Bagehot emerges as the pioneer formulator of modern central bank practice (including that of the Bank of England) in using variations in the discount rate to *anticipate* the business cycle and to damp it down.[3] His position is thus significantly closer to modern central bank practice than that of Wicksell, who is often cited as a forerunner of it. Wicksell was concerned to match the bank lending rate with the underlying marginal rate of profit and was only peripherally concerned with an endogenous cycle.[4]

Bagehot's contribution is important in the context of modern central bank procedures in another respect. The 1844 Bank Charter Act made the monetary base – the Bank of England note issue – the focus of control, substituting rules for discretion, and linking it directly to the balance of payments. This posed serious problems for the financial sector which had

ceased to compete aggressively with the discount market, following the crisis of 1847, are evidence of the support for the market which it provided especially when other discounters were turning away all but their regular customers (Appendices 6, 7). Before 1844 the Bank could fulfil this role by issuing new notes, a practice prevented by the 1844 Act.

[3] The policy of seeking a 'soft landing' in the recent jargon. As the then Deputy Governor of the Bank of England put it: 'The message for policy is that it is important not to let domestic demand grow too rapidly. The longer the correction is left, the sharper the required adjustment will be ... By acting pre-emptively, and trying to anticipate developments, the MPC [Monetary Policy Committee] has been able to maintain overall stability in the economy ... Pre-emptive action to slow domestic demand growth to a more sustainable level is the key to avoiding a larger and more painful adjustment at a later date' (King 2000, p. 2).

[4] See the material in O'Brien (1997a, II, pp. 3–62, especially pp. 57–62). See also Wicksell ([1907] 1953) and Uhr (1960, pp. 25–6, 133–7). Humphrey (1992) has shown that if Wicksell's policy prescription is modelled as a lagged response of the lending rate to the rate of inflation, the result will be regular fluctuation of the price level.

previously, especially during the 1830s, relied on an elastic supply of Bank of England notes in times of pressure. By switching the focus of control from the monetary base to the discount rate, Bagehot anticipated a similar switch in the 1980s, following a modern experiment with monetary base control (Goodhart, 1989, pp. 217–8, 235–7).

The model is set out formally in this chapter. Care has been taken to be as faithful as possible to Bagehot's intentions, and thus page references are provided throughout, indicating the material in *Lombard Street* which lies behind an equation. Section 8.1 develops the formal version of Bagehot's model. Having set up the complete model, section 8.2 examines the question of stability. Bagehot's recommendations for the use of Bank Rate are explained and a formal treatment of stability is provided. It turns out that Bagehot was correct: an active policy of using Bank Rate would provide stability while simply following the market rate produces a recurrent cycle of prices.

8.1 Bagehot's Model

This section presents a formal version of Bagehot's model. The framework of the trade cycle is described in subsection 8.1.1. Subsection 8.1.2 examines the details of harvest variation, the demand for other kinds of subsistence, and Bagehot's multiplier. These elements combined to produce a complete cycle of national income. The behaviour of the market rate of interest through the cycle is examined in subsection 8.1.3, and savings, investment and the money supply in subsection 8.1.4. The associated price level changes are examined in subsection 8.1.5, and the consequences for the balance of payments in subsection 8.1.6. Subsection 8.1.7 looks at the effects on both the gold holdings of the Bank and its Banking Department reserve, with the implications for the Bank Rate in subsection 8.1.8.

8.1.1 The Cycle

At the heart of Bagehot's analysis is a trade cycle. However it is not an exogenous income cycle, as it was for Overstone (O'Brien, 1995), but a cycle resulting from regular exogenous agricultural shocks. Around this cycle is built the rest of the analysis. Bagehot's vision of the cycle can most easily be explained with Figure 8.1.

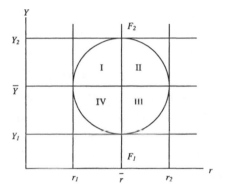

Figure 8.1: The Circular Fluctuation of Income and Interest

Income, Y, fluctuates between a maximum of Y_2 at the peak of the cycle and a minimum of Y_1 at the bottom of the cycle. The market rate of interest, r, ranges between a maximum at r_2 and a minimum at r_1. The equilibrium rate of interest at which the money supply is constant is $\bar{r}$; when r is below $\bar{r}$ there is net bank lending, and when r exceeds $\bar{r}$ there is net accumulation of idle balances within the banking system. $\bar{Y}$ is the equilibrium level of income (here treated for simplicity as a constant) around which actual income fluctuates cyclically. The path followed by the economy can be divided into four phases, indicated in the diagram by the labels for quadrants I, II, III and IV. Starting from the bottom of the cycle at F_1, the interest rate falls below its equilibrium value $\bar{r}$, and income rises. As it rises towards its equilibrium value

$\bar{Y}$, the interest rate continues to fall. Beyond $\bar{Y}$, however, the interest rate begins rising again towards its equilibrium value, though income continues to rise. Once the peak of the cycle is reached at F_2, however, income begins to fall while interest rates rise above $\bar{r}$. The rise in interest rates continues until income has returned to the equilibrium value, after which rates begin to fall again until they again reach $\bar{r}$ at the bottom of the cycle.

The four quadrants thus correspond to boom (I), downturn (II), depression (III) and recovery (IV). In recovery and boom we have rising income and low interest rates; and in downturn and slump we have falling income and high interest rates.

We can now examine in turn the behaviour of income, interest rates, savings, investment and the money supply, prices, the balance of payments, the Bank of England reserve, and Bank Rate. Finally the question of stability is addressed.

8.1.2   Income

The Harvest

The harvest fluctuates in an agricultural cycle of good and bad years (Bagehot, 1873, pp. 123, 158). Writing H for harvest:

$$\begin{aligned} H &= H^* + \bar{H} \\ &= A_1 \cos bt + A_2 \sin bt + \bar{H} \end{aligned} \qquad (8.1)$$

where $\bar{H}$ is the average level of harvest around which fluctuations, H^*, take place.

The demand function for corn is:

$$q = a_0 p_c^{-\alpha_1} \qquad (8.2)$$

with $0 < \alpha_1 < 1$. Inversely, the price of corn depends on the harvest. Neglecting grain storage, as Bagehot does, and setting a_0 at unity, we may write:

$$H = q \tag{8.3}$$

Then:

$$\frac{dp_c}{dH} = \frac{-p_c^{1+\alpha_1}}{\alpha_1} \tag{8.4}$$

Expenditure on corn is:

$$T = qp_c \tag{8.5}$$

and

$$
\begin{aligned}
\frac{dT}{dp_c} &= q + p_c\frac{dq}{dp_c} \\
&= p_c^{-\alpha_1} + p_c\left[\frac{-\alpha_1}{p_c^{\alpha_1}p_c}\right] \\
&= p_c^{-\alpha_1} - \frac{\alpha_1}{p_c^{\alpha_1}} = \frac{1-\alpha_1}{p_c^{\alpha_1}}
\end{aligned} \tag{8.6}
$$

This is positive for $0 < \alpha_1 < 1$.

Then the effect of harvest variation on total revenue can be written:

$$
\begin{aligned}
\frac{dT}{dH} &= \frac{dT}{dp_c}\frac{dp_c}{dH} \\
&= -\frac{(1-\alpha_1)\,p_c}{\alpha_1}
\end{aligned} \tag{8.7}
$$

This is negative for $o < \alpha_1 < 1$, so that expenditure on corn decreases as the harvest improves. The elasticity of corn expenditure with respect to the harvest is thus $\frac{dT}{dH}\frac{H}{T} = -\frac{(1-\alpha_1)p_c}{\alpha_1}\frac{H}{p_c q} = -\frac{(1-\alpha_1)}{\alpha_1}$, since the whole harvest is assumed to come on the market and thus $H = q$.

This in turn has implications for expenditure on other commodities, which will fall in the event of a poor harvest and rise in good years.

Other Subsistence

Let f represent the proportion of the budget spent on corn and c the proportion spent on other basic items such as clothing.

Treating $\frac{1}{T}\frac{dT}{dH}$ as the proportional change in corn expenditure resulting from a harvest change (setting H at unity), we can obtain the corresponding proportional change in expenditure on other basics, denoted by τ:

$$\left(\frac{1}{T}\frac{dT}{dH}\right)\frac{f}{c} = \frac{1}{\tau}\frac{d\tau}{dH} \tag{8.8}$$

where the two sides are opposite in sign.

The proportional change in expenditure on τ can thus be translated into an absolute change in spending on non-food items by multiplying the right hand side of equation (8.8) by τ. Thus the absolute change is $d\tau/dH$.

The Multiplier

Bagehot pioneered the idea of a kind of multiplier (Wright, 1956). He explains (1873, pp. 125-8) the multiplier effect working through the rest of the economy, as the decreased prosperity of the suppliers of basics, after a poor harvest, reduces, in turn, the demand for the output of the other industries. Thus:

$$\frac{dY}{dH} = \mu\frac{d\tau}{dH} \tag{8.9}$$

where μ is Bagehot's multiplier.

Bagehot posits, for illustrative purposes, 26 industries (including agriculture) from A to Z. Writing:

$$\frac{d\tau}{dH} = \beta \tag{8.10}$$

to simplify the notation, β represents the reduction in demand for articles like clothing following a decrease in the harvest. This reduces demand in the next industry in the alphabetic sequence, by a proportion denoted here by z_3. Demand for the output of the industry represented by D in the sequence can then be reduced by z_4. The successive reductions in demand would then be, where T is the total reduction in demand:

$$
\begin{aligned}
T &= \beta + z_3\beta + z_3 z_4\beta + ... + z_3....z_{26}\beta \\
&= \beta\left(1 + z_3 + z_3 z_4 + ... + z_3....z_{26}\right)
\end{aligned}
\tag{8.11}
$$

Denoting the term in brackets by $(1 + s_{24})$:

$$\frac{dT}{d\beta} = (1 + s_{24}) \tag{8.12}$$

This is Bagehot's multiplier, denoted above for convenience by μ.[5]

The Income Cycle

$$\frac{dY}{dt} = \frac{dY}{dH}\frac{dH}{dt} \tag{8.13}$$

Substituting from equations (8.9), (8.8), (8.7), (8.5) and (8.3) for dY/dH and from equation (8.1) for dH/dt:

$$
\begin{aligned}
\frac{dY}{dt} &= \mu\frac{d\tau}{dH}\frac{dH}{dt} = \mu\left(\frac{dT}{dH}\frac{1}{T}\right)\frac{f}{c}\tau\frac{dH}{dt} \\
&= \mu\left(\frac{1-\alpha_1}{\alpha_1}\right)p_c\frac{1}{p_cq}\frac{f}{c}\tau\frac{dH}{dt} \\
&= \frac{\mu\tau}{H}\left(\frac{1-\alpha_1}{\alpha_1}\right)\frac{f}{c}\left(-A_1\sin bt + A_2\cos bt\right) \tag{8.14}
\end{aligned}
$$

Bagehot had thus provided a theory of the trade cycle building up from harvest variations and involving a multiplier.

8.1.3 Interest Rates

Although as a banker Bagehot recognised the existence of a structure of interest rates, he writes habitually about *the* market rate of interest. Thus we can deal with a single rate without doing violence to his vision.

---

[5]While this is not strictly a Keynesian multiplier, it does, as the s_{24} term indicates, show how a series of products of fractional terms cumulates to produce a final change in income greater – in Bagehot's view significantly greater – than the initial one. Strictly, equation (8.9) should contain an additional term representing the change in national income represented by an initial alteration in agricultural output, its size partially dependent on that of the agricultural sector, but it is not part of Bagehot's argument. What he does stress is the *multiple* effect of an initial change: 'under a system in which everyone is dependent on the labour of everyone else, the loss of one spreads and multiplies through all, and spreads and multiplies the faster the higher the previous perfection of the system of divided labour, and the more nice and effectual the mode of interchange' (1873, pp. 126-7).

Movements in the market rate of interest depend on changes in the level of income through the cycle, resulting in changes in investment opportunities (1873, pp. 123, 131, 149). Both the change in the level of income, and the divergence of income from its equilibrium, seem to influence the rate of interest, which varies around its equilibrium value, only attaining that value at the top and bottom of the cycle.

Cyclical movements give rise not only to changes in income but also to changes in prices (Bagehot, 1873, pp. 138, 140-8, 150-3). As demand for capital becomes keener, in the face of rising prices, the market rate of interest rises (1873, pp. 154-6). If we posit an equilibrium price level $\bar{P}$, corresponding to the equilibrium level of income $\bar{Y}$, the prices above equilibrium will involve rising interest rates and vice versa. Thus we may write, with P as the general price level:

$$\frac{dr}{dt} = \alpha_2 \frac{dY}{dt} - \alpha_3(\bar{Y} - Y) - \alpha_4\left(\bar{P} - P\right) \tag{8.15}$$

with $\alpha_2, \alpha_3, \alpha_4 > 1$. This can be related to the quadrants of the cycle discussed above. Thus in quadrant I, $dY/dt > 0$ and both $(\bar{Y} - Y)$ and $\left(\bar{P} - P\right)$ are negative. Interest rates rise.

In quadrant II, $dY/dt < 0$, but $(\bar{Y} - Y)$ and $\left(\bar{P} - P\right)$ are both negative: the market rate of interest rises towards r_2, with the positive values of $-\alpha_3\left(\bar{Y} - Y\right)$ and $-\alpha_4\left(\bar{P} - P\right)$ sufficient to outweigh the negative influence of dY/dt until both $(\bar{Y} - Y)$ and $\left(\bar{P} - P\right)$ reach zero.

In quadrant III, the interest rate falls away from its maximum under the combined influence of a negative value for dY/dt and positive values for $(\bar{Y} - Y)$ and $\left(\bar{P} - P\right)$.

Finally, in quadrant IV, dY/dt is positive as the economy recovers from the bottom of the cycle, but this is outweighed by the continued influence of positive values for the Y and P bracketed terms, so that the market rate of interest continues to fall until it reaches r_1 and these influences disappear, to be replaced, as the cycle continues, by negative values within the brackets, so that the interest rate rises towards the peak of the cycle, reaching its equilibrium rate as the cycle turns.

8.1.4 Savings, Investment and the Money Supply

Bagehot argues that in the downswing of the cycle savings (S) exceed investment (I) (1873, pp. 131, 137-8, 142-3, 145, 149-50, 156). Idle balances accumulate in the banking system, awaiting investment.[6] Then, in the following upswing, investment exceeds saving and the gap, after the activation of the idle balances, is filled by additions to the money supply (M^s).

But, as we have already seen, the rate of interest is above its equilibrium rate in the downswing and below it in the upswing. Thus changes in the money supply depend on the relationship of the current market rate to the equilibrium one. In summary, then:

$$I = S + \frac{dM^s}{dt}$$

and:

$$I - S = \frac{dM^s}{dt} = \alpha_5 (\bar{r} - r) \qquad (8.16)$$

with $\alpha_5 > 0$.

8.1.5 The Price Level

Changes in the price level (P) are associated with both changes in the money supply (M^s) and, as already noted, changes in the level of income (Y). In the upswing, not only are loans and discounts cheap, with the market rate of interest below its equilibrium rate, but the availability of credit increases – there is a greater willingness to discount bills (1873, pp. 137-8). Bagehot

---

[6]'During a depressed period the savings of the country increase considerably faster than the outlet for them. A person who has made savings does not know what to do with them ... Till a saving is invested or employed it exists only in the form of money: a farmer who has sold his wheat ... holds [the money], or some equivalent for money, till he sees some advantageous use to be made of it. Probably he places it in a bank' (1873, pp. 142–3). The treatment anticipates Hawtrey (1928, pp. 60–3).

thus expressly distinguishes 'cheap money' from improved credit (1873, p. 141); but both increase the call on resources, leading to higher prices:

> The rise of prices is quickest in an improving state of credit ... In times of good credit there are a great number of strong purchasers, and in times of bad credit only a smaller number of weak ones; and, therefore, years of improving credit ... are years of rising price, and years of decaying credit, years of falling price. (1873, p. 138)[7]

The price level is also influenced by Bank Rate, which can be used to check an upswing. Bagehot explains this quite clearly. The Bank has to have available large sums in bullion, at call, in the event of a balance of payments deficit:

> In order to find such great sums, the Bank of England requires the steady use of an effectual instrument. That instrument is the rate of interest. (1873, p. 45)

This acts primarily on the capital account. However it also operates on the price level (and thus, after a lag, on the current account):

> And there is also a slower mercantile operation. The rise in the rate of discount acts immediately on the trade of this country. Prices fall here; in consequence imports are diminished, exports are increased, and, therefore, there is more likelihood of a balance in bullion coming to this country after the rise in the rate than there was before. (1873, p. 46)

---

[7]Bagehot did not explicitly consider the question of inflationary expectations, reasonably enough in an economy anchored by the gold standard (though he makes passing reference to Jevons's work (1863) on the gold discoveries – 1873, p. 1389). Rather he treats changes in the price level as signals of the strength of demand.

Taking all these influences together, we may write:

$$\frac{dP}{dt} = \alpha_6 \left(\frac{dM^s}{dt}\right) + \alpha_7 \left(\frac{dY}{dt}\right) - \alpha_8 (r_b - \bar{r}_b) \qquad (8.17)$$

where r_b is Bank Rate, the Bank of England's minimum discount rate, and $\bar{r}_b$ represents the average or 'normal' rate as perceived by the money market. Then substituting equations (8.14) and (8.16) into equation (8.17) we have:

$$\begin{aligned} \frac{dP}{dt} &= \alpha_6 \left\{\alpha_5(\bar{r} - r)\right\} + \alpha_7 \left\{\frac{\mu\tau}{H}\left(\frac{1-\alpha_1}{\alpha_1}\right)\frac{f}{c}(-A_1 \sin bt + A_2 \cos bt)\right\} \\ &\quad -\alpha_8 (r_b - \bar{r}_b) \end{aligned} \qquad (8.18)$$

8.1.6 The Balance of Payments

Bagehot envisages the balance of payments on both current and capital accounts as varying with the cycle. The current account depends on the home price level relative to the long-term equilibrium price level $\bar{P}$, which is consistent with current account balance (1873, pp. 117-118).

With prices moving pro-cyclically, it is reasonable to interpret Bagehot as envisaging current account deficits in the upper part of the cycle, where income rises above its equilibrium level $\bar{Y}$. Correspondingly, the lower part of the cycle, with income below $\bar{Y}$, will involve a current account surplus.

The capital account depends on relative interest rates at home and abroad (1873, p. 146). For simplicity the equilibrium rate of interest, $\bar{r}$, is identified here with the world rate of interest, though in practice the greater security of Britain, in Bagehot's day, would have allowed the capital account to balance at a slightly lower long-run rate. Thus, in the model, the capital account would be in deficit whenever the market rate of interest fell below this benchmark, and vice versa.

The fact that the overall payments balance is made up of two separate accounts, driven by different forces, means that the state of the overall account in two of the four quadrants of the cycle is dependent on the relative strengths of different influences. In quadrant I of the cycle, with $Y > \bar{Y}$

and $r < \bar{r}$, there would be a deficit on both current and capital account. Correspondingly, in quadrant III, with $Y < \bar{Y}$ and $r > \bar{r}$, there would be a surplus on both parts of the overall account. But in quadrant II with $Y > \bar{Y}$ and $r > \bar{r}$ we have an uncertain outcome which may vary in overall balance as income falls towards $\bar{Y}$ and interest rises towards r_2; the current account will be in deficit but the capital account in surplus. Similarly in quadrant IV, with $r < \bar{r}$ and $Y < \bar{Y}$, a capital account deficit will be accompanied by a current account surplus.

The current account balance B_c can be written:

$$B_c = X - M \tag{8.19}$$

So that:

$$\frac{dB_c}{dt} = \frac{dX}{dt} - \frac{dM}{dt} \tag{8.20}$$

$$\frac{dX}{dt} = \alpha_9 \left(\bar{P} - P \right) \tag{8.21}$$

$$\frac{dM}{dt} = \alpha_{10} \left(\bar{P} - P \right) \tag{8.22}$$

with $\alpha_9 > 0$ and $\alpha_{10} < 0$. So:

$$\frac{dB_c}{dt} = (\alpha_9 - \alpha_{10}) \left(\bar{P} - P \right)$$

and writing $(\alpha_9 - \alpha_{10}) = \alpha_{11}$:

$$\frac{dB_c}{dt} = \alpha_{11} \left(\bar{P} - P \right) \tag{8.23}$$

Then, writing B_k for the balance on capital account:

$$\frac{dB_k}{dt} = \alpha_{12} \left(\bar{r} - r \right) \tag{8.24}$$

with $\alpha_{12} < 0$. So the variation in the overall balance of payments in response to endogenous forces may be written:

$$\frac{dB}{dt} = \frac{dB_c}{dt} + \frac{dB_k}{dt} = \alpha_{11} \left(\bar{P} - P \right) + \alpha_{12} \left(\bar{r} - r \right) \tag{8.25}$$

In addition, as mentioned in subsection 8.1.5, it was open to the Bank to influence both capital account and current account by the use of Bank Rate. Where this policy is followed, the equation becomes:

$$\frac{dB}{dt} = \frac{dB_c}{dt} + \frac{dB_k}{dt} = \alpha_{11}\left(\bar{P} - P\right) + \alpha_{12}\left(\bar{r} - r\right) + \alpha_{13}\left(r_b - \bar{r}_b\right) \qquad (8.26)$$

with $\alpha_{13} > 0$.

8.1.7 Bullion and the Banking Department Reserve

The gold in the Issue Department of the Bank, and the notes in the Banking Department reserve both varied, under the 1844 Bank Charter Act, with the state of the balance of payments. Under that Act, the only source of gold to meet a balance of payments deficit was, in practice, the holding in the Issue Department of the Bank (Bagehot, 1873, p. 34).

To obtain gold for overseas payment, Bank of England notes had first to be obtained – normally from the Banking Department of the Bank, rather than from circulation – either by discounting bills at the Bank or by withdrawing deposits from it. Thus a balance of payments deficit would reduce both the Bank's notes (designedly the core of the high-powered money base of the system) and holdings of bullion. Conversely, a net inflow of gold would result in a rise in the Bank's gold holding; and since the note issue of the Bank was constrained, under the 1844 Act, both by its balance sheet and by an upper limit on security-backed note issue of £14m, the gold inflow provided the backing for extra note issue.

The size of the Banking Department reserve would also vary with Bank Rate, the Bank of England's discount rate. Firstly, as was indicated in subsection 8.1.5, Bagehot expected a rise in Bank Rate to operate directly on the balance of payments, affecting both the capital account and the current account. Secondly, the further Bank Rate rose above its normal level, the more that the banking system would increase its own reserves as a precaution against a liquidity squeeze. But, as witnesses before official committees testified (including Alderman Salomons whose evidence is reproduced by Bagehot in Appendix B of *Lombard Street* – 1873, pp. 337-49), and as Bagehot himself emphasised (1873, pp. 27-30, 66-71) those extra reserves were held at the Bank of England.[8]

The continued influences of the balance of payments, and of the level of Bank Rate, on these precautionary reserves held by the banking system of the Bank, can thus be written, where R represents the Banking Department reserve:

$$\frac{dR}{dt} = \alpha_{14}\frac{dB}{dt} + \alpha_{15}\left(r_b - \bar{r}_b\right) \tag{8.27}$$

with $\alpha_{14}, \alpha_{15} > 0$. ($\alpha_{14}$ would be less than unity if, as anticipated by the framers of the 1844 Act, a gold inflow resulted in some extra notes in circulation, as well as increased reserves in the Banking Department of the Bank).

Substituting from equation (8.26):

$$\frac{dR}{dt} = \alpha_{14}\left\{\alpha_{11}\left(\bar{P} - P\right) + \alpha_{12}\left(\bar{r} - r\right) + \alpha_{13}\left(r_b - \bar{r}_b\right)\right\} + \alpha_{15}\left(r_b - \bar{r}_b\right)$$

and writing $\alpha_{16} = (\alpha_{14}\alpha_{13} + \alpha_{15})$:

$$\frac{dR}{dt} = \alpha_{14}\left\{\alpha_{11}\left(\bar{P} - P\right) + \alpha_{12}\left(\bar{r} - r\right)\right\} + \alpha_{16}\left(r_b - \bar{r}_b\right) \tag{8.28}$$

8.1.8 Bank Rate

The minimum rate charged for assistance by the Bank, normally a discount rate rather than a lending rate, was known as Bank Rate. The Bank varied it according to the state of the reserves in the Banking Department of the Bank. The lowest rate charged was normally 1.75 per cent (though the Bank

---

[8]'It was precisely this view which led me in 1847 resolutely to maintain an apparently extravagant balance at the Bank of England. I was determined that at the critical moment my funds should not be in jeopardy – that I would float or sink with the Bk of E. but with no body else. that I would be free and prepared to meet every call. let all the bill brokers in London go *in coelum*.' Overstone to G.W. Norman, 8 November 1857 in O'Brien (1971, II, p.774). Overstone was in 1847 still a leading private banker in the firm Jones Loyd.

went as low as 1.5 per cent in 1852) and the maximum rate was normally 7 per cent, though higher rates occurred at times of severe pressure, reaching 8, 9, and even 10 per cent.[9] This was charged when reserves were at or near their minimum.

The reserves in the Banking Department of the Bank ranged in size up to about £14 million;[10] and Bagehot's key proposal was that the lower limit at which the Bank should aim should be £10 million. Then the level of Bank Rate (r_b) would be determined as:

$$r_b = \frac{K}{R} \tag{8.29}$$

where K is an arbitrary constant and the above figures imply a K value of 90.[11]

Then:

$$\frac{dr_b}{dt} = \frac{dr_b}{dR}\frac{dR}{dt} \tag{8.30}$$

Differentiating equation (8.29) and substituting for dR/dt from equation

---

[9]Committee on Bank Acts, Parliamentary Papers, 1857, Sess 2, vol. X, part II, appendix 6. The rate did not rise above 7 per cent, even in the crisis of October 1847, between 1844 and October 1857. However when the Act had been suspended in 1857, and the limits imposed by the Act of 1844 had been breached (which did not happen in 1847), the rate rose to 8, 9 and even (from 9 November to 24 December 1857) 10 per cent. Again in 1866, the year of the Overend crisis, the rate rose as high as 10 per cent and remained at that level from 12 May to 16 August. There were also higher rates in 1863 and 1864, of which Bagehot seems to have approved (1873, p. 183). The figures are from Clapham (1944, II, Appendix B, pp. 429–30).

[10]*Parliamentary Papers*, 1857, Sess 2, vol. X, part II, appendices 12, 14; *Parliamentary Papers* 1873, vol. XXXIX, p. 161. In June 1871 they rose briefly above £17m.

[11]If we take 9 per cent as the maximum rate charged by the Bank except when the 1844 Act had been suspended, then this rate would, under Bagehot's plan, be charged when the Banking Department reserve fell as low as £10m. Equation (8.29) then implies a K value of 90. Then when the Banking Department reserve reached what Bagehot regarded as the desirable rather than the minimum level, which was, as we shall see in subsection 8.2.1, £15m, this implies a Bank Rate of 6 per cent which is reasonable given both Bagehot's aim of strengthening that reserve and the range within which Bank rate typically varied, though it implied a higher level on average than hitherto. (The Bank had already, during the 1860s, increased the average holding of notes and coin in the Banking Department, compared with the period 1844–1858.)

(10.36)

$$\frac{dr_b}{dt} = -\frac{K}{R^2}\left\{\alpha_{14}\alpha_{11}\left(\bar{P}-P\right) + \alpha_{14}\alpha_{12}\left(\bar{r}-r\right) + \alpha_{14}\alpha_{16}\left(r_b - \bar{r}_b\right)\right\} \quad (8.31)$$

8.2   The Question of Stability

8.2.1   Bagehot's Recommendations

Bagehot emphasised that, while it was not a desirable arrangement, the plain fact was that the Bank of England held the reserve for the entire banking system (1873, pp. 66, 110-12, 189-92, 249, 253-4, 294-8, 329-31). This forced the Bank to provide assistance to the whole system – to be the lender of last resort (1873, pp. 64,73). The Bank should formally accept the role, lending freely at times of monetary pressure, though at high rates of interest (1873, pp. 197-9).

But to be in a position to lend in this way, the Bank must itself be possessed of adequate reserves. The key proposal which Bagehot stressed, to achieve a sufficient level of reserves, was to use Bank Rate as an active weapon of policy. Up to 1857 the Bank had failed to protect its reserve in this way, according to Bagehot (1873, pp. 46-7), simply following the changes in the market rate of interest. But active use of Bank Rate as a policy tool had proved successful in the years 1862-5 (the Bank had failed to act correctly during the Overend and Gurney crisis of 1866) and again from 1870 onwards (1873, pp. 182-4). From 1860 onwards the Bank, under the influence of Goschen's calculations concerning the gold points, had adopted the policy of changing Bank Rate by a full percentage point, which was, in Bagehot's view, 'a particular mode of raising the rate of interest, which is far more efficient than any other mode' (1873, p. 181).

Bank Rate was the key weapon of monetary control. It was futile, Bagehot argued, to attempt to control the money supply through rationing discounts, as the Currency School envisaged; such a policy, if attempted, would bring the financial system to a halt and leave the Bank itself holding dishonoured bills (1873, pp. 189-90).[12] But Bagehot did agree, strongly, with the Currency School view (O'Brien, 1971, I, p. 95) that *early* use of monetary restriction – though in his case this meant raising Bank Rate – was necessary to stabilise the system (1873, pp. 185-6, 197). Bank Rate must not follow the market rate; its level must be dictated by reserve considerations (1873, pp. 319-20).

But at what level of reserve should the Bank aim? Bagehot hesitated to give a precise numerical answer – as a practical banker he knew that the reserve required by a bank depended on the structure of its liabilities (1873, pp. 301-6). Thus "no certain or fixed proportion of its liabilities can in the present times be laid down as that which the Bank ought to keep in reserve" (1873, p. 318). But he knew that there was another consideration what he called the 'apprehension minimum', the level of reserve below which panic might ensue, had to be taken into account (1873, pp. 322-4). This too was variable, depending on recent monetary history (1873, p. 324). Nonetheless Bagehot knew that some sort of numerical answer should be given (1873, p. 325).

With reluctance he put forward the following levels. The minimum reserve should be £10 million; to this should be added £1.5 million as the size of random shock which could hit the Bank at any time (1873, pp. 327-8), and a further £3 or £3.5 million for what may be broadly characterised as implementation lags.

When his plan is analysed formally, using the model developed in preceding sections, Bagehot's intuition, based as it was on a profound understanding

---

[12]'It is alleged that the Bank of England can keep aloof in a panic ... The holders of this opinion in its most extreme form say, that in a panic the Bank of England can stay its hand at any time; that, though it has advanced much, it may refuse to advance more; ... that it can refuse to make any further discounts ... But in this form the notion scarcely merits serious refutation ... if the Bank declines to discount, the holders of the bills previously discounted cannot pay ... The notion that the Bank of England can stop discounting in a panic, and so obtain fresh money, is a delusion ... if it does ... its bill case will daily be more and more packed with bills "returned unpaid"' (1873, pp. 188–90).

of the factual basis of his argument, proves to be correct.

8.2.2   A Formal Treatment of Stability

From the preceding section it is evident that the key equations, in the context
of stability, are (8.14), (8.15), (8.18) and (8.31). For convenience these are
reproduced here as the following four equations:

$$\frac{dY}{dt} = \frac{\mu\tau}{H}\left(\frac{1-\alpha_1}{\alpha_1}\right)\frac{f}{c}\left(-A_1 \sin bt + A_2 \cos bt\right) \tag{8.32}$$

$$\frac{dr}{dt} = \alpha_2\frac{dY}{dt} - \alpha_3(\bar{Y}-Y) - \alpha_4\left(\bar{P}-P\right) \tag{8.33}$$

$$
\begin{aligned}
\frac{dP}{dt} &= \alpha_6\left\{\alpha_5(\bar{r}-r)\right\} + \alpha_7\left\{\frac{\mu\tau}{H}\left(\frac{1-\alpha_1}{\alpha_1}\right)\frac{f}{c}\left(-A_1 \sin bt + A_2 \cos bt\right)\right\} \\
&\quad -\alpha_8\left(r_b - \bar{r}_b\right)
\end{aligned}
\tag{8.34}
$$

$$\frac{dr_b}{dt} = -\frac{K}{R^2}\left\{\alpha_{14}\alpha_{11}\left(\bar{P}-P\right) + \alpha_{14}\alpha_{12}\left(\bar{r}-r\right) + \alpha_{14}\alpha_{16}\left(r_b-\bar{r}_b\right)\right\} \tag{8.35}$$

Equation (8.32) shows that there is an inbuilt cycle of income. Nothing can
be done about that. But the behaviour of prices around that cycle can be
stable, unstable or they can exhibit regular fluctuations of their own. Which
outcome is to be anticipated depends, according to Bagehot, on whether a
boom is halted quickly enough by the early use of Bank Rate. If the Bank
simply follows the behaviour of the market rate of interest, contraction will
occur too late and, in all probability, a financial panic will ensue. Thus we
need to use equations (8.34), (8.33) and (8.35) to investigate stability.

   If we then apply the standard analysis of the stability of a differential
equation system (Chiang, 1984, pp. 638-45)[13], we obtain two Jacobians of
partial derivatives of the differential equations. The first involves the partials
from equations (8.34) and (8.33), and relates to the case where the Bank

---

[13]Further details of the approach followed here can be found in chapter 10 and in O'Brien
(1995).

follows the market rate. Writing P' for equation (8.34) and r' for equation (8.33), we have:

$$J_1 = \begin{bmatrix} \frac{\partial P'}{\partial P} & \frac{\partial P'}{\partial r} \\ \frac{\partial r'}{\partial P} & \frac{\partial r'}{\partial r} \end{bmatrix} = \begin{bmatrix} 0 & -\alpha_6\alpha_5 \\ \alpha_4 & 0 \end{bmatrix} \tag{8.36}$$

J_1 thus has a zero trace and a positive determinant, yielding a vortex. If the Bank simply follows the market rate, prices will fluctuate around the cycle, with no tendency to move towards equilibrium.

The second Jacobian involves the partials from equations (8.34) and (8.35), with Bank Rate used as a positive tool of monetary control. Writing P' for equation (8.34) as before, and r_b' for equation (8.35), we have:

$$J_2 = \begin{bmatrix} \frac{\partial P'}{\partial P} & \frac{\partial P'}{\partial r_b} \\ \frac{\partial r_b'}{\partial P} & \frac{\partial r_b'}{\partial r_b} \end{bmatrix} - \begin{bmatrix} 0 & -\alpha_8 \\ \frac{K}{R^2}\alpha_{14}\alpha_{11} & \frac{-K}{R^2}\alpha_{16} \end{bmatrix}$$

This has a negative trace and a positive determinant, implying a stable equilibrium. Unless $(\alpha_{16})^2 > 4(\alpha_8\alpha_{11}\alpha_{14})$, which seems inherently unlikely, this would yield a stable focus rather than a stable node, which contrasts with the vortex implied by the first Jacobian.

Fluctuations in real income were unavoidable; but the price level could be, under a Bank Rate regime, so regulated that overlarge fluctuations of the kind which Bagehot feared (1873, pp. 150-1) could be avoided.

8.3 Conclusions

In this chapter we have explored Bagehot's macroeconomic model, setting out the equations for the trade cycle, built around harvest variations, interest rates, savings, investment and the money supply, the price level, the balance of payments, the Bank of England reserve and Bank Rate. These equations then form the basis of an analysis of the stability of Bagehot's model; and the conclusion emerges that his emphasis on the fundamental importance of Bank Rate management is vindicated.

Bagehot is chiefly famous as the proponent of the concept of the Bank as lender of last resort. In point of fact he was not truly responsible for this – the credit should go to Thomas Joplin; see chapter 7 and O'Brien (1993, pp. 17-19, 116-7, 172)[14]. But Bagehot should be credited with articulating, and working out in detail, a theory of monetary control which was to prove of fundamental importance in the development of central banking. This development was a necessary pre-requisite for the exercise of the last resort role.

---

[14]Wood points out that the concept was also advanced by witnesses before the 1832 Committee on the Bank Charter, and later by members of the Banking School (1939, pp. 85, 102, 103, 165n). However, it is argued in chapter 7 that Joplin has priority.

Chapter 9

Joplin's Model: A Formal Statement

Thomas Joplin was born, probably in 1790, in Newcastle upon Tyne, and died in Silesia in 1847. Though very much an outsider as far as the London financial establishment – which no doubt regarded him with disdain as a rough man from the North East of England – was concerned, Joplin is an important figure in British banking history. For he was the tireless, and ultimately successful, pioneer of joint stock banking in England. Indeed he was the founder of the National Provincial Bank, though he was driven from this and left uncompensated.

However, Joplin has additional claims to fame. Though he was excluded from the metropolitan network of those influential in the contemporary discussions of monetary theory, policy and institutions, his contributions to macroeconomic theory, though ignored during his lifetime, have turned out to be extremely forward looking. In addition, as mentioned in chapter 7, he made a key contribution to the theory of central bank policy through his priority in the development of the concept of the lender of last resort.

A full length study of Joplin was published in 1993 (O'Brien, 1993). This covered the full range of his intellectual and business achievements. However, the focus of the present chapter is the macroeconomic model which is at the core of his writings. This model displays a sophistication which places it well ahead of that of his contemporaries in either the Currency School or the Banking School, even though the monetary theorists of both camps were men of great ability whose own contributions were far from trivial.

Joplin's macroeconomic model has much in common with the literature which developed following the publication of Keynes's *General Theory* in 1936. It is an income-expenditure model. For equilibrium, expenditure must equal income. Income in turn arises from production. Expenditure is made up of consumption and investment. Savings are equal to investment plus consumption borrowing, when the market for loans clears.

Joplin's model, however, unlike many Keynesian models, is set firmly in the context of an open economy. Thus expenditure is equal to output plus net imports. However, going beyond a Keynesian model to what has become known as the neo-Keynesian synthesis, Joplin has aggregate demand depending upon the money supply, with changes in aggregate demand, due to changes in the money supply, having multiple effects on the level of income. In turn, Joplin included in his model changes in the level of inventories, a consideration which was later to be emphasised by Keynes's contemporary and critic Ralph Hawtrey (1928).

An increase in the money supply would increase both employment (Joplin did not assume constant labour market clearing at full employment) and the price level – the labour supply was less than perfectly elastic. But a rise in the price level could raise it above the one appropriate for balance of payments equilibrium, leading to a balance of payments deficit, with a consequent reduction in the money supply, aggregate demand and the price level which would return to equilibrium. Conversely, a fall in the money supply would produce a balance of payments surplus and a return to equilibrium.

However Joplin identified a number of problems with this equilibration, given the monetary institutions of the contemporary British economy. In particular, he argued cogently that a gold outflow, consequent upon a balance of payments deficit, fell upon the Bank of England, which however supplied the financial circulation, rather than the money supply which determined the price level of goods and services. The Bank was not in a position to produce downward pressure on the domestic price level with a view to correcting the balance of payments.

The basis for this argument was a dual-circulation hypothesis. There were two separate money markets to clear – that relating to the goods market and that relating to the financial market. The market for goods and services was serviced by the money supply provided by the country bank note issue, which was not directly affected by a gold outflow. Indeed the country banks, by keeping their lending rate fixed and varying the note issue, rather than allowing the supply of and demand for loans to clear at an equilibrium rate of interest, varied the money supply in ways which bore no relation to the balance of payments.

Joplin argued – correctly, as was to become apparent in 1847 and 1857 – that reducing the Bank of England note issue pari passu with an outflow of gold would have no effect on the price level of goods and services, which was what was relevant to the balance of payments, but would instead produce a liquidity crisis in the London money market.

In all this Joplin's position stands in sharp contrast to that of the Currency School and to that of the Banking School. On the one hand the Currency School persisted in the view that the Bank of England supplied the high powered monetary base for means of payment in the country as a whole and thus enjoyed unique leverage over the price level and, through this, the balance of payments. On the other hand the Banking School, as we saw in chapter 5, felt unable to recognise that disturbances to the balance of payments could result from changes in the domestic money supply.

Joplin's model is certainly worth taking seriously. In what follows here it emerges that it fits effortlessly into a neo-Keynesian open-economy framework. Taking the general framework of Argy's (1981) model as a starting point has three particular advantages. Firstly, it shows how well Joplin's work fits into a model of this kind, incorporating both output changes and price level changes. Secondly, it shows how much more complex was Joplin's approach than even a mainstream neo-Keynesian model, in certain key respects. Clearly the most important of these aspects is the treatment of the money market. Since these aspects only become clear when changes in the money supply are involved, difference equation versions are included in this chapter as well as equations for levels. Thirdly, this treatment enables us to see how vividly a model which is as faithful as possible to Joplin's own macroeconomics contrasts with the standard account of what 19th century economists were supposed to believe about macroeconomics; see, for example, Copeland (1994, chapter 5).

After listing the variables employed in this model, we obtain, in turn, equations for both levels and first differences in the goods market, corresponding to the standard IS equation; corresponding equations for the money market relating to transactions in goods, and for financial transactions (so that the model has two LM equations for levels, and correspondingly for differences); a balance of payments equation corresponding to the standard BP line (and its difference equivalent); and an aggregate supply function, and an aggregate demand function and corresponding difference versions. Using these we can obtain output, the interest rate, the money supply, the general price level, and the separate price levels for agricultural and non-agricultural output.

9.1   List of Variables

Y_t real income
C_t real consumption
I_t real investment
$P_{h,t}$ home (domestic) prices
$P_{f,t}$ foreign prices
R fixed (gold parity) exchange rate
P_t weighted average of $P_{h,t}$ and $P_{f,t}R$
X_t real exports
M_t real imports
$Y_{f,t}$ foreign income
P_a price level of home-produced agricultural output
P_m price level of home-produced non-agricultural output
$M_{c,t}^D$ demand for money for transactions in the goods market
$M_{c,t}^S$ supply of money for this purpose
$M_{F,t}^D$ demand for money for financial transactions ('abstract circulation')
$M_{F,t}^S$ supply of money for financial transactions
$P_{F,t}$ price level of financial transactions
r_t market rate of interest
$\bar{r}$ fixed rate of interest charged by the country banks
r_e notional equilibrium interest rate which would clear the loan market
r_f foreign interest rate
B_t balance of payments deficit: $B_t = X_t - M_t$
G_t government expenditure
T_t government revenue
L^D demand for loans from the country banks
L^S supply of savings deposits held with the country banks
BEN_t note issue by the Bank of England
W_t wage rate

Some further symbols are introduced at the appropriate points in the argument. Joplin does not (though he easily could have done) incorporate capital flows into his balance of payments analysis.

9.2   The Goods Market

Goods market equilibrium requires that income equals absorption:

$$Y_t P_{h,t} = (C_t + I_t) P_t + X P_{h,t} - M P_{f,t} R \qquad (9.1)$$

$$C_t P_t = (\alpha_1 Y_t + \alpha_2 \Delta Y_t - \alpha_3 r_t) P_t \tag{9.2}$$

where $\Delta Y_t = Y_t - Y_{t-1}$ is an accelerator embodying induced inventory changes. Demand for goods is also affected, Joplin argued, by the effects of the interest rate on stockholding.

$$I_t P_t = (\alpha_4 \Delta Y_t - \alpha_5 r_t) P_t = (\alpha_4 Y_t - \alpha_4 Y_{t-1} - \alpha_5 r_t) P_t \tag{9.3}$$

$$X_t P_{h,t} = \left(\frac{\alpha_6 P_{f,t} R}{P_{h,t}} + \alpha_7 Y_{f,t} \right) P_{h,t} = \alpha_6 P_{f,t} R + \alpha_7 Y_{f,t} P_{h,t} \tag{9.4}$$

$$M_t P_{f,t} R = \left(\alpha_8 Y_t + \frac{\alpha_9 P_{h,t}}{P_{f,t} R} \right) P_{f,t} R = \alpha_8 Y_t P_{f,t} R + \alpha_9 P_{h,t} \tag{9.5}$$

$$P_t = \gamma_t P_{h,t} + (1 - \gamma_t) P_{f,t} R \tag{9.6}$$

where γ_t is the proportion of income spent on home-produced goods. Thus:

$$(1 - \gamma_t) = \frac{M_t P_{f,t} R}{Y_t P_{h,t}} \tag{9.7}$$

and substituting for $M_t P_{f,t} R$ from (9.5) and rearranging we obtain:

$$\gamma_t = \alpha_8 R \left(\frac{P_{f,t}}{P_{h,t}} \right) + \frac{\alpha_9}{Y_t} - 1 \tag{9.8}$$

$$P_{h,t} = \beta_t P_{a,t} + (1 - \beta_t) P_{m,t} \tag{9.9}$$

where:

$$\beta_t = \frac{Y_{a,t}}{Y_t}$$

the ratio of agricultural output to total output.

But the price level of non-agricultural output is sticky. If we posit an equilibrium ratio of non-agricultural output prices to agricultural prices, K, we can write:

$$\Delta P_{m,t} = \alpha_{10} \left(\frac{P_{a,t-1}}{P_{m,t-1}} - K \right)$$

Thus:

$$P_{m,t} = P_{m,t-1} + \alpha_{10} \left(\frac{P_{a,t-1}}{P_{m,t-1}} - K \right) \tag{9.10}$$

Then substitution of (9.10) into (9.9), (9.9) into (9.4), (9.5) and (9.6), (9.6) into (9.2) and (9.3), followed by substitution of (9.2), (9.3), (9.4) and (9.5) into (9.1) yield an equation of r in Y for given prices, or the familiar IS curve.

$$
r_t = Y_t \left(\frac{\alpha_1 + \alpha_2 + \alpha_4}{(\alpha_3 + \alpha_5)} - \frac{\alpha_8 P_{f,t} R}{(\alpha_3 + \alpha_5)} \frac{1}{P_t} - \frac{P_{h,t}}{P_t} \frac{1}{(\alpha_3 + \alpha_5)} \right)
$$
$$
- Y_{t-1} \left(\frac{\alpha_2 - \alpha_4}{\alpha_3 + \alpha_5} \right) + \frac{\alpha_6 P_{f,t} R}{P_t} + (\alpha_7 Y_{f,t} - \alpha_9) \frac{P_{h,t}}{P_{f,t}} \tag{9.11}
$$

where

$$
P_{h,t} = \beta_t P_{a,t} + (1 - \beta_t) \left[P_{m,t-1} + \alpha_{10} \left(\frac{P_{a,t-1}}{P_{m,t-1}} - K \right) \right]
$$

and

$$
P_t = \gamma_t \left[\beta_t P_{a,t} + (1 - \beta_t) \left\{ P_{m,t-1} + \alpha_{10} \left(\frac{P_{a,t-1}}{P_{m,t-1}} - K \right) \right\} \right] + (1 - \gamma_t) P_{f,t} R
$$

In difference form, with all initial prices at unity, and foreign income treated as being constant, this can be written:

$$
\Delta r_t = \Delta Y_t \left(\frac{\alpha_1 + \alpha_2 + \alpha_4 + \alpha_8 R - 1}{\alpha_3 + \alpha_5} \right) - Y_t \left(\frac{\alpha_8 R \Delta P_t + \Delta P_{h,t} - \Delta P_t}{\alpha_3 + \alpha_5} \right)
$$
$$
+ \Delta Y_{t-1} \left(\frac{\alpha_2 - \alpha_4}{\alpha_3 + \alpha_5} \right) + \Delta P_t \alpha_6 R
$$
$$
+ (\alpha_7 Y_{f,t} - \alpha_9)(\Delta P_{h,t} - \Delta P_t) \tag{9.12}
$$

where, with changes in the foreign price level ignored,

$$
\Delta P_t = \gamma_t \Delta P_{h,t} + \Delta \gamma_t (P_{h,t} - P_{f,t} R) \tag{9.13}
$$

and, in turn,

$$
\Delta P_{h,t} = (1 - \beta_t) \left[\Delta P_{m,t-1} + \frac{\alpha_{10}}{P_{m,t-1}} \left\{ \frac{P_{m,t-1} \Delta P_{a,t-1} - P_{a,t-1} \Delta P_{m,t-1}}{P_{m,t-1}} \right\} \right]
$$
$$
+ \beta_t \Delta P_{a,t} + P_{a,t} \Delta \beta_t \tag{9.14}
$$

9.3   The Money Market

9.3.1   Goods Market Transactions

Joplin believed that a rise in income raised velocity of circulation, as did a rise in the interest rate. Hence:

$$\frac{M_{c,t}^D}{P_t} = (\alpha_{10} Y_t - \alpha_{11} \Delta Y_t - \alpha_{12} r_t) \tag{9.15}$$

For money market equilibrium we have:

$$\frac{M_{c,t}^D}{P_t} = \frac{M_{c,t}^S}{P_t}$$

yielding

$$r_t = \left(\frac{\alpha_{10} - \alpha_{11}}{\alpha_{12}}\right) Y_t + \left(\frac{\alpha_{11}}{\alpha_{12}}\right) Y_{t-1} - \left(\frac{M_{c,t}^S}{\alpha_{12}}\right)\left(\frac{1}{\alpha_{12}}\right) \tag{9.16}$$

which is the familiar LM curve, here called the LM_c curve, as it relates only to consumption transactions.

However, the interesting part of Joplin's analysis of this part of the money market is highlighted writing the equation in differential form. With initial prices at unity,

$$\Delta r_t = \left(\frac{\alpha_{10} - \alpha_{11}}{\alpha_{12}}\right) \Delta Y_t + \left(\frac{\alpha_{11}}{\alpha_{12}}\right) \Delta Y_{t-1} - \left(\frac{\Delta M_{c,t}^S}{\alpha_{12}}\right) - \left(\frac{\Delta M_{c,t}^S \Delta P_t}{\alpha_{12}}\right) \tag{9.17}$$

It is the term $\Delta M_{c,t}^S$, which reflects particularly Joplin's individual approach, which can nevertheless be captured within this general framework. For

$$\Delta M_{c,t}^S = M_{c,t}^S - M_{c,t-1}^S$$

is made up of the following elements.

1. $(B_t/4) + B_{t-1}$, representing the balance of payments as affecting Bank of England notes immediately and country bank notes after a lag. The

(1/4) weight is Joplin's.[1] The proposition is that the financial circulation (or 'abstract circulation' as Joplin called it) affected the price of financial assets but not the balance of payments. Joplin concluded that the 'consumptive circulation' – the money supply involved in demanding goods – was the note issue of the country banks and one quarter of the note issue of the Bank of England. He arrives at the one quarter weighting from two different considerations: firstly, the denominations of the notes circulated by these two sources of issue (adjusted by an allowance for till money); and, secondly, relative consumption of goods in London and Lancashire which he puts at one fifth of total UK consumption. Since the note issues of the Bank of England and the combined country banks were about equal, and writing 100 for each, we have $\left(\frac{4}{5}\right) M_c^S = 100CBN$, and $\left(\frac{1}{5}\right) M_c^S = 100BEN$, so that $M_c^S = 500BEN = 125CBN$. Hence a weighting of $\left(\frac{1}{4}\right)$ on Bank of England issues is required.

2. $\frac{\varsigma}{4}\left(G_t - T_t\right)$, where ς is the proportion of the government deficit borrowed from the central bank ((3/4) of the money thus created however goes into the financial circulation).[2]

3. $\left(1 - \varsigma\right)\left(G_t - T_t\right)$, where the remainder of the government deficit is borrowed directly or indirectly via customers from the country banks.

4. $\left(L^D - L^S\right)$, representing net money created by the country banks as a result of charging $\bar{r}$ rather than varying the interest rate so as to allow the loan market to clear.

This last term can be expressed as a function of the difference between the market clearing rate of interest, r_e, and the fixed rate $\bar{r}$.

---

[1]See Joplin (1823, pp. 156-7; 1825, pp. xxv, 23-6; 1826, pp. 48-9; 1828, pp. 28-32; 1831, p. 8; 1832, pp. 87-98, 113-14).

[2]In view of the importance of property taxation during this period, and the fact that there was no income tax between 1816 and 1842, it seems best to treat tax revenue as exogenous and not as a function of income.

Writing I for L^D and S for L^S, since the demand for and supply of loans relate to the savings/investment discrepancy in O'Brien (1993, chapter 7):

$$I - S = I - I_e - (S - S_e)$$

where I_e and S_e represent the (equal) amount of demand for and supply of loans if the country banks allowed the loan market to clear (as they would with a properly regulated paper currency). In setting this up we can take account of Joplin's contention that the demand by the agricultural sector for loans was negatively related to its income (the harvest).

Writing, as before, β_t as the agricultural proportion of GNP and $(1 - \beta_t)$ as the non-agricultural proportion we have:

$$I = \alpha_{13} \left(1 - \beta_t\right) Y_t - \alpha_{14} \beta_t Y_t - \alpha_{15} \bar{r}$$

$$I_e = \alpha_{13} \left(1 - \beta_t\right) Y_t - \alpha_{14} \beta_t Y_t - \alpha_{15} r_e$$

$$S = \alpha_{16} Y_t + \alpha_{17} \bar{r}$$

$$S_e = \alpha_{16} Y_t + \alpha_{17} r_e$$

where the country bank spread between lending and borrowing rates is ignored. Then:

$$I - I_e = \alpha_{15} \left(r_e - \bar{r}\right) \tag{9.18}$$

$$S - S_e = \alpha_{17} \left(\bar{r} - r_e\right)$$

$$L^D - L^S = \left(\alpha_{15} + \alpha_{17}\right) \left(r_e - \bar{r}\right)$$

Thus:

$$
\begin{aligned}
M_{c,t}^S - M_{c,t-1}^S &= \Delta M_{c,t}^S \\
&= \left(\frac{B_t}{4}\right) + B_{t-1} + \left(\frac{\zeta}{4}\right) (G_t - T_t) + (1 - \zeta) (G_t - T_t) \\
&\quad + (\alpha_{15} + \alpha_{17}) (r_e - \bar{r})
\end{aligned}
$$

which simplifies to

$$M^S_{c,t} - M^S_{c,t-1} = \left(\frac{B_t}{4}\right) + B_{t-1} + \left(1 - \left(\frac{3}{4}\right)\zeta\right)(G_t - T_t) + (\alpha_{15} + \alpha_{17})(r_e - \bar{r})$$

(9.19)

Equation (9.19) can be substituted into (9.17), the differential form of the *LM* curve, to obtain a curve of money market equilibrium for consumption transactions which incorporates Joplin's view of the factors responsible for variations in the money supply.

For the purpose of solving the system as a whole, r_e can be replaced by r_t, since the equilibrium rate for the economy as a whole would require satisfaction of goods market equilibrium with savings equal to investment.

9.3.2 Financial Market Transactions

The equation of demand for balances for financial transactions can be written:

$$\frac{M^D_{F,t}}{P_{F,t}} = \alpha_{17}Y_t - \alpha_{18}\Delta BEN_t - \alpha_{19}\Delta Y_t - \alpha_{20}r_t$$

(9.20)

where inclusion of the item ΔBEN_t indicates that contraction of the Bank of England note issue is taken as a signal by the financial sector that it is necessary to increase precautionary balances, and ΔY_t is included because Joplin believed that a rise in national income increased velocity of both the 'consumptive' and the 'abstract' circulation.

$$\frac{M^D_{F,t}}{P_{F,t}} = \frac{M^S_{F t}}{P_{F,t}}$$

(9.21)

for equilibrium in the financial money market.

Substituting from (9.21) into (9.20) we obtain the locus of equilibrium in the financial money market:

$$r_t = \frac{\alpha_{17}}{\alpha_{20}}Y_t - \frac{\alpha_{18}}{\alpha_{20}}\Delta BEN_t - \frac{\alpha_{12}}{\alpha_{20}}\Delta Y_t - \frac{M^S_{F,t}}{P_{F,t}}\frac{1}{\alpha_{20}}$$

(9.22)

However it is necessary to write the equation in difference form to pick up Joplin's particular perspective on changes in the supply of funds to financial markets.

In difference form, taking the initial value of $P_{F,t}$ as unity:

$$\Delta r_t = \frac{\alpha_{17}}{\alpha_{20}}\Delta Y_t - \frac{\alpha_{18}}{\alpha_{20}}\Delta\left(\Delta BEN_t\right) - \frac{\alpha_{12}}{\alpha_{20}}\Delta\left(\Delta Y_t\right) - \frac{1}{\alpha_{20}}\Delta M_{F,t}^S + \frac{1}{\alpha_{20}}M_{F,t}^S\Delta P_{F,t}$$

$$(9.23)$$

where

$$\Delta\left(\Delta BEN_t\right) = BEN_t - 2BEN_{t-1} + BEN_{t-2}$$

$$\Delta\left(\Delta Y_t\right) = Y_t - 2Y_{t-1} + Y_{t-2}$$

and

$$\Delta M_{F,t}^S = \left(\frac{3}{4}\right)B_t + \left(\frac{3}{4}\right)\zeta\left(G_t - T_t\right) + \mu\left[\left(\frac{3}{4}\right)B_t + \left(\frac{3}{4}\right)\zeta\left(G_t - T_t\right)\right]$$

$$(9.24)$$

where μ is the deposit multiplier in the London money market. The weight of $(3/4)$, on a change in the Bank of England circulation resulting from a balance of payments or government surplus or deficit, corresponds to the weighting of $(1/4)$ for the 'consumptive circulation'.

As before, ζ is the proportion of the government deficit borrowed from the central bank. Joplin estimated μ at 5. On this basis, equation (9.24) simplifies to:

$$\Delta M_{F,t}^S = \frac{9}{2}\left[B_t + \zeta\left(G_t - T_t\right)\right] \qquad (9.25)$$

which can be substituted into equation (9.23) to yield the alternative (difference) form of the LM_F curve for financial money market equilibrium.

9.3.3   The Balance of Payments

$$B_t = XP_{h,t} - M_t P_{f,t}R \qquad (9.26)$$

$$M_t = \alpha_6 Y_t + \frac{\alpha_7 P_{h,t}}{P_{f,t}R} \qquad (9.27)$$

$$X_t = \alpha_8\frac{P_{f,t}R}{P_{h,t}} + \alpha_9 Y_{f,t} \qquad (9.28)$$

Substituting (9.28) and (9.27) into (9.26) yields:

$$B_t = \alpha_8 P_{f,t}R + \alpha_9 Y_{f,t}P_{h,t} - \alpha_6 Y_t P_{f,t}R - \alpha_7 P_{h,t} \qquad (9.29)$$

Setting $B_t = 0$ as required for equilibrium,

$$Y_t = \frac{\alpha_8 P_{f,t} R - \alpha_7 P_{h,t}}{\alpha_6 P_{f,t} R - \alpha_9 P_{h,t}} \qquad (9.30)$$

which is an analogue of the conventional BP line although, since there are no capital flows in equation (9.26) this will be vertical for given prices (including the gold price).

If we include capital flows – which would certainly be reasonable in the context of the 19th century gold standard – the balance of payments equation would become:

$$B_t = X P_{h,t} - M P_{f,t} + \alpha_{21} (r_t - r_f) \qquad (9.31)$$

which yields after substitution of the export and import equations (9.28) and (9.27).

$$B_t = \alpha_8 P_{f,t} R + \alpha_9 Y_{f,t} P_t - \alpha_6 Y_t P_{f,t} R - \alpha_7 P_{h,t} + \alpha_{21} (r_t - r_f) \qquad (9.32)$$

Setting $B_t = 0$ as required for equilibrium, we obtain the standard equation of r in Y for a BP line with given prices:

$$r_t = \frac{\alpha_6}{\alpha_{21}} Y_t P_{f,t} R + \frac{\alpha_7}{\alpha_{21}} P_{h,t} + r_f - \frac{\alpha_8}{\alpha_{21}} P_{f,t} R - \frac{\alpha_9}{\alpha_{21}} Y_{f,t} P_{h,t} \qquad (9.33)$$

If we ignore secondary effects on foreign prices, interest rates and income (Joplin does not do so entirely but they are peripheral to his story except in the context of reciprocal demand – O'Brien (1993, chapter 12) we can obtain the difference version of the BP line:

$$\begin{aligned} \Delta r_t &= \frac{\alpha_6}{\alpha_{21}} P_{f,t} R \Delta Y + \frac{\alpha_7}{\alpha_{21}} \Delta P_{h,t} - \frac{\alpha_9}{\alpha_{21}} Y_{f,t} \Delta P_{h,t} \\ &= \left(\frac{\alpha_6}{\alpha_{21}} P_{f,t} R \right) \Delta Y + \left(\frac{\alpha_7 - \alpha_9}{\alpha_{21}} Y_{f,t} \right) \Delta P_{h,t} \qquad (9.34) \end{aligned}$$

9.3.4 Aggregate Supply and the Labour Market

Joplin does not assume that real wages are constant during macroeconomic fluctuations. The labour demand and supply equations are as follows. The equation for the quantity of labour demanded is:

$$Q^D_{L,t} = \delta_1 - \varepsilon_1 W_t + \varepsilon_2 Y_t \tag{9.35}$$

The equation for the quantity of labour supplied is:

$$Q^S_{L,t} = \delta_2 + \varepsilon_3 W_t + \varepsilon_4 Y_t \tag{9.36}$$

Labour market clearing yields:

$$W_t = \frac{\delta_1 - \delta_2}{\varepsilon_1 + \varepsilon_3} + \frac{\varepsilon_2 - \varepsilon_4}{\varepsilon_1 + \varepsilon_3} Y_t \tag{9.37}$$

Then GNP rises if wages rise or if domestic prices rise (producing increased profit opportunities):

$$Y_t = \rho P_{h,t} W_t \tag{9.38}$$

Writing a for

$$\frac{\delta_1 - \delta_2}{\varepsilon_1 + \varepsilon_3}$$

and b for

$$\frac{\varepsilon_2 - \varepsilon_4}{\varepsilon_1 + \varepsilon_3}$$

$$Y_t = \rho P_{h,t} \left(a + b Y_t \right) \tag{9.39}$$

which after collection of terms yields:

$$Y_t = \frac{\rho a P_{h,t}}{(1 - \rho b P_{h,t})} \tag{9.40}$$

Writing α_{22} for ρa and α_{23} for ρb to simplify notation:

$$Y_t = \frac{\alpha_{22} P_{h,t}}{(1 - \alpha_{23} P_{h,t})} \tag{9.41}$$

which is the aggregate supply function. Differencing then yields:

$$\Delta Y_t = \frac{(1 - \alpha_{23} P_{h,t}) \alpha_{22} \Delta P_{h,t} + \alpha_{22} \alpha_{23} P_{h,t} \Delta P_{h,t}}{(1 - \alpha_{23} P_{h,t})^2} \tag{9.42}$$

which, after clearing of brackets and setting the initial price level to unity, yields:

$$\Delta Y_t = \frac{\alpha_{22} \Delta P_{h,t}}{(1 - \alpha_{23})^2} \tag{9.43}$$

We have then an aggregate supply function with output functionally dependent on the domestic price level P_h. The output level (with the interest rate) is determined by the $IS = LM$ aggregate demand condition (section 9.3.5 below), and thus we solve for the domestic price level using the aggregate supply equation.

In turn, P_h is related to the two domestic price levels P_a and P_m by (9.9). Given output we can solve equation (9.37) for W_t, and replace P_a in (9.9) by:

$$\frac{\beta_t Y}{\alpha W}$$

Let L_a and L_m denote the agricultural and non-agricultural labour force respectively, and write the value of agricultural output as proportional to the labour cost of production, so that:

$$Y_a P_a = \theta_1 W L_a \tag{9.44}$$

Hence:

$$Y_a = \frac{\theta_1 W L_a}{P_a} = Y\beta \tag{9.45}$$

and the agricultural price level is:

$$P_a = \frac{\theta_1 W L_a}{Y\beta}$$

Furthermore:

$$Y_m P_m = \theta_2 W L_m \tag{9.46}$$

and using (9.9) yields P_m for a given P_h.

It seems reasonable to treat β as exogenous for the purposes of monetary analysis. The main change in agricultural output which Joplin considers is a harvest failure. In rejecting the agricultural cobweb (see O'Brien, 1993, chapter 11) he opted for the view that acreage was static. He does not regard substitution in the consumption basket between agricultural and non-agricultural output as being of significance for his model. By contrast γ_t is endogenous; but from (9.8) it is determined given output and the domestic price level (since the price of gold is fixed and the foreign price level is treated as exogenous).

9.3.5   Aggregate Demand

For the purpose of considering equilibrium levels, the aggregate demand curve for Joplin's model can be derived using the IS and the LMc curves (9.11) and (9.16) as the financial circulation does not affect demand for output except during a financial crisis.

Combining the two equations we have:

$$
\begin{aligned}
Y_t &\left(\frac{\alpha_1 + \alpha_2 + \alpha_4}{\alpha_3 + \alpha_5} - \frac{\alpha_8 P_{f,t} R}{\alpha_3 + \alpha_5} \frac{1}{P_t} - \frac{1}{\alpha_3 + \alpha_5} \frac{P_{h,t}}{P_t} - \frac{(\alpha_{10} - \alpha_{11})}{\alpha_{12}} \right) \\
= \ & Y_{t-1} \left(\frac{\alpha_2 - \alpha_4}{\alpha_3 + \alpha_5} + \frac{\alpha_{11}}{\alpha_{12}} \right) - \alpha_6 \left(\frac{P_{f,t} R}{P_t} \right) \\
& - (\alpha_7 Y_{f,t} - \alpha_9) \frac{P_{h,t}}{P_t} - \frac{M_{c,t}^S}{P_t} \frac{1}{\alpha_{12}}
\end{aligned}
\tag{9.47}
$$

Given that, by (9.19):

$$
P_{h,t} = \frac{P_t - (1 - \gamma) P_{f,t} R}{\gamma_t}
$$

the ratio $P_{h,t}/P_t$ can be written as

$$
\frac{P_t - (1 - \gamma) P_{f,t} R}{\gamma_t P_t}
\tag{9.48}
$$

Substituting (9.48) into (9.47), dividing through by the coefficient on Y_t, and letting:

$$
\begin{aligned}
A \ = \ & Y_{t-1} \left(\frac{\alpha_2 - \alpha_4}{\alpha_3 + \alpha_5} + \frac{\alpha_{11}}{\alpha_{12}} \right) - \left(\frac{\alpha_8 P_{f,t} R}{P_t} \right) \\
& - (\alpha_7 Y_{f,t} - \alpha_9) \left(\frac{P_t - (1 - \gamma) P_{f,t} R}{\gamma_t P_t} \right)
\end{aligned}
\tag{9.49}
$$

and:

$$
\begin{aligned}
B \ = \ & (\alpha_3 + \alpha_5) \left(\frac{1}{\alpha_1 + \alpha_2 + \alpha_4} \right) - \frac{P_t}{P_{f,t} R} \left(\frac{\gamma_t}{\alpha_8 - P_t (1 - \gamma_t)} \right) \\
& - \left(\frac{\alpha_{12}}{(\alpha_{10} - \alpha_{11})(\alpha_3 + \alpha_5)} \right)
\end{aligned}
\tag{9.50}
$$

we obtain:

$$
Y_t = AB
\tag{9.51}
$$

The corresponding difference version, letting:

$$C = Y_t \left(\frac{\alpha_8 R \Delta P_t + \Delta P_{h,t} - \Delta P_t}{\alpha_3 + \alpha_5} \right) - \Delta Y_{t-1} \left(\frac{\alpha_2 - \alpha_4}{\alpha_3 + \alpha_5} + \frac{\alpha_{11}}{\alpha_{12}} \right)$$
$$- \Delta P_t \alpha_6 R - (\alpha_7 Y f - \alpha_9) (\Delta P_{h,t} - \Delta P_t)$$
$$- \left(\frac{\Delta M_{c,t}^S + M_{c,t}^S \Delta P_t}{\alpha_{12}} \right) \tag{9.52}$$

and:

$$D = \left(\frac{\alpha_3 + \alpha_5}{\alpha_1 + \alpha_2 + \alpha_4 + \alpha_8 R - 1} \right) - \left(\frac{\alpha_{12}}{\alpha_{10} - \alpha_{11}} \right) \tag{9.53}$$

is:

$$\Delta Y_t = CD \tag{9.54}$$

where, as before, $\Delta P_{h,t}$ is defined as in (9.14).

The difference version has the advantage over (9.51) that the slope of the relationship between the price level and output is unambiguously negative.

9.4 Conclusions

This chapter has demonstrated that it is possible to state Joplin's model in terms recognisable to those familiar with a standard neo-Keynesian model, although it is apparent that Joplin's model is considerably more elaborate in key respects. We have obtained, following Joplin's analysis, a version of the familiar IS curve of goods market equilibrium and two LM curves, one for equilibrium in the money market relating to goods market transactions and one for equilibrium in the money market relating to financial transactions. When these equations are expressed in difference form the full complexity (and potential for instability) involved in Joplin's complex analysis become clear. We have also obtained the analogue in Joplin's analysis of the conventional BP line, and developed an aggregate supply function which captures Joplin's treatment so that aggregate supply is dependent on the domestic price level. Combining aggregate supply with aggregate demand, as determined by the $IS = LM$ condition, yields the domestic price level. Joplin's model is thus complete.

Chapter 10

Stability With an Inbuilt Cycle

In chapter 5, the debate between the Currency School and the Banking School over the proper response of monetary policy to disturbances, and the kind of monetary regime required, were discussed. It was argued there that the stability of the adjustment process was extremely important. The Banking School (and the modern free banking movement) device of citing long-run equilibrium as a solution to a short-run problem – the Ricardian telescope – proved unhelpful. In particular, given the existence of endogenous fluctuations in real income, there was a choice (with which governments remain faced both in this context and in that of an exogenous disturbance such as a rise in the price of oil) between responding according to 'currency' (counter-cyclical) or 'banking' (pro-cyclical) policies. In this chapter we explore formally the stability properties of the two contrasting approaches.

This chapter is divided into three sections, each of which explores one aspect of the debate over stability. In section 10.1 it is shown that adherence to the Currency School monetary rule should normally (that is, in the absence of an implausibly violent trade cycle) result in economic stability. Section 10.2 explores the implications of the Banking School 'passive money supply' prescription and concludes that there is no determinate equilibrium in this case. If the Banking School position is strengthened by an attempt to rectify this indeterminacy, the best that can be obtained is a saddle point. Section

10.3 demonstrates that, even where the Banking School ultimately has to face reality (in the form of the balance of payments constraint on monetary passivity implied by a convertible currency), the amplitude of fluctuations will, as the Currency School maintained, be greater where bankers respond to 'the needs of trade'. We concentrate on price fluctuations, treating income variation as exogenous, though in the Currency School writings some feedback from price to income variation is not ruled out.

10.1   The Currency School: Metallic Fluctuation

According to the Currency School view, the price level would rise or fall as a result of two factors. Firstly, there were changes in prices inherent in the trade cycle, reflecting, in particular, the level of capacity utilisation. Secondly, the price level would rise or fall with net increases or decreases in the money supply. Such changes would occur where the money supply exceeded, or fell short of, the demand for money which, at least in the debates up to 1844, was held to depend on the levels of income and prices. (After 1844 the existence of precautionary balances, changing with confidence, was also recognised.)

$$\frac{dP}{dt} = \alpha_1 \left(M^S - M^D \right) + \alpha_2 \frac{dT}{dt} \qquad (10.1)$$

with $\alpha_1 \alpha_2 > 0$ and where P is the domestic price level, M^S is the money supply, M^D is demand for money and T is an index of capacity utilisation in the economy, taking a value of unity when the level of national income is at its long-run equilibrium value. Changes in capacity utilisation are positively related to changes in the level of income.

$$\frac{dT}{dt} = f \left(\frac{dY}{dt} \right) \qquad (10.2)$$

with $f' > 0$. The Currency School (especially Overstone) argued that there was an inbuilt trade cycle so that income fluctuated around its steady state value. Total income Y_t is thus made up of two components, a steady state value and a fluctuating component. Such a view can be represented by a function of the form $Y_t = Y_c + Y_p$, where Y_p represents steady state income and Y_c is the term representing fluctuation around that steady state. Then Y_c may be written:

$$Y_c = e^{ht} \left(A_1 \cos vt + A_2 \sin vt \right) \tag{10.3}$$

where h and v are the real parts of the complex numbers $h \pm vi$.[1] For steady fluctuation, neither increasing nor damped, $h = 0$.

For a differential equation of the form:

$$y''(t) + a_1 y'(t) + a_2 y = d \tag{10.4}$$

$$h = -\frac{1}{2} a_1 \tag{10.5}$$

In this case, $a_1 = 0$ as $h = 0$. Furthermore:

$$v = \frac{1}{2} \sqrt{4a_2 - a_1^2} \tag{10.6}$$

In this case, where $h = a_1 = 0$, $v = \sqrt{a_2}$. For simplification of notation we write $\sqrt{a_2} = b$, and income with an inbuilt trade cycle may be written:

$$Y_t = A_1 \cos bt + A_2 \sin bt + Y_p \tag{10.7}$$

Thus differentiating and substituting into (10.2) gives:

$$\frac{dT}{dt} = f \left(-A_1 \sin bt + A_2 \cos bt \right) \tag{10.8}$$

---

[1]See Chiang (1984, p. 524). Given $Y_c = e^{ht} \left(A_1 e^{vit} + A_2 e^{-vit} \right)$, the Euler relations are $e^{vit} = \cos vt + i \sin vt$ and $e^{-vit} = \cos vt - i \sin vt$. Using

$$
\begin{aligned}
Y_c &= e^{ht} \left[A_1 \left(\cos vt + i \sin vt \right) + A_2 \left(\cos vt - i \sin vt \right) \right] \\
&\quad e^{ht} \left[\left(A_1 + A_2 \right) \cos vt + \left(A_1 - A_2 \right) i \sin vt \right]
\end{aligned}
$$

and writing $A_5 = (A_1 + A_2)$ and $A_6 = (A_1 - A_2 i)$, $Y_c = e^{ht} \left(A_5 \cos vt + A_6 \sin vt \right)$. Since the numbering of constants is arbitrary, A_5 and A_6 have been replaced by A_1 and A_2 in the text.

Demand for money can be written:

$$M^D = \alpha_3 kPY = \alpha_3 kP\left(Y_c + Y_p\right) \tag{10.9}$$

where k is, as usual, demand for balances. Thus substituting for M^D in (10.1) yields:

$$\frac{dP}{dt} = \alpha_1 M^S - \alpha_1 \alpha_3 kP\left(Y_c + Y_p\right) + \alpha_2 \frac{dT}{dt} \tag{10.10}$$

Substituting for Y_t from (10.7) and dT/dt from (10.8) and collecting terms:

$$\begin{aligned}\frac{dP}{dt} &= \alpha_1 M^S - \alpha_1 \alpha_3 kP\left(A_1 \cos bt + A_2 \sin bt\right) - \alpha_1 \alpha_3 kPY_p \\ &\quad + \alpha_2 f\left(-A_1 \sin bt + A_2 \cos bt\right)\end{aligned} \tag{10.11}$$

The money supply itself changed, if the principle of metallic fluctuation were adhered to, with the balance of payment, which in turn depended on the relationship between the home price level and the foreign price level (without necessarily assuming purchasing power parity). Gold flows across the exchanges would affect the reserves of the Bank of England: these in turn would, under metallic fluctuation, directly affect the note issue; and the change in the Bank of England note issue, as the high-powered monetary base, would alter the total money supply. Thus:

$$\frac{dG}{dt} = \alpha_4\left(P^* - P\right) \tag{10.12}$$

with $\alpha_4 > 0$ and where G is gold reserves, P^* is the home price level which ensures balance of payments equilibrium (and, as above, P is the existing home price level).

$$\frac{dR}{dt} = \alpha_5 \frac{dG}{dt} \tag{10.13}$$

with $\alpha_5 > 0$ and where R represents Bank of England reserves.

$$\frac{dN}{dt} = \alpha_6 \frac{dR}{dt} \tag{10.14}$$

with $\alpha_6 > 0$ and where N is Bank of England notes and, under the Currency School proposals, as realised in the Bank Charter Act of 1844, notes above the £14 million 'fiduciary issue' had to be backed by 100 per cent gold reserves.

The change in money supply can thus be written as:

$$\frac{dM^S}{dt} = \alpha_7 \frac{dN}{dt} \tag{10.15}$$

with $\alpha_7 > 0$ and where $\alpha_7 > 1/r$, the implied reserve ratio of the financial system.

Substituting (10.12), (10.13) and (10.14) into (10.15) and amalgamating the α_i coefficients into α_8 we have:

$$\frac{dM^S}{dt} = \alpha_8 (P^* - P) \tag{10.16}$$

with $\alpha_8 > 0$. Equations (10.11) and (10.16) can be examined for stability using the Jacobian (and writing P' and M' for $\frac{dP}{dt}$ and $\frac{dM^S}{dt}$):[2]

$$J = \begin{bmatrix} \frac{\partial P'}{\partial P} & \frac{\partial P'}{\partial M^S} \\ \frac{\partial M'}{\partial P} & \frac{\partial M'}{\partial M^S} \end{bmatrix} \tag{10.17}$$

where for stability we require that the trace $\operatorname{tr} J < 0$ and the determinant $|J| > 0$. Here:

$$\frac{\partial P'}{\partial P} = -\alpha_1 \alpha_3 k \{A_1 \cos bt + A_2 \sin bt\} - \alpha_1 \alpha_3 k Y_p \tag{10.18}$$

$$\frac{\partial P'}{\partial M^S} = \alpha_1 \tag{10.19}$$

$$\frac{\partial M'}{\partial P} = -\alpha_8 \tag{10.20}$$

$$\frac{\partial M'}{\partial M^S} = 0 \tag{10.21}$$

Thus $|J| = -(\alpha_1)(-\alpha_8) > 0$ and $\operatorname{tr} J = -\alpha_1 \alpha_3 k \{A_1 \cos bt + A_2 \sin bt\} - \alpha_1 \alpha_3 k Y_p$.

---

[2]Strictly, this technique is appropriate to investigation of local stability (Chiang, 1984, pp. 638-645). However for the particular functions involved there is no need to evaluate the partials in the Jacobian at $\frac{dP}{dt} = \frac{dM}{dt} = 0$ since the conditions these imply ($M^S = kPy, P = P^*$) do not affect the evaluation of the partial derivatives in the Jacobian.

The trigonometric part of $\mathrm{tr} J$ will fluctuate in sign, but is unlikely to be more than (perhaps) 10 per cent of Y_p. Thus $\mathrm{tr} J < 0$ and we have stability as long as the inbuilt cycle in Y_c is not too large in relation to steady state income. However in the event of fluctuations in Y_p which are large enough to dominate steady state income, an unstable node or unstable focus would result.

10.2   The Banking School

The essential difficulty faced by anyone attempting to model the Banking School position is that its members consistently avoided discussing the problem of the determination of the price level in the short run, appealing instead to the proposition that, in the long run, the price level was fixed by the international price of gold. As Humphrey (1990) has explained, in a different context, the proposition was that:

$$P = P_G P_{FG} \tag{10.22}$$

where P is the home price of goods (£/Goods), P_G is fixed gold price (£/Gold) and P_{FG} is the world price of goods in terms of gold (Gold/Goods).

The nearest approach to an explanation is that to be found in Tooke's critique (1844) of Overstone in which he appears to be arguing that the price level depends upon aggregate demand and aggregate supply. But unfortunately both aggregate demand and aggregate supply turn out to be of the same form. If PY is money income, w is the wage rate, L the labour force, r the profit rate and K the capital stock, this form is:

$$PY = wL + rK \tag{10.23}$$

so that instead of two equations we have only one, with $wL+rK$ representing not only the value of output but also the level of factor income expended on that output – which would be true only in equilibrium.

Thus the Currency School were able to charge the Banking School with holding a model in which the price level determined the money supply while neglecting the (short run) influence of the money supply on the price level.

Using the same notation as in the Currency School case, we can model the Banking School proposition that the money supply should respond to 'the needs of trade' as follows:

$$\frac{dM^S}{dt} = \alpha_9 \left(M^D - M^S\right) + \alpha_{10}\frac{dT}{dt} \tag{10.24}$$

with $\alpha_9, \alpha_{10} > 0$. Then using equations (10.7), (10.8) and (10.9):

$$\begin{aligned}\frac{dM^S}{dt} &= \alpha_9\alpha_3 kP\left(A_1\cos bt + A_2\sin bt\right) + \alpha_9\alpha_3 kPY_p - \alpha_9 M^S \\ &\quad + \alpha_{10}f\left(-A_1\sin bt + A_2\cos bt\right)\end{aligned} \tag{10.25}$$

Equation (10.25) is however proportional to equation (10.11) as can be demonstrated by differentiating it with respect to P. Writing, as before, M' for $\frac{dM^S}{dt}$, we have:

$$\frac{dM'}{dP} = \alpha_9\alpha_3 k\left\{A_1\cos bt + A_2\sin bt\right\} + \alpha_9\alpha_3 kY_p \tag{10.26}$$

which is merely equation (10.18) multiplied by $\left(-\frac{\alpha_9}{\alpha_1}\right)$. Thus the charge levelled by the Currency School against the Banking School – that the latter's theoretical framework involved no determinate equilibrium – is supported.[3]

The Jacobian of partials from equations 10.11 and 10.25 thus has a zero determinant - there is only one equation for the two endogenous variables, the price level and the money supply.

If we attempt to supply the deficiency by crediting the Banking School with acceptance of the two equilibrium conditions:

$$M^S = kPY \tag{10.27}$$

$$P = P^* \tag{10.28}$$

---

[3]The same conclusion was reached by Humphrey (1993, pp. 22-5) in his elegantly simple model of the Real Bills doctrine.

the difference between the Currency and Banking School positions can be summarised as follows. Given a disturbance so that:

$$M^S < kPY \qquad (10.29)$$

$$P > P^* \qquad (10.30)$$

the Currency School rule involved:

$$\frac{dM^S}{dP} < 0 \qquad (10.31)$$

while the Banking School 'needs of trade' response implied:

$$\frac{dM^S}{dP} > 0 \qquad (10.32)$$

This can be captured by multiplying equation (10.16) by minus one. The resulting Jacobian will have a negative trace and a negative determinant so that, at best, the Banking School position implied a saddle point.

10.3   The Amplitude of Fluctuations

A significant part of the Currency School case against the Banking School was that adherence to its precepts would increase the amplitude of fluctuation. While a convertible currency and the constraints imposed by the price-specie-flow mechanism would ultimately call the issuing banks to heel, adherence to the Banking principle in the upturn would undoubtedly increase the magnitude of fluctuations. Throughout this discussion we concentrate on price fluctuations, treating income variation as inherent in the system. Thus we do not deal with possible feedback from price to income variation, though in the 19th century literature this is certainly not ruled out.

We start with the proposition that:

$$P = \frac{M^S T}{kY} \qquad (10.33)$$

where, as before, P is the home price level and M^S is the money supply, with k as demand for balances and Y as income. Again we have T, representing capacity utilisation which pushes up prices in the cycle, independently of monetary causes, thus ensuring the existence of a tendency for prices to move with the cycle – the fluctuations of income, by increasing the ratio of output to any given money supply would otherwise tend to move prices counter-cyclically.

By equation (10.12) we require for balance of payments equilibrium that $P = P^*$.

If we define $P^* = M/kY_p$ (with T at unity and Y_c at zero) the economy will ultimately have to return to this position which is dictated by convertibility. But the amplitude of fluctuations around that equilibrium will differ according to whether the Currency School 'counter-cyclical' or the Banking School 'passive money supply' policy is followed.

From equation (10.33):

$$\frac{dP}{dt}\frac{1}{P} = \frac{dM^S}{dt}\frac{1}{M^S} + \frac{dT}{dt}\frac{1}{T} - \frac{dk}{dt}\frac{1}{k} - \frac{dY}{dt}\frac{1}{Y} \tag{10.34}$$

If changes in capacity utilisation affect the price level and thus the balance of payments, we can capture the relative positions of the two schools as follows. For the Currency School the (proportionate) change in the money supply would be negatively related to the (proportionate) change in capacity utilisation, since the deterioration in the balance of payments would be allowed to affect monetary growth:

$$\frac{dM^S}{dt}\frac{1}{M^S} = -\alpha_{11}\frac{dT}{dt}\frac{1}{T} \tag{10.35}$$

with $\alpha_{11} > 0$. Thus:

$$\frac{dP}{dt}\frac{1}{P} = (1 - \alpha_{11})\frac{dT}{dt}\frac{1}{T} - \frac{dk}{dt}\frac{1}{k} - \frac{dY}{dt}\frac{1}{Y} \tag{10.36}$$

For the Banking School the money supply should respond to the 'needs of trade' and thus:

$$\frac{dM^S}{dt}\frac{1}{M^S} = \alpha_{12}\frac{dT}{dt}\frac{1}{T} \tag{10.37}$$

with $\alpha_{12} > 0$. In this case:

$$\frac{dP}{dt} = (1 + \alpha_{12}) \frac{dT}{dt}\frac{1}{T} - \frac{dk}{dt}\frac{1}{k} - \frac{dY}{dt}\frac{1}{Y} \qquad (10.38)$$

Given $\alpha_{11}, \alpha_{12} > 0$, it must follow that $(1 + \alpha_{12}) > (1 - \alpha_{11})$ and so fluctuations would be greater than in the Currency School case.

Given (10.2) and (10.7) above, so that:

$$\frac{dT}{dt}\frac{1}{T} = f\left(\frac{dY}{dt}\frac{1}{T}\right)$$

$$= f\frac{(-A_1 \sin bt + A_2 \cos bt)}{T} \qquad (10.39)$$

the fluctuations inherent in income would be magnified or damped in the price fluctuations dependent on whether a Banking School or Currency School regime was being followed. The Currency School could, and did, advocate further damping of the cycle through the term $\frac{dk}{dt}\frac{1}{k}$, which could also be negatively related to $\frac{dT}{dt}\frac{1}{T}$ via the information/velocity of circulation mechanism discussed in chapter 5.

10.4   Conclusions

We have shown that the prescriptions of the Currency School, at least if they had been targeting the right money supply (Joplin had established that they were not, but he was ignored), produced negative feedback to a disturbance, and stabilisation of the price level. Under normal circumstances, where fluctuations of real income around the steady state value are not extreme, the Currency School rules for response would produce stability. By contrast, the Banking School, handicapped by having no adequate theory of the determination of the domestic price level in the short run, effectively left the price level indeterminate in that short run. Even if we attempt to supply this deficiency, by crediting the Banking School with some loose adherence to a quantity theory of money, the best that we can achieve is a saddle point, while the amplitude of fluctuations will be significantly greater if Banking School prescriptions are followed.

Bibliography

[1] Argy, V. (1981) *The Postwar International Money Crisis - an Analysis*. London: Allen & Unwin.

[2] Ashton, T.S. and Sayers, R.S. (1953) *Papers in English Monetary History*. Oxford: Clarendon.

[3] Bagehot, W. (1873) *Lombard Street: A Description of the Money Market*. London: King.

[4] Barbon, N. (1690) *A Discourse of Trade*. London: Milbourn. Reprinted (ed. by J.H. Hollander) (1903). Baltimore: Johns Hopkins Press.

[5] Baring, Sir F. (1797) *Observations on the Establishment of the Bank of England and the Paper Circulation of the Country*. Reprinted (1967). New York: Kelley.

[6] Baudrillart, H. (1853) *Jean Bodin et son Temps*. Paris: Guillaumin.

[7] Blaug, M. (1995) Why is the quantity theory of money the oldest surviving theory in economics? In M. Blaug, W. Eltis, D.P. O'Brien, D. Patinkin, R. Skidelsky and G.E. Wood *The Quantity Theory of Money: From Locke to Keynes and Friedman*, pp. 27-49. Aldershot: Edward Elgar.

[8] Bodin de St Laurent, J. (1907) *Les Idées Monétaires et Commerciales de Jean Bodin*. Bordeaux: Cadoret. Reprinted (1970). New York: Burt Franklin.

[9] Bodin, J. (1568a) *La Response de Maistre Jean Bodin Advocat en la Cour au Paradoxe de Monsieur de Malestroit, Touchant L'encherissement de Toutes Choses, & le Moyen d'y Remedier*. Paris: Martin le Jeune.

[10] Bodin, J. (1568b) *Response to the Paradoxes of Malestroit*. Translated by H. Tudor and R.W. Dyson (1997). Bristol: Thoemmes Press.

[11] Bodin, J. (1578) *Les Paradoxes du Seigneur de Malestroit, Conseiller du Roy, & Maistre ordinaire de ses comptes, sur le faict des Monnoyes, presentez à sa Majesté, au moys de Mars, M.D.LXVI. Avec la responce de Jean Bodin aus dicts Paradoxes*. Paris: Jacques du Puys.

[12] Bonney, R. (2004) John Law (bap. 1671, d. 1729), finance minister in France. In *Oxford Dictionary of National Biography* (ed. by B. Harrison). Oxford: Oxford University Press.

[13] Bowley, M.E.A. (1973) *Studies in the History of Economic Theory Before 1870*. London: Macmillan.

[14] Boyer-Xambeu, M.T., Deleplace, G. and Gillard, L. (1988) Métaux d'Amérique et Monnaies d'Europe. *Annales Economies Sociétés Civilisations*, 43, pp. 959-67.

[15] Boyer-Xambeu, M.T., Deleplace, G. and Gillard, L. (1994) *Private Money and Public Currencies: The Sixteenth Century Challenge*. Translated by A. Azodi. New York: M.E. Sharpe.

[16] Buchan, A. (1959) *The Spare Chancellor: The Life of Walter Bagehot*. London: Chatto and Windus.

[17] Cannan, E. (ed.) (1810) *The Paper Pound of 1797-1821: The Bullion Report 8th June 1810*. London: P.S. King, 1919. 2nd ed. (1925). Reprinted (1969), London: Frank Cass.

[18] Cantillon, R. (1730) *Essai sur la Nature du Commerce en Général.* London: Fletcher Gyles. Edited and translated by H. Higgs (1931). London: Macmillan. Reprinted (1964). New York: A.M. Kelley.

[19] Chiang, A.C. (1984) *Fundamental Methods of Mathematical Economics*, 3rd ed. London: McGraw Hill.

[20] Child, J.C. (1668) *Brief Observations Concerning Trade, and Interest of Money.* London: Elizabeth Calvert.

[21] Clapham, J.H. (1944) *The Bank of England: A History*, 2 vols. Cambridge: Cambridge University Press.

[22] Copeland, L.S. (1994) *Exchange Rates and International Finance*, 2nd ed. London: Addison-Wesley.

[23] Craig, J. (1953) *The Mint.* Cambridge: Cambridge University Press.

[24] D'Avenel, G. (1894) *Histoire Economique de la Propriété, des Salaires, des Denrées et de Tous les Prix en Général depuis l'an 1200 jusqu'en l'an 1800.* Paris: Imprimerie Nationale.

[25] Davies, G. (1994) *A History of Money.* Cardiff: University of Wales Press.

[26] De Roover, R. (1949) *Gresham on Foreign Exchange.* Cambridge, Mass.: Harvard University Press.

[27] De Roover, R. (1953) *L'evolution de la Lettre de Change*, XIVe-XVIIe *Siècle.* Paris: Colin.

[28] Dempsey, B.W. (1935) The historical emergence of quantity theory. *Quarterly Journal of Economics*, 50, pp. 174-84.

[29] Dixon, E. (1925) Massie, J. (d. 1784). In *Palgrave's Dictionary of Political Economy* (ed. by H. Higgs), II, pp. 707-9. London: Macmillan.

[30] Feaveryear, A. (1963) *The Pound Sterling*, 2nd ed. Revised by E.V. Morgan. Oxford: Clarendon.

[31] Feinstein, C.H. (1995) Changes in nominal wages, the cost of living and real wages in the United Kingdom over two centuries, 1780-1990. In *Labour's Reward. Real Wages and Economic Change in 19th and 20th-century Europe* (ed. by P. Scholliers and V. Zamagni), pp. 3-36. Aldershot: Edward Elgar.

[32] Fetter, F.W. (1965) *The Development of British Monetary Orthodoxy 1797-1875*. Cambridge, Mass.: Harvard University Press.

[33] Franklin, J.H. (1968) Bodin, Jean. In *International Encyclopaedia of the Social Sciences, Vol. 3* (ed. by D.L. Sills), pp. 110-112. New York: Macmillan.

[34] Fullarton, J. (1845) *On the Regulation of Currencies*. 2nd ed. reprinted (1969). New York: Kelley.

[35] Gayer, A., Rostow, W. and Schwartz, A. (1953) *The Growth and Fluctuation of the British Economy 1790-1850*, 2 vols. Oxford: Clarendon.

[36] Gazier, M. and Gazier, B. (1978) *Or et Monnaie chez Martin de Azpilcueta*. Paris: Economica.

[37] Geary, R.C. and Leser, C.E.V. (1968) Significance tests in multiple regression. *The American Statistician*, 22, pp. 20-1.

[38] Gilbart, J.W. (1854) The laws of the currency, as exemplified in the circulation of country bank notes in England, since the passing of the Act of 1844. *Journal of The [Royal] Statistical Society*, 17, pp. 289-321.

[39] Gillard, L. (1994) Y a-t-il Étalon-Or à la Renaissance? In *Or, Monnaie, Échange dans la Culture de la Renaissance* (ed. by A. Tournon and G.-A. Pérouse), pp. 59-69. St. Etienne: University of St. Etienne.

[40] Glasner, D. (1985) A reinterpretation of classical monetary theory. *Southern Economic Journal*, 52, pp. 46-67. Reprinted in *Pioneers in Economics* (ed. by M. Blaug), 20, pp. 217-38 (1991). Aldershot: Edward Elgar.

[41] Glasner, D. (1989) On some classical monetary controversies. *History of Political Economy*, 21, pp. 201-29. Reprinted in *Pioneers in Economics* (ed. by M. Blaug), 20, pp. 257-85 (1991). Aldershot: Edward Elgar.

[42] Gómez Camacho, F. (1998) Later scholastics: Spanish economic thought in the sixteenth and seventeenth centuries. In *Ancient and Medieval Economic Ideas and Concepts of Social Justice* (ed. by S. Todd Lowry and B. Gordon). Leiden: Brill.

[43] Goodhart, C.A.E. (1989) *Money, Information and Uncertainty*, 2nd ed. London: Macmillan.

[44] Gordon, B. (1975) *Economic Analysis before Adam Smith*. London: Macmillan.

[45] Grassby, R. (1969) The rate of profit in seventeenth century England. *English Historical Review*, 84, pp. 721-51.

[46] Gregory, T.E. (1929) *Select Statutes, Documents and Reports Relating to British Banking, 1832-1928*, 2 vols. London: Milford.

[47] Gregory, T.E. (1936) *The Westminster Bank through a Century*, 2 vols. London: Oxford University Press/H. Milford.

[48] Grice-Hutchinson, M. (1952) *The School of Salamanca: Readings in Spanish Monetary Theory 1544-1605*. Oxford: Clarendon.

[49] Grice-Hutchinson, M. (1978) *Early Economic Thought in Spain, 1177-1740*. London: Allen and Unwin.

[50] Habakkuk, H.J. (1952) The long-term rate of interest and the price of land in the seventeenth century. *Economic History Review*, 5, pp. 26-45.

[51] Hamilton, E.J. (1934) *American Treasure and the Price Revolution in Spain.* Cambridge, Mass.: Harvard University Press.

[52] Hankey, T. (1867) *The Principles of Banking*, 4th ed. (1887). London: Effingham Wilson.

[53] Harsin, P. (1928) *Les Doctrines Monétaires et Financières en France du XVIe au XVIIIe Siècle.* Paris: Félix Alcan.

[54] Hauser, H. (ed. and introd.) (1932) *La Response de Jean Bodin.* Paris: Librairie Armand Colin.

[55] Hawtrey, R.G. (1928) *Currency and Credit*, 3rd ed. London: Longman.

[56] Hawtrey, R.G. (1932) *The Art of Central Banking.* London: Longman.

[57] Heaton, H. (1948) *Economic History of Europe.* Revised ed. New York: Harper.

[58] Hegeland, H. (1951) *The Quantity Theory of Money.* Göteborg: Elanders Boktryckeri.

[59] Horner, F. (1802) Thornton on the nature and effects of the paper credit of Great Britain. *Edinburgh Review*, 1, pp. 172-201. Reprinted in *Foundations of Monetary Economics* (ed. by D.P. O'Brien) (1994), II, pp. 113-43. London: William Pickering.

[60] Horsefield, J.K. (1960) *British Monetary Experiments.* Cambridge, Mass.: Harvard University Press.

[61] Hughes, J.R.T. (1960) *Fluctuations in Trade, Industry and Finance.* Oxford: Clarendon.

[62] Hume, D. (1752) *Writings on Economics* (ed. by E. Rotwein) (1955). Edinburgh: Nelson.

[63] Humphrey, T.M. (1987) Lender of the last resort. In *The New Palgrave Dictionary of Money and Finance, vol. II* (ed. by P. Newman, M. Milgate and J. Eatwell), pp. 571–4. London: Macmillan.

[64] Humphrey, T.M. (1989). Lender of last resort: the concept in history. Reprinted in *Money, Banking and Inflation*, pp. 12-20 (1993). Aldershot: Edward Elgar.

[65] Humphrey, T.M. (1990) Fisherian and Wicksellian price-stabilisation models in the history of monetary thought. *Federal Reserve Bank of Richmond Economic Review*, 76(3), pp. 3-12.

[66] Humphrey, T.M. (1992). Price-level stabilization rules in a Wicksellian model of the cumulative process. *Scandinavian Journal of Economics*, 94, pp. 509–18.

[67] Humphrey, T.M. (1993) *Money, Banking and Inflation*. Aldershot: Edward Elgar.

[68] Humphrey, T.M. (1997). Lender of last resort. In *Business Cycles and Depressions* (ed. by D. Glasner), pp. 391–2. New York: Garland.

[69] Humphrey, T.M. and Keleher, R.E. (1984) The lender of last resort: a historical perspective. *Cato Journal*, 4, pp. 275-318.

[70] Jevons, W.S. (1863) *A Serious Fall in the Value of Gold Ascertained and its Social Effects Set Forth*. London: Stanford.

[71] Johnston, J. (1984) *Econometric Methods*, 3rd ed. London: McGraw Hill.

[72] Joplin, T. (1823) *Outlines of a System of Political Economy written with a View to Prove to Government and Country that the cause of the Present Agricultural Distress is Entirely Artificial.* London: Baldwin, Cradock and Joy. Reprinted (1970), New York: Kelley.

[73] Joplin, T. (1825) *An Illustration of Mr. Joplin's Views on Currency, and Plan for Its Improvement; together with Observations applicable to the Present State of the Money Market; in a series of Letters* [which appeared in the *Courier*]. London: Baldwin, Cradock and Joy.

[74] Joplin, T. (1826) *Views on the Subject of Corn and Currency.* London: Baldwin, Cradock and Joy.

[75] Joplin, T. (1828) *Views on the Corn Bill of 1827, and Other Measures of Government.* London: Ridgway.

[76] Joplin, T. (1831) *The Plan of a National Establishment for Country Banking and the Principles by which it is recommended.* London: Ruffy.

[77] Joplin, T. (1832) *An Analysis and History of the Currency Question.* London: Ridgway.

[78] Joplin, T. (1833) *A Digest of the Evidence on the Bank Charter taken before the Committee of 1832.* London: Ridgway.

[79] Joplin, T. (1835) *Case for Parliamentary Enquiry into the Circumstances of the Panic: in a Letter to Thomas Gisborne, Esq, M.P.* London: Ridgway.

[80] Joplin, T. (1839) *On Our Monetary System.* London: Ridgway.

[81] Joplin, T. (1841) *The Cause and Cure of Our Commercial Embarrassments.* London: Ridgway.

[82] Joplin, T. (1844) An Examination of Sir Robert Peel's Currency Bill of 1844, in a Letter to the Bankers of the United Kingdom. London: Richardson.

[83] Kelly, P.H. (ed.) *Locke on Money*, 2 vols. Oxford: Clarendon.

[84] Keynes, J.M. (1936) *The General Theory of Employment, Interest and Money*. London: Macmillan. Reprinted for the Royal Economic Society (1973). London: Macmillan.

[85] King, M. (2000). *Balancing the Economic See-Saw*. London: Bank of England.

[86] King, W.T.C. (1936) *History of the London Discount Market*. London: Routledge.

[87] Klein, L.R. (1992) Smith's use of data. In *Adam Smith's Legacy* (ed. by M. Fry), pp. 15-28. London: Routledge.

[88] Kravis, I. (1956) Availability and other influences on the commodity composition of trade. *Journal of Political Economy*, 64, pp. 143-155.

[89] Laidler, D. (1990) Alfred Marshall and the development of monetary economics. In *Centenary Essays on Alfred Marshall* (ed. by J.K. Whitaker), pp. 44-78. Cambridge: Cambridge University Press.

[90] Laidler, D. (1991) *The Golden Age of the Quantity Theory*. London: Harvester Wheatsheaf.

[91] Law, J. (1705) *Money and Trade Considered with a Proposal for Supplying the Nation with Money*. Edinburgh: Andrew Anderson. Reprinted (1966), New York: A.M. Kelley.

[92] Leatham, W. (1840) *Letters on the Currency... Ascertaining for the First Time, on True Principles, the Amount of Inland and Foreign*

Bills of Exchange in Circulation for Several Consecutive Years, and Out at One Time. London: Privately Printed.

[93] Lee, G. (1975) The concept of profit in British accounting, 1760-1900. *Business History Review*, 49, pp. 6-36.

[94] Leigh, A.H. (1974) John Locke and the quantity theory of money. *History of Political Economy*, 6, pp. 200-219.

[95] Letwin, W. (1963) *The Origins of Scientific Economics*. London: Methuen.

[96] Locke, J. (1691) *Some Considerations of the Consequences of the Lowering of Interest, and Raising the Value of Money*, 2nd ed. (1696). London: A. and J. Churchill. Reprinted in *Monetary Theory: 1601-1758, Vol. IV* (ed. by A.E. Murphy) (1997), pp. 1-98. London: Routledge.

[97] Lowry, S. Todd (1996) Review of M.T. Boyer-Xambeau, G. Deleplace and L. Gillard *Private Money and Public Currencies: The Sixteenth and Seventeenth Century Challenge. History of Political Economy*, 28, pp. 310-13.

[98] MacIver, R.M. (1930) Bodin, Jean. In *Encyclopaedia of the Social Sciences, Vol. 2* (ed. by E.R.A. Seligman with Alvin Johnson), pp. 614-16. New York: Macmillan.

[99] Maddala, G.S. (1977) *Econometrics*. Tokyo: McGraw-Hill Kogakusha.

[100] Malynes, G. de (1603) *Englands View, in the Unmasking of Two Paradoxes*. Reprinted (1972), New York: Arno Press.

[101] Massie, J. (1750) *The Natural Rate of Interest*. London: Owen. Reprinted (1970), New York: Johnson.

[102] Mathias, P. (1957) The social structure in the eighteenth century: a calculation by Joseph Massie. *Economic History Review*, 10, pp. 30-45.

[103] Matthews, R. (1954) *A Study in Trade-Cycle History*. Cambridge: Cambridge University Press.

[104] Mayer, T. (1995) *Doing Economic Research*. Aldershot: Edward Elgar.

[105] McCulloch, J.R. (1862) *A Catalogue of Books, the Property of a Political Economist*. Reprinted (1995), London: Routledge/Thoemmes.

[106] Meier, G. (1980) *International Economics*. Oxford: Oxford University Press.

[107] Mill, J.S. (1829-30/1844) *Essays on Some Unsettled Questions of Political Economy*. Reprinted in *Essays on Economics and Society* (ed. by J.M. Robson) (1967). Toronto: Toronto University Press.

[108] Mill, J.S. (1844) The currency question. *Westminster Review*, 41, pp. 579-98.

[109] Mill, J.S. (1848) *Principles of Political Economy* (ed. by W.J. Ashley) (1923). London: Longmans.

[110] Mirowski, P. (1982) Adam Smith, empiricism, and the rate of profit in eighteenth century England. *History of Political Economy*, 14, pp. 178-98.

[111] Mishkin, F.S. (1986) *The Economics of Money, Banking, and Financial Markets*. Boston: Little Brown.

[112] Mitchell, B.R. with Deane, P. (1962) *Abstract of British Historical Statistics*. Cambridge: Cambridge University Press.

[113] Monroe, A.E. (1924) *Monetary Theory before Adam Smith*. Reprinted (1966). New York: A.M. Kelley.

[114] Monroe, A.E. (ed.) (1951) *Early Economic Thought: Selections from Economic Literature prior to Adam Smith.* Cambridge, Mass.: Harvard University Press.

[115] Moore, G.A. (1948) Introduction to and translation of *The Response of Jean Bodin to the Paradoxes of Malestroit and the Paradoxes.* Chevy Chase, Md.: Country Dollar Press.

[116] Moosa, I. (1993) Did the gold standard really work? *Sheffield University Management School Discussion Paper,* No. 93.43.

[117] Morgan, E.V. (1943) *The Theory and Practice of Central Banking 1797-1913.* Reprinted (1965). London: Frank Cass.

[118] Morineau, M. (1985) *Incroyables Gazettes et Fabuluex Métaux.* Paris: Maison des Sciences de l'Homme.

[119] Murphy, A.E. (1986) *Richard Cantillon: Entrepreneur and Economist.* Oxford: Clarendon.

[120] Murphy, A.E. (1997) *John Law: Economic Theorist and Policy-Maker.* Oxford: Clarendon.

[121] Murphy, A.E. (2000) Canons of monetary orthodoxy and John Law. In *Contributions to the History of Economic Thought: Essays in Honour of R.D.C. Black* (ed. by A.E. Murphy and R. Prendergast), pp. 294-317. London: Routledge.

[122] Myint, H. (1958) The 'classical' theory of international trade and the underdeveloped countries. *Economic Journal,* 68, pp. 317-37.

[123] Newmarch, W. (1851) An attempt to ascertain the magnitude and fluctuations of the amount of bills of exchange (inland and foreign) in circulation at one time in Great Britain, in England, in Scotland, in

Lancashire, and in Cheshire, respectively, during each of the twenty years 1828-1847, both inclusive; and also embracing in the inquiry bills drawn up on foreign countries. *Journal of the [Royal] Statistical Society*, 14, pp. 143-83.

[124] Norman, G.W. (1841) *Letter to Charles Wood... on Money and the Means of Economizing the Use of It.* London: Richardson.

[125] North, D. (1691) *Discourses upon Trade.* London: Basset. Reprinted in *Early English Tracts on Commerce* (ed. by J.R. McCulloch) (1856) and Reprinted (1954). Cambridge: Cambridge University Press.

[126] O'Brien, D.P. (1971) *The Correspondence of Lord Overstone*, 3 vols. Cambridge: Cambridge University Press.

[127] O'Brien, D.P. (1975) *The Classical Economists.* Oxford: Clarendon.

[128] O'Brien, D.P. (1990) Marshall's work in relation to classical economics. In *Centenary Essays on Alfred Marshall* (ed. by J.K. Whitaker), pp. 127-163. Cambridge: Cambridge University Press.

[129] O'Brien, D.P. (1992) Petty's political Arithmetick. Reprinted in *Methodology, Money and the Firm*, vol. 2, pp. 99-106 (1994), Aldershot: Edward Elgar.

[130] O'Brien, D.P. (1993) *Thomas Joplin and Classical Macroeconomics.* Aldershot: Edward Elgar.

[131] O'Brien, D.P. (1995) Long-run equilibrium and cyclical disturbances: the currency, and banking controversy over monetary control. In M. Blaug, W. Eltis, D.P. O'Brien, D. Patinkin, R. Skidelsky and G.E. Wood, *The Quantity Theory of Money*, pp. 50-79. Aldershot: Edward Elgar.

[132] O'Brien, D.P. (1996) Monetary base control and the Bank Charter Act of 1844. *University of Durham Department of Economics Working Paper*, No. 159.

[133] O'Brien, D.P. (1997a) *The Foundations of Business Cycle Theory*, 3 vols. Cheltenham: Edward Elgar.

[134] O'Brien, D.P. (1997b) Introduction. In J. Bodin *Response to the Paradoxes of Malestroit*. Translated by H. Tudor and R.W. Dyson. Bristol: Thoemmes.

[135] O'Brien, D.P. (2004) *The Classical Economists Revisited*. Princeton: Princeton University Press.

[136] O'Brien, G. (1920) *An Essay on Mediaeval Economic Teaching*. London: Longman.

[137] Overstone, Lord (1837) *Reflections suggested by a perusal of Mr. J. Horsley Palmer's pamphlet on the causes and consequences of the pressure on the money market*. Reprinted in *Tracts and Other Publications on Metallic and Paper Currency*, pp. 1-40 (1857). London: Privately Printed.

[138] Overstone, Lord (1840a) *Remarks on the management of the circulation; and on the condition and conduct of the Bank of England and of the country issuers*. Reprinted in *Tracts and Other Publications on Metallic and Paper Currency*, (1857). London: Privately Printed.

[139] Overstone, Lord (1840b) *Effects of the administration of the Bank of England: a second letter to J.B. Smith*. Reprinted in *Tracts and Other Publications on Metallic and Paper Currency*, (1857). London: Privately Printed.

[140] Overstone, Lord (1857) *Tracts and Other Publications on Metallic and Paper Currency*. London: Privately Printed.

[141] Palliser, D.M. (1992) *The Age of Elizabeth*. London: Longman.

[142] Parliamentary Papers (1832) *Report from the Secret Committee appointed to inquire into the expediency of renewing the Charter of the Bank of England, and into the System on which Banks of Issue in England and Wales are conducted*. 1831-2 (722) VI, 1.

[143] Parliamentary Papers (1840) *Report from the Select Committee appointed to inquire into the effects produced on the Circulation of the Country by the Various Banking Establishments issuing Notes payable on demand*. 1840 (602) IV, 1.

[144] Parliamentary Papers (1841) *Report from the Committee of Secrecy appointed to consider the effects produced on the circulation of the Country by the Various Banking Establishments issuing Notes payable on demand*, 1841 Session I (366, 410) V, 1, 5.

[145] Parliamentary Papers (1847-8a) *Report from the Select Committee on Commercial Distress* (584, 395) VIII Part I, 505, Part II, 1, 379.

[146] Parliamentary Papers (1847-8b) *Report from the Lords' Secret Committee appointed to inquire into the Cause of the Distress among the Commercial Classes* (565) (565-II) VIII Part III, 1, 537.

[147] Parliamentary Papers (1857) *Report from the Select Committee appointed to Inquire into the operation of the Bank Act of 1844 and of the Bank Acts of Scotland and Ireland 1845* (220 Sess.2) X Part I, 1 (220-I Sess 2) X Part II, 1.

[148] Parliamentary Papers (1857-8) *Report from the Select Committee appointed to inquire into the operation of the Bank Act of 1844, and of*

the Bank Acts for Ireland and Scotland of 1845, and into the causes of the recent commercial distress, and to investigate how far it has been affected by the laws for regulating the issue of Bank notes payable on demand. (381) V, 1.

[149] Parliamentary Papers (1873) *Return of the Bank of England on the last day of each week from 3rd January to 24th December 1872.* (229) XXXIX, 161.

[150] Pennington, J. (1838) Appendix C of Tooke, T. and Newmarch, W. A *History of Prices and of the State of the Circulation, Vol. 2*, pp. 369-78. London: Longman.

[151] Peronnet, M. (1994) De L'Or Splendeur Immortelle... In *Or, Monnaie, Échange dans la Culture de la Renaissance* (ed. by A. Tournon and G.A. Pérouse), pp. 45-58. St. Etienne: University of St. Etienne.

[152] Petty, W. (1662) *A Treatise of Taxes and Contributions.* London: Brooke. Reprinted in *Monetary Theory: 1601-1758*, vol. II (ed. by A.E. Murphy), London: Routledge.

[153] Petty, W. (1690) *Political Arithmetick.* London: Robert Clavel and Henry Mortlock. Reprinted (1992), Düsseldorf: Verlagsgruppe Handelsblatt.

[154] Phelps Brown, E.H. and Hopkins, S.V. (1959) Builders' wage-rates, prices and population: some further evidence. *Economica*, 27, pp. 18-29.

[155] Pollard, S. (1972) Capital accounting in the industrial revolution. In *Capital Formation in the Industrial Revolution* (ed. by F. Crouzet), pp. 94-118. London: Methuen.

[156] Popescu, O. (1998) Latin American scholars. In *Ancient and Medieval Economic Ideas and Concepts of Social Justice* (ed. by S. Todd Lowry and B. Gordon). Leiden: Brill.

[157] Potter, W. (1650) *The Key of Wealth.* London: Nicholas Bourne. Reprinted in *Monetary Theory: 1601-1758, vol. II* (ed. by A.E. Murphy) (1997), pp. 15-137. London: Routledge.

[158] Reynolds, B. (1945) Introduction to and translation of J. Bodin, *Method for the Easy Comprehension of History.* New York: Columbia University Press.

[159] Ricardo, D. (1810) *The High Price of Bullion, a Proof of the Depreciation of Banknotes* (ed. by P. Sraffa) (1951). Cambridge: Cambridge University Press.

[160] Ricardo, D. (1817) *On the Principles of Political Economy and Taxation* (ed. by P. Sraffa) (1951). Cambridge: Cambridge University Press.

[161] Robbins, L. (1958) *Robert Torrens and the Evolution of Classical Economics.* London: Macmillan.

[162] Sabine, G.H. (1951) *A History of Political Theory*, 3rd ed. London: Harrap.

[163] Samuelson, P.A. (1980) A corrected version of Hume's equilibrating mechanisms for international trade. In *Flexible Exchange Rates and the Balance of Payments* (ed. by J.S. Chipman and C.P. Kindleberger), pp. 141-158. Amsterdam: North Holland.

[164] Samuelson, P.A. (1986) *The Collected Scientific Papers of Paul A. Samuelson, Vol. V.* (ed. by K. Crowley). Cambridge, Mass.: MIT Press.

[165] Sayers, R.S. (ed.) (1963) *The Economic Writings of James Pennington.* London: London School of Economics.

[166] Schumpeter, J.A. (1954) *History of Economic Analysis*. London: Allen and Unwin.

[167] Seligman, E.R.A. (1930) Bullionists. In *Encyclopaedia of the Social Sciences*, vol. 3 (ed. by E.R.A. Seligman with A. Johnson), pp. 60-64. New York: Macmillan.

[168] Senior, N.W. (1830) *Three Lectures on the Cost of Obtaining Money, and on Some Effects of Private and Government Paper Money.* London: John Murray.

[169] Servet, J.M. (1994) Les paradoxes des paradoxes de Malestroit. In *Or, Monnaie, Échange dans la Culture de la Renaissance* (ed. by A. Tournon and G.A. Pérouse), pp. 71-79. St. Etienne: University of St. Etienne.

[170] Shaw, W.A. (1937) *Bibliography of the Collection of Books and Tracts on Commerce, Currency and Poor Law, 1557 to 1763, formed by Joseph Massie.* London: Harding's Bookshop.

[171] Silk, M. (1972) Introduction. In G. de Malynes, *England's View, in the Unmasking of Two Paradoxes* (1603). New York: Arno Press.

[172] Skaggs, N.T. (1995) Henry Thornton and the development of classical monetary economics. *Canadian Journal of Economics*, 28, pp. 1212-27.

[173] Smith, A. (1776) *An Inquiry into the Nature and Causes of the Wealth of Nations* (ed. by R.H. Campbell, A.S. Skinner and W.B. Todd) (1976). Oxford: Oxford University Press.

[174] Spiegel, H.W. (1991) *The Growth of Economic Thought*, 3rd ed. Durham, N.C.: Duke University Press.

[175] Spooner, F.C. (1972) *The International Economy and Monetary Movements.* Cambridge, Mass.: Harvard University Press.

[176] Thompson, E.A. (1974) The theory of money and income consistent with orthodox value theory. In *Trade, Stability and Macroeconomics* (ed. by G. Horwich and P. Samuelson), pp. 427-453. New York: Academic Press.

[177] Thornton, H. (1802) *An Enquiry into the Nature and Effects of the Paper Credit of Great Britain.* Reprinted (ed. by F.A. Hayek) (1939), London: Allen and Unwin.

[178] Thornton, H. (1811) *Speech of 7 May 1811.* Reprinted in Thornton (1802), pp. 327-346.

[179] Tooke, T. (1840) *A History of Prices, and of the State of the Circulation*, vol. III. London: Longman.

[180] Tooke, T. (1844) *An Inquiry into the Currency Principle.* London: Longman.

[181] Tooke, T. and Newmarch, W. (1838-57) *A History of Prices and of the State of the Circulation from 1792 to 1856.* London: Longman. Reprinted (1925). London: P.S. King.

[182] Tooley, J. (1955) Introduction to and translation of *J. Bodin Six Books of the Commonwealth.* Oxford: Blackwell.

[183] Torrens, R. (1837) *A Letter to the Right Honourable Lord Viscount Melbourne on the Causes of the Recent Derangements in the Money Market and on Bank Reform.* London: Longman.

[184] Torrens, R. (1844) *An Inquiry into the Practical Working of the Proposed Arrangements for the Renewal of the Charter of the Bank of England, and the Regulation of the Currency: with a Refutation of the Fallacies Advanced by Mr. Tooke.* London: Smith Elder.

[185] Torrens, R. (1848) *The Principles and Practical Operation of Sir Robert Peel's Bill of 1844 Explained and Defended Against the Objections of Tooke, Fullarton and Wilson.* London: Longman.

[186] Torrens, R. (1852) Review of J. Lalor, *Money and Morals: A Book for the Times. Globe*, 13 October, p. 1.

[187] Torrens, R. (1857) *The Principles and Practical Operation of Sir Robert Peel's Act of 1844 Explained and Defended: Second Edition with Additional Chapters on Money, the Gold Discoveries, and International Exchange; and a Critical Examination of the Chapter 'on the Regulation of a Convertible Paper Currency' in Mr. J.S. Mill's Principles of Political Economy.* London: Longman.

[188] Tucker, G. (1960) *Progress and Profits in British Economic Thought 1650-1850.* Cambridge: Cambridge University Press.

[189] Uhr, C.G. (1960) *Economic Doctrines of Knut Wicksell.* Berkeley, Calif.: University of California Press.

[190] Vaughn, K. (1980) *John Locke:. Economist and Social Scientist.* London: Athlone Press.

[191] Vickers, D. (1960) *Studies in the Theory of Money 1690-1776.* London: Peter Owen.

[192] Vilar, P. (1976) *A History of Gold and Money, 1450-1920.* Translated by J. White. London: NLB.

[193] Viner, J. (1937) *Studies in the Theory of International Trade.* London: Allen and Unwin.

[194] Wasserman, M.J. and Beach, F.H. (1934) Some neglected monetary theories of John Law. *American Economic Review*, 24, pp. 646-57.

[195] White, L. (1984) *Free Banking in Britain.* Cambridge: Cambridge University Press.

[196] Wicksell, K. (1907) *The Enigma of Business Cycles.* London: Macmillan. Translated in *International Economic Papers* (ed. by A.T. Peacock, R. Turvey and E. Henderson), 1953, 3, pp. 58–74.

[197] Wood, E. (1939) *English Theories of Central Banking Control 1819-58.* Cambridge, Mass.: Harvard University Press.

[198] Wright, A.L. (1956) The genesis of the multiplier. *Oxford Economic Papers*, 8, pp. 181-93.

[199] Zallio, F. (1990) Adam Smith's dual circulation framework. *Royal Bank of Scotland Review*, 166, pp. 34-43.

Index